TARGET HIROSHIMA

TARGE⊕HIROSHIMA

**DEAK PARSONS
AND THE
CREATION
OF THE
ATOMIC BOMB**

Al Christman

Naval Institute Press
Annapolis, Maryland

Library of Congress Cataloging-in-Publication Data
Christman, Albert B.
    Target Hiroshima : Deak Parsons and the creation of the atomic
  bomb / Al Christman
        p.   cm.
    Includes bibliographical references and index.
    ISBN 1-55750-120-3 (alk. paper)
    1. Parsons, William Sterling, 1901–1953. 2. Admirals—United
States—Biography. 3. United States. Navy—Biography. I. Title.
V63.P35C47   1998
359'.0092—dc21
    [B]   98-2553

Printed in the United States of America on acid-free paper ∞
05 04 03 02 01 00 99 98   9 8 7 6 5 4 3 2
First printing

Frontispiece: Foreground figures in shipboard scene at Bikini (*left to right*): Vice Adm. W. H. P. Blandy, commander, Operation Crossroads; Rear Adm. William Parsons, deputy commander for Technical Direction; Roger Warner, Los Alamos leader for bomb assembly; and Maj. Gen. William Kepner, deputy commander for Air Operations
Harlow W. Russ, Los Alamos Historical Museum

The following publishers have granted permission to quote from copyrighted works.

Curtis Brown, Ltd.: From *Seven Hours to Zero,* by Joseph L. Marx. © 1967 by Joseph L. Marx.

Kluwer Academic Publishers: From *Reminiscences of Los Alamos, 1943–1945,* edited by Lawrence Badash, Joseph Hirschfelder, and Herbert Broida. © 1980 by D. Reidel Publishing Co., Dardrecht, Holland.

Simon and Schuster, Inc.: From *The Making of the Atomic Bomb,* by Richard Rhodes. © 1986 by Richard Rhodes.

William Morrow and Co., Inc.: From *Pieces of the Action,* by Vannevar Bush. © 1970 by Vannevar Bush.

Contents

Preface

Thirty-two years ago I began the quest to separate Deak Parsons the man from Captain Parsons the wartime legend. Between 1965 and 1971 I interviewed forty former Parsons associates about his unusual naval career, including his leading roles in the three military-scientific programs crucial to American victory in World War II: radar, the proximity fuze, and the atomic bomb. Among those interviewed were Vannevar Bush, the chief mobilizer of science for the war; Lt. Gen. Leslie Groves, director of the Manhattan Project; and most of the Los Alamos scientists and officers who worked with Parsons in the weaponization and overseas assembly of the wartime bombs.

The interviews confirmed that Deak Parsons was indeed, as some described him, a new breed of officer, a breed much needed in the expanded military technology of the nuclear age. Even so, there was little possibility of producing a Parsons biography at that time. Most of the records that could give substance to his achievements remained classified for security reasons. Moreover, the interviewing on Parsons had been conducted as an adjunct to research for the history I was writing of the Naval Weapons Center, China Lake. While the work on the China Lake history continued, the research on Parsons ended with the interviews. My task was completed when I furnished tapes and transcripts of the Parsons interviews to the Naval Historical Center's Operational Archives, where they are preserved for posterity and are available for scholars. At least, I believed that my work was over.

However, two decades later, following my government retirement, I crossed paths with Vice Adm. F. L. Ashworth, USN (Ret.), one of the principal persons interviewed earlier. We were scarcely through dinner before he struck a nerve. He said, "The Parsons story still needs to be told, now more than ever." I agreed to at least try an article and soon after queried *Naval History* magazine. The editor, then Paul Stillwell, replied, "First the article, then the book."

In several important ways the three-decade delay between start of interviews and completion of book has enhanced the final biography. Many of the interviews would be unavailable today. Conversely, crucial records not available then have been declassified in recent years.

In addition, the delay has improved our perspective on the technological advances of Deak Parsons' day. In particular, the radiation hazards and the moral issues of the atomic bomb are seen in a more discerning light now than when still under the shadow of World War II. These issues, plus revisionist efforts to reshape nuclear history, make it all the more important to examine the circumstances that brought the atomic bomb into being and into combat use.

In the Parsons odyssey we view the World War II landscape from the perspective of the military officer who worked most intimately with the Los Alamos scientists. We accompany him as he plans for and then takes charge of the overseas assembly of the combat bombs. We accompany him as bomb commander on the Hiroshima mission. We enter the nuclear age with Parsons as the Atomic Admiral who did the initial planning for Operation Crossroads and then provided technical direction in its execution. Through him we see the problems, the possibilities, and the limitations not only of nuclear energy but of other technological advances that came out of the World War II scientific mobilization.

The search for Parsons the man—and the basis for his effectiveness—has been more difficult than tracking his military and scientific achievements. He was interested in results, not personal credit. Only in letters to family and close friends did he allow glimpses of the inner man. His uncommon brilliance and intense commitment to mission explain much. But his reputation for success, sometimes seen as the Midas touch, is also explained by his natural way of working with fellow officers as shipmates, whether at sea or ashore, and with scientists as equal partners. He was a "network" man before the word gained its current meaning. The challenge of this biography has been to illuminate the personal strengths that Parsons himself hid through innate modesty.

After thirty-two years it is hard to stop and let the story speak for itself. But first, I invite your attention to the Acknowledgments. As Deak Parsons would have me say, this book is not something I produced alone; it is the product of the combined efforts, talents, and encouragement of many people. Without them Deak Parsons would be but a fading legend. I salute them all.

Acknowledgments

Thanks first to those whose support goes back to the beginning of this thirty-two-year quest: Vice Adm. Frederick L. Ashworth, USN (Ret.); Vice Adm. John T. Hayward, USN (Ret.); and Adm. Horacio Rivero, USN (Ret.)—all close associates of Parsons who have both inspired and helped me in this long effort to bring the Deak Parsons legacy and lessons into national consciousness. On the civilian side, my hearty thanks to Dean Allard, who as head of the navy's Operational Archives and later director of Naval History supported and advised me through the task from beginning to end. From the 1965 endorsement of director of Naval History Rear Adm. E. M. Eller, USN (Ret.), to today's director, William Dudley, I have had invaluable support from the Naval Historical Center (formerly Naval History Division).

Special appreciation is due Parsons family members. This biography would not have been possible without the help of Deak Parsons' sister, Clarissa Fuller; his late wife, Martha Parsons Burroughs; his daughters, Clara Parsons and Margaret Parsons Bowditch; and his brother Harry Parsons Jr.

I am indebted to all the scientists, officers, and other Parsons associates who shared their recollections in interviews. Among these, special thanks are due Norris Bradbury, Norman Ramsey, and Charles Critchfield for their insights into Parsons' Los Alamos years. The full list of persons interviewed is provided in the Bibliography.

The institutional services received have come through the generous help of staff members and archivists, including, among others, Bernard Cavalcante, Catherine Lloyd, and Judith Short, Operational Archives, Naval Historical Center; Elizabeth Babcock and Leroy Doig, Naval Air Weapons Station, China Lake, Calif.; Roger Meade, archivist/historian, Los Alamos National Laboratory; Rebecca Collinsworth, curator, Los

Alamos Museum; Marjorie Ciarlanti, Civil Reference Branch, National Archives; Alice S. Creighton, Nimitz Library Archives, U.S. Naval Academy; and Gerald A. Bennett, Applied Physics Laboratory, the Johns Hopkins University.

Two journal articles served as major stepping stones toward the book manuscript: "Deak Parsons, Officer-Scientist," U.S. Naval Institute *Proceedings,* January 1992; and "Making It Happen," *American Heritage of Invention and Technology,* Summer 1995.

The final archival research for this project was made possible by a Helen Hawkins Memorial Research Grant administered by the San Diego Independent Scholars. For this I am grateful not only in my own behalf but also for the recognition this fund provides for independent scholarship.

I have attempted to portray in this account some of the century's greatest technological events without drowning the reader in technical detail. In striving for readability I have had a great deal of help. My sincerest personal thanks in this regard are due Janet Kunert—my life partner, chief critic, and closest supporter. Thanks, too, go to Karen O'Connor—writing specialist extraordinary. I have also received invaluable help and continuous encouragement from my peers of the Writers Studio of Encinitas; thanks to each of you. And I extend a snappy salute to Mary V. Yates for masterful editorial assistance.

Invaluable help has been received from manuscript reviews, both partial and full, by Roger Meade, Los Alamos National Laboratory; Stanley Middleman, University of California, San Diego; and Vice Adm. Gerald Miller, USN (Ret.). Earlier reviews of sample chapters by Vice Admiral Ashworth and Jonathan Weisgall, author of *Operation Crossroads,* were valuable in establishing the style and framework for the final work. The late Stanley Goldberg, authority on Lt. Gen. Leslie Groves and the Manhattan Project, generously shared his research and historical insights.

I am grateful to Paul Stillwell of the Naval Institute for his encouragement when it was most needed to go forward with a full biography and for his subsequent help and counsel.

From these acknowledgments it is clear that I have received help from many able people, who in the spirit of Deak Parsons have given for the sake of knowledge, not personal credit. And although final responsibility rests with me for any errors or omissions, the finished product is not that of one person but of many.

·1·

A New Kind of Warrior

He was the finest technical officer the navy has had in this century.
Vice Adm. John T. Hayward, USN (Ret.)

Military Police, carbines in hand, ringed the barnlike briefing hut. Security officers checked the identification of each person entering. Crews of seven B-29 bombers from the Army Air Forces 509th Composite Group filed in and sat on unpainted wooden benches among scientists and technicians wearing military uniforms.

Expectations ran high at this meeting of 4 August 1945 on the island of Tinian, fifty-eight hundred miles from San Francisco and fifteen hundred from mainland Japan. At 1500 (military time), group commander Col. Paul Tibbets informed the mixed military and civilian group that orders had arrived to deliver upon the enemy "the gadget" that had been the object of their secret tests and practice bombings of the past ten months.[1] Tibbets announced there was one person present who had witnessed the gadget's awesome power: Capt. William Parsons.

A tall, thin naval officer known as "Deak" stepped forward. His penetrating brown eyes engaged the audience. The eagles on his khaki collar reminded the airmen present that as a navy captain he was equivalent in rank to Tibbets, a "bird colonel." Receding hair and high forehead gave an impression of uncommon cerebral capacity. His forty-four years made him fourteen years older than Tibbets and nearly twice the age of most of the airmen and scientists present.

Even the airmen knew Deak Parsons to be the leader of a mixed group of officers, enlisted men, and civilians at the heart of the hush-hush mission on Tinian. But none among the aircrews except Tibbets knew that this naval officer in their midst was the ordnance chief and associate director of a secret weapons laboratory at Los Alamos, New Mexico, where the gadget had been designed and developed.

Parsons told the crews, "The bomb you are going to drop is something new in the history of warfare. It is the most destructive weapon ever produced. We think it will knock out everything within a three mile area." He then signaled for a film of the weapon exploding from the top of a tower in New Mexico. When the projector began chewing up the film, Parsons had it stopped. With characteristic dryness he said, "The film you are now *not* about to see was made of the only test we performed."[2]

Instead of showing the film of the Trinity test, Parsons described what he had seen less than three weeks earlier: "I was in a B-29 looking down at the flash in the darkness and I can say it is the brightest and hottest thing on this earth since creation."[3] He described the churning mushroom and dust column that rose to the stratosphere. The combat version of that bomb was now assembled and ready, he said. All they were waiting for was the end of a rainstorm then raging over Japan.

The airmen departed, many of them proud to be part of a mission that could shorten, if not end, the war. They had been selected to deliver the gadget. Deak Parsons, who knew all the details of this revolutionary weapon, would be with them.

That evening Parsons retired to his tent among those of the fifty civilians and officers he had brought from Los Alamos to direct the technical work of the mission.[4] The tents were pitched alongside the four parallel runways of Tinian's North Field. The island had been captured ten months earlier. Rush construction had made it, in essence, a giant aircraft carrier. Bomb-laden B-29s now used it for mass air raids on Japan. One of these raids occurred the night after the briefing. Every fifteen seconds for an hour and a half another B-29 would start down one of the runways, the four Wright 2,200-horsepower engines revved up to bring the plane to flying speed before the end of the runway. Of those from previous runs that had not made it, only burned hulls remained.

This night four bombers in a row crashed on takeoff.[5] Parsons watched the night sky turn bright with flames fed by exploding ammunition and fuel for the three-thousand-mile round trip. These accidents were tragic, but Parsons could envision far worse. The bomber on the nuclear mission would be fifteen thousand pounds overweight. If it crashed, fire could ignite the bomb's powder charge and propel the uranium-235 bullet into a uranium-235 sleeve, creating some level of nuclear explosion.[6]

Parsons was not a man to change an agreed-upon plan without good reason. He and General Groves had decided earlier that the bomb should be completely assembled before takeoff because of the difficulty of doing so in the cramped space of the plane's bomb bay.[7] But that decision came before Parsons witnessed plane crashes that turned the early morning bright with flame.

Shortly after sunup on Sunday, 5 August, Parsons shared his concerns with Brig. Gen. Thomas Farrell, Groves' deputy at Tinian. Parsons warned that if the overloaded bombing plane crashed and burned on takeoff, "we'd make a terrible mess of things around here."[8] He did not have to explain to Farrell that the cookoff of an atomic bomb of that early design could cause untold damage and loss of life on the island.

To avoid such a risk, Parsons advocated that he load the powder charges to the Little Boy gun after the plane took off and was clear of the island. Farrell, aware of Groves' opposition to in-flight tinkering, asked whether Parsons had made the assembly with the powder charges before. "No," Parsons responded, "but I've got all day to try it."[9]

By 1500 the 9,700-pound bomb, 10.5 feet long and 29 inches in diameter, hung from its hook in the bomb bay of the *Enola Gay,* sway braces attached. Parsons crawled into the bomb bay, squeezing himself into the narrow space at the tail of this weapon so innocuously named Little Boy. He held a checklist covering the steps for loading the high explosives and the detonator for triggering the nuclear explosion. Perched on a narrow catwalk hastily constructed that morning, he endured the sweltering heat, cramped quarters, and poor lighting within the bomb bay. Time and time again he repeated the eleven steps on the list.

When General Farrell dropped by, he noticed that Parsons' graphite-blackened hands were nicked from working with sharp-edged parts within the bomb. "For God's sakes, man," Farrell urged, "let me loan you a pair of pigskin gloves."

"I wouldn't dare," Parsons replied. "I've got to feel the touch."[10]

Who was this navy captain in the bomb bay of an air force bomber working intently on a nuclear device dreamed up by civilians? What brought him to Tinian and a pivotal role in a military-scientific mission that would change the world?

Deak Parsons was a new kind of warrior in the midst of a weapons revolution. He fought his battles in the laboratory and on the proving grounds. When he went into combat he did so with new and radical weapons he had helped create.

Parsons proclaimed himself a sailor at heart, but it was the allure of science that took control of his career and set him on a nuclear odyssey. During World War II this odyssey took him to Los Alamos, Trinity, Tinian, and—as bomb commander—the Hiroshima mission of the *Enola Gay*. After the war it would take him to Operations Crossroads and the nuclear tests at Eniwetok. As the Atomic Admiral of the postwar world, he led the navy into the nuclear age.[11] He did more than any other officer of his time to shape the navy's nuclear policies and capabilities. He was an early advocate of nuclear power for ships and submarines, and his initiatives gave nuclear-strike capabilities to carrier aircraft. As the military's foremost nuclear expert, he provided technical leadership for, and witnessed, seven of the first eight atomic explosions.

Parsons' achievements and influence went beyond the nuclear. As a lieutenant in the early 1930s he had been the first officer of any service to recognize the full military potential of high-frequency radio experiments at the Naval Research Laboratory. These were the beginnings of radar in the United States.

Early in World War II Parsons provided military leadership in the creation of the proximity fuze, essentially a miniature radar installed in projectiles so that they can sense when they are within lethal distance of their target. As with the atomic bomb, he accompanied the proximity fuze during its first use in combat.

As one of the navy's foremost ordnance experts, Parsons pushed the

·2·

Cow Town to Crab Town

The convivial young savior from Fort Sumner . . . is as persevering as a starved mosquito . . . [and] is possessed of a well-oiled, double-jointed tongue.

Naval Academy class of 1922, *The Lucky Bag*

In many ways William Sterling Parsons was a younger copy of his father, Harry Robert Parsons. On the surface they both appeared to be uncommonly reserved and mild-mannered; beneath they were strong-willed and determined.

Born in South Side Chicago in April 1872, the senior Parsons grew up in a tough neighborhood. To come home from school he had to go with his brothers' gang or take elusive back routes; otherwise he could expect, as he said, "a guaranteed beating."[1] To survive, he built himself up physically and took boxing lessons. Thereafter, when provoked, he used his boxing skills with a thoroughness that belied his unassuming appearance.

Harry worked days and attended law school at night, gaining admittance to the bar in 1896. Meanwhile, his fine bass-baritone voice made him a favorite soloist throughout Chicago.[2] At a dance he met Clara Doolittle, a graduate of Smith College fluent in French and German. Her notable ancestry included her grandfather, Senator James R. Doolittle, who as a presidential emissary visited the courts of Napoleon II and Alexander of Russia.[3]

postwar transition from big guns to guided missiles and other rocket-propelled weapons. He left an enduring mark on the navy's laboratory system, particularly through the promotion of military-scientific partnerships in research and development management.

Deak Parsons' naval career spanned the years 1918 to 1953, a full cycle from post–World War I to post–World War II. During that time the relationship between American science and the military changed from indifference to collaboration. The result was a weapons revolution that perfected radar and created the first mass-produced smart weapons, modern military rockets, guided missiles, and the atomic bomb. Parsons played active roles, both military and technical, in these major advances. His is a life that reveals both lessons and cautions concerning the use of science for military purposes. It is the life of a new kind of warrior.

Harry and Clara married during May 1900 and settled in the Evanston suburb of Chicago. Born on 26 November 1901, William Sterling Parsons entered a world largely free of war (the British and the Boers still had problems to settle). Few, if any, looking down upon the auburn-haired baby boy at Chicago Baptist Hospital could have foreseen the deadly world wars that lay ahead within the lifetime of the newborn child, or the pivotal role he would play in ending the worst of them. Indeed, as a boy, William seemed anything but a fighter. He was unusually shy and not at all aggressive.

Twenty months after William's birth, baby sister Clarissa arrived, also auburn haired, but by no means shy or passive. William and Clarissa grew up inseparable. While adults wondered about William's quiet ways, Clarissa saw "Boy," as she called him, as a master of adventure. He taught her how to place crossed pins on the track of the nearby electric railway. After the train passed, William would rush back to the track to pick up their scissorslike creations.[4] Even then he did not hesitate to take risks in the name of innovation.

Clarissa also saw her brother as a fount of wisdom. When she asked Boy what was on the other side of Lake Michigan, he solemnly responded, "Europe."[5] It was not the content but the profundity and brevity of Boy's pronouncements that impressed Clarissa.

If Europe seemed to be just on the other side of the lake, the Territory of New Mexico sounded to the Chicago siblings like a wilderness at the far ends of the earth. They heard relatives respond with shock when their father announced plans to move to the Territory. Clarissa and William heard agitated voices asking their father how he could contemplate taking his family to a place not even, to their way of thinking, in the United States.[6]

But the children received a different impression when Mr. Fishback the land promoter visited their home. Fishback sought to develop a community of orchard homes on irrigated land along the Pecos River at the town of Fort Sumner. He conjured up visions of apple, peach, and pear orchards flanked by grape-laden vineyards and rich fields of celery, sweet potatoes, and cantaloupes. This irrigated valley would make everybody rich.[7] Fishback's scheme fit Harry Parsons' dreams of future wealth and country living. These desires were strengthened as the family grew. On 9 July 1908 the third auburn-haired child,

Critchell, was born. Harry Parsons, who had had to fight for his own space in the big city, wanted his children to have the freedom of the new West.

The prospective move to the Territory hung over the family for two years. This and William's shyness seem to account for the decision not to enter him in elementary school until the move was completed. This meant that William at eight years of age would enter first grade with his six-year-old sister—a strange beginning indeed for the education of a future admiral.[8]

In the fall of 1909 Harry Parsons had one railway boxcar into which he had to fit the family's furniture and carriage, Queenie the carriage horse, a registered Jersey bull and cow, and several dozen cackling chickens—all the while leaving space for himself to sleep and cook.

Of the thousands of people enticed into New Mexico by the promotional claims of railroads, land developers, and the territorial government itself, few obtained as much value from the $35 emigrant boxcar fee as this urban lawyer in quest of his rural dream. Despite a diet consisting largely of eggs—very fresh—Harry appreciated the marvel of railroad travel and its advantages over the wagon trains of earlier western settlers. But after five days and nights with Queenie and the two reluctant bovine travelers, the would-be gentleman-rancher welcomed the whistle signaling the journey's end. The Fort Sumner depot with its red-tiled roof and poured-concrete walls was the town's architectural pride, having withstood the full might of a tornado a year earlier.[9]

Clara, the children, and Grandmother Doolittle traveled west in November, having given Harry time to rent a house and get settled. When the train pulled into Fort Sumner, William and Clarissa could see their father waiting for them with Queenie and the family carriage. The ensuing carriage ride over dirt roads and two-rut trails revealed no sign of the fabled riches to be plucked. Clara and Grandmother Doolittle looked out on the rubble of businesses destroyed in the tornado, a happenstance scattering of patched-up wood-frame homes, broad expanses of sage, and a pervading flatness crying for hills. Whatever misgivings the women may have had, they dutifully hid them. As Clarissa Fuller recalls, "It was a beautiful sunny day and all the way across the old [dry] lake my grandmother and my mother kept re-echoing each other, 'Oh what wonderful air, what wonderful air! Oh, yes, what wonderful air!'" The enchantment had begun.[10]

More than distance and latitude separated Chicago from Fort Sumner in 1909. A time warp set them apart, Chicago boldly charging into the twentieth century, Fort Sumner still drifting in the nineteenth. Automobiles were replacing horse-drawn buggies and wagons in Chicago, but horses still owned the streets of Fort Sumner. Here, "sanitation" meant outhouses; improved streets meant fewer ruts. Household water did not flow in pipes but was pumped from cisterns, dipped from irrigation ditches, or purchased from the water cart pulled by Mr. Edward's burro.[11]

The town had neither school bell nor even schoolhouse. Each year town authorities looked around for the empty house or store with the lowest rent. Volunteers then nailed up blackboards, attached roll-down maps, installed seats and desks—each with its own inkwell—and hung coatracks near the door. A pot-bellied wood stove provided heat, and a water pail with a single dipper served teacher and children alike.[12] In 1909 the transformation had occurred in a vacated harness shop. The school year was well under way that November when William, eight, and Clarissa, six, set out together for their first day in first grade. Their route went along the main canal, crossed the dike, and circled a field of mesquite and cactus. After passing several stores the inseparable brother and sister entered the former harness shop. New classmates, grades one through eight, stared.

The teacher asked of the newcomers, "And who do we have here?"

To which Clarissa promptly replied, "I am Clarissa and this is my brother William."

The teacher asked, "And can your brother speak for himself?"

"Oh, yes," Clarissa responded, "he talks when it's important."[13]

Harry rented the Old Garvey Place, a simple wood-frame house with its back door a dozen steps from a six-foot irrigation ditch and the front looking out over uninterrupted brushland as far as the eye could see.

The infinite view outside did little to solve the inside problems of fitting the married couple, grandmother, two children, and baby Critchell into three rooms: two bedrooms and a combined kitchen–living room. Harry and Clara accepted this, believing it to be temporary, and so it was for the next six years.

The five homes on the east side of the irrigation ditch teemed with children, none more important in William Parsons' youth than Kenneth Wilkinson, an exuberant and happy-go-lucky boy who was quite the opposite of the quiet and contemplative William.[14]

At school, William skipped grade after grade, catching up and then passing his own age group. Fellow pupils sought him for competitive teams in arithmetic, geography, and grammar. In his early teens he became the star of Fort Sumner spelling bees. After winning first prize in his district, William carried the hopes of the town to the 1914 State Spelling Contest at Albuquerque, only to lose by leaving the *e* out of *potatoes*.[15]

William's pursuit of knowledge went beyond the classroom to the canals, ditches, dams, pumps, and waterwheels that provided Fort Sumner's lifeblood. Fuller's waterwheel intrigued him most. He would point out to Clarissa how power was transferred from the burro walking in circles to the wheel that lifted pans of water from the canal into a collecting ditch.

Clarissa thought it more important to know about horses. In Pecos River country, a horse of one's own was nearly every child's dream. Her father, who rode a beautiful filly to his law office every day, understood. He bought ponies for William and Clarissa. But it soon became clear that William preferred making intricate structures with his Erector Set to riding and grooming his horse.[16]

Harry Parsons encouraged William and Clarissa in animal husbandry even as his own dream of fruit-laden orchards faded. Although the soil was fertile and the water adequate, there was a problem in the cumulative buildup of salts from irrigation. Harry Parsons expressed no regrets. He had a law practice—not large, but a living. A modest man with modest means, he was gaining the respect of the Fort Sumner community.

Clara Parsons did not gain community acceptance as readily. Her degree and mastery of languages meant nothing to the old-timers. One of these, Mrs. J. V. Stearns, said, "Mrs. Parsons thought . . . because she was from Chicago and there was a long line of blue blood back of her that the rest of us didn't amount to a whole lot."[17]

The Parsons family's early friends in Fort Sumner were mainly newcomers like themselves, but many of the newcomers moved on when their orchard dreams turned sour and the difficulties of raising a family under frontier conditions became apparent. The town was haunted by its legacy as the site of the Bosque Redondo Indian Reservation, which claimed the lives of thousands of Native Americans in the 1860s, and as the place where Billy the Kid was gunned down in 1881.[18] Nevertheless, Harry and Clara stayed, believing that a new era of prosperity and justice still lay ahead.

During the family's early years in Fort Sumner, the troublemakers were the North Fourth Street ruffians with their guns and booze. In opposition, Harry Parsons and other reformers had the force of community action, the law, and if need be their fists. The reformers purged the town of saloons, first by voting in local option, and later by campaigning for prohibition. As the sole lawyer among the reformers, Harry Parsons gained the enmity of saloon keepers and their customers along North Fourth Street.

One of these, described merely as "Mr. X" by Clarissa, once cast vile names upon Harry Parsons in a public area. Harry turned. "Don't say that again, Mr. X." The man, unfamiliar with Harry's boxing reputation in South Side Chicago, spit out an even stronger invective. Whereupon, Clarissa tells us, "Mr. X found himself flying out in the street from a powerful left to the jaw! As he crawled to the opposite sidewalk, and pulled himself up to sit on the curb, he looked very embarrassed and at the same time respectful of the polite Mr. Parsons."[19]

Harry Parsons strolled calmly on to his office. But he was no longer that outsider from Chicago; he was a man to be respected by everyone in Fort Sumner.

As William the child became Bill the youth, the world changed dramatically. In 1914 the assassination of Austria's Archduke Ferdinand triggered World War I. In 1915 Alexander Graham Bell made the first transcontinental telephone call. Also that year, Robert Goddard, whom Bill would later come to know, proposed a "rocket apparatus," and Albert Einstein postulated his general theory of relativity. World wars and technological advances would in time set the course of Bill Parsons' life, but the big change he faced in the summer of 1915 was the family's move from the Old Garvey Place to the Parsons homestead two and a half miles east of town. Although small by New Mexico standards, the 287-acre ranch provided space aplenty for the growing family. Besides the rambling eight-room main house, the outbuildings included a small house for Grandmother Doolittle.

Little brother Critchell, now an unmistakable presence in the family, was big framed for his seven years, a rough-and-tumble boy with none of the quiet ways that characterized Bill. Critch reveled in galloping his pony at a dangerous pace across the prairie and in releasing the bull when he saw his sister coming down the lane.[20]

Unlike Critch, who sought audiences for his antics, Bill preferred walks alone on the prairie with his .22 rifle in hand, relentlessly pursuing the homestead's enemies: chicken hawks and prairie rattlers. However, it was Bill the thinker, not Bill the hunter, whom Grandmother Doolittle nourished with her wisdom and love of literature. At the ranch, Bill and Clarissa slept in Grandmother Doolittle's little house. She read to them every evening, first a chapter of the Bible, then from a book of their choice, including Dickens, Scott, O. Henry, George Eliot, Jane Austen, Shakespeare, Harold Bell Wright, Robert Louis Stevenson, and Mark Twain. Although Bill became deeply absorbed in the readings, part of his interest lay elsewhere. He craved the drama of physical discovery: the secrets of electrical creation, schematics of engines, the wonders of the vacuum tube, the principles of flight.[21]

Bill learned more on his own and from his mother and Grandmother Doolittle than in the storefront schools of Fort Sumner, where teachers—some good, many not—came and went. In the winter of 1914–15 a teacher of great religious fervor regularly invited members of his church to speak to the class. This irked Clarissa, and when the speaker droned on past dismissal time, Clarissa shook her fist—and the teacher saw the gesture. That evening the enraged teacher called on Clara Parsons, saying, "That girl of yours has no manners. She's going to apologize, or not come back to school."[22]

Clara made her choice: Neither Clarissa nor Bill would go back to that school. Instead, through regular assignments and recitations they finished grade school at home. High school posed a more difficult problem, but Clara took it in stride. She obtained a position teaching English and Spanish at the Santa Rosa High School, forty-six miles north of Fort Sumner. In the fall of 1916 she left Critchell in the care of Harry and Grandmother Doolittle and rented a small house in Santa Rosa. There she entered both William and Clarissa as freshmen. Bill soon advanced to sophomore, then junior—all in the same year.

Bill's brilliance quickly caught the attention of his nineteen-year old mathematics teacher, Volney Poulson. Poulson encouraged Bill to take the Naval Academy exam, which Senator A. A. Jones had opened up to competition between his principal appointee and two alternates. Poulson, as a Jones appointee to West Point, took Bill under his wing, and the two of them studied mathematics together in preparation for their exams for the separate academies.[23]

In the spring of 1917 Bill Parsons, the class shrimp with less than a year's time in high school, journeyed to Roswell to take an exam for which sons of admirals prepared themselves by attending special preparatory schools. He completed the exam oblivious to the keenness of the competition. He saw only educational opportunity and, now that the United States had entered the war, a chance to serve. With his examination papers handed in there was nothing more he could do except return home and eat bananas and more bananas, his formula for gaining the weight he needed to meet the academy's minimum requirement.[24]

While awaiting results from the Naval Academy, Bill entered Fort Sumner High School as a senior in the fall of 1917. Clara had lost her teaching position. The senior class in the new Fort Sumner High School consisted of two burly males, two females, and the little Parsons boy with all the answers. "He really wasn't very popular in school because he was so much brighter," according to one old-timer, who added, "He was not an especially friendly person; he was rather withdrawn."[25] Bill did participate in the Spanish club, the literary society, and the yearbook staff. But he might have qualified as a complete square had not his chum Ken Wilkinson, now a junior, kept him from being completely solemn. The school year 1917–18 had serious overtones, with American troops beginning to join their European allies in deadly trench warfare against Germany. Bill and Ken experienced a surge of patriotism and joined in schoolyard denunciations, as stated in the yearbook, of the "insidious Hun and his damnable hate propaganda."[26]

Harry Parsons' purchase of a Model T Ford complicated family life, even though he himself eschewed the mechanical monster and continued to ride his filly back and forth to his law office. "Whenever the car was out at the house," Clarissa later reported, "it was a battle with the three of us. One had the key, one was in the car, and one was on the phone to our parents to straighten out on who was going where."[27]

When possible, Clara and the children combined their missions, cranked up the Ford, and went to town together. Such a day occurred in late June 1918. On this occasion they had made their last stop at the post office. Awaiting them was an impressive letter to William S. Parsons from the United States Naval Academy. Bill, then a half-year beyond his sixteenth birthday, had passed the Naval Academy exam; the principal appointee and first alternate had not. Clarissa and Critchell thought, "Oh my, this is going to be wonderful. He's going to come back in uniform!" But, she reported, "I remember my mother crying. That was the first time I ever saw her cry."[28]

Bill, who had never been further away from home than Albuquerque (125 miles), revealed his thoughts in action. Still underweight, he asked to stop at the general store on the way home: he had to pick up more bananas.

The slight sixteen-year-old boy traveling alone to Annapolis in the railroad coach felt none of the fear that had brought tears to his mother's eyes. By nature Bill Parsons was an optimist. He had a right to be: In eight years he had advanced through twelve grades of school. He had passed the Naval Academy exam at age sixteen. He wanted an education, a profession, a wartime patriotic opportunity, and adventure. All four were now within reach. What he lacked in weight and physical stature, he made up for in confidence—a quiet, inner self-esteem.

Bill arrived at the Naval Academy a week before the required reporting date. He used the time to eat as much as possible, including more bananas, before the physical examination. After stepping onto the storefront penny scales, he would telegraph his progress home.[29]

But on the appointed day, he failed to move the needle of the academy's precise scales to the required number of pounds. And stretch though he might, he could not bring the top of his head to the critical inch mark. The examiner expressed regret, but the requirement was firm; regulations were regulations.

Had Bill been as shy as some in Fort Sumner thought him, he would have accepted the examiner's pronouncement. But this was no time for shyness. The small, red-headed applicant from the western plains appealed. He presented his case to the officials: Being two years younger than most entering cadets, he was necessarily shorter and lighter; to be otherwise would not be normal. Being normal, he should be accepted. His logic impressed the authorities. On 21 June 1918 the examining board found "William Sterling Parsons a candidate from New Mexico in their opinion physically sound, well formed, of robust condition."[30]

Bill Parsons and nearly six hundred other entering cadets learned rather quickly that the academy grounds with their austere edifices of stone and massive green lawns should not be referred to as a campus but as "the Yard." They learned that upperclassmen graduating in June should be called not the senior class but "the First Class." Most important, they themselves were not freshmen but "plebes." One plebe writing for the *Lucky Bag* annual described their plight: "We lost our individuality and became laundry numbers." Moreover, the writer observed, "soon we were discovering that we had chests, and that whisk brooms were made to be worn out, and that our straight and narrow path was exceedingly narrow and geometric in shape." Compliance to the narrow path was enforced by the ubiquitous upperclassmen with their demands to "brace up" and "get your guts up and pull in that chin."[31]

The humbling experiences of plebe year provided new beginnings and new identities. Playing on the name Parsons, the midshipmen bestowed upon the serious young man from New Mexico the moniker Deacon.[32] Deacon soon contracted to Deke or Deak—a nickname that would cling to him even as he went to sea, to naval proving grounds, and into scientific laboratories. It followed him into World War II combat, to the nuclear climax of that war, to Operations Crossroads, and beyond.

By the midpoint of Deak's plebe year, it appeared unlikely that he would ever be engaged in war. The 11 November 1918 Armistice silenced the guns of the "war to end all wars." Germany was smashed. Ironically, Deak's class of 1922, whose graduates would feel the full brunt of the next world war, was identified as the "Disarmament Class."[33]

At Annapolis, Deak excelled in the sciences, led his class in Spanish, and relished laboratory experiments. He whizzed through the weekly exams in mathematics, which classmates described as "nightmares of semi-ann[ual] proportions."[34] Unlike Albert Michelson, the academy's all-time superstar in science, Deak Parsons had goals that went beyond an Annapolis science education, however.[35] He wanted an active career in the fleet. While he needed financial support for his education as much as Michelson had, Deak did not subordinate seamanship to other studies. He eagerly awaited the "Youngsters' Cruise," which would mark not only the end of plebe year and promotion to midshipman third class but also his first opportunity to go to sea.

Deak seems to have savored every moment of the Youngsters' Cruise. After the first night aboard ship in a hammock, he listened to the welcome command, "All Hands up anchor!" Along with several hundred other midshipmen, Deak watched the familiar structures of the Yard fade before his eyes, the distinctive dome of the chapel disappearing behind the fantail last. By nightfall the bow of the ship sliced through open sea, and a shipmate noted, "The decks had a sure enough heave."[36]

Sixteen-hour duty shifts, even with the stoking of furnaces and holystoning of decks, did not diminish the view of verdant Guantánamo Bay or the thrill of watching the flying fish in a seeming race with the ship as she approached the Virgin Islands. To celebrate the Fourth of July, the duty shifts were cut to twelve hours, and the midshipmen staged a pie-eating contest. The excitement of going through the Panama Canal was enhanced by what a shipmate described as the sensations of the cruise: a freshwater shower and liberty in Colón. Heavy weather on the return gave an unforgettable lesson on the power of an angry sea over man and his floating machines.[37]

At New York City, Deak had four days and nights in which to see everything from Coney Island to the Follies. But he found more pleasure in observing the coaling of the ship in Boston and the firing of its big guns in the drill grounds of the Chesapeake.

At the end of the cruise, as the chapel dome reemerged on the shore of the Severn, the new midshipman third class from New Mexico had gained his sea legs. Now he was truly a sailor.

Deak returned home on furlough, filled with the excitement of the cruise and his new position in the world. Clarissa and Critch were quite entranced, at first, with their big brother's exploits. To learn what a sailor's life was like, they even accepted the role of crew and went along with mock commands. But after two mornings of holystoning the kitchen floor and polishing Deak's brass buttons, they mutinied.[38]

•

The class of 1922 produced the two admirals most involved in the beginnings of today's nuclear navy: William S. "Deak" Parsons and Hyman George "Rickie" Rickover.

Rickover, born in Russia in January 1900, was two years older than Parsons. Rickover's father, a tailor, brought his family to Chicago about the time Harry Parsons was preparing to move his family from the Windy City to the Territory of New Mexico. Both youths hungered for knowledge and knew that their parents did not have money to send them to college. Thus, scoring well on the Naval Academy entrance examination was important to each. They understood that anything less than 2.5 out a possible 4.0 on any subject would disqualify them. Their scores:

	Parsons	Rickover
English	2.9	3.4
Geography	2.9	3.0
History	2.6	2.7
Arithmetic	3.4	3.8
Geometry	3.5	2.6

Slightly lower scores in history might, ironically, have changed history itself. By their third year, Parsons' and Rickover's class standings (among 562 students) were:

	Parsons	Rickover
General merit	34	90
Ordnance	174	53
Navigation	23	167
Math	14	200
Electrical engineering	81	70
Military character	118	415
Practice cruise	219	414
English	211	18
Languages	5	52

While Parsons' high standing in math, languages (notably Spanish, in which he was fluent), and navigation (his favorite subject) fit the expected pattern, his midlevel position in ordnance, especially in comparison with Rickover, is hard to fathom for the officer who would one day be described as the "premier ordnance expert of the modern navy."[39]

For his four years at the academy, Parsons stood 48th in conduct out of a graduating class of 539. All of his demerits were for "minor offenses" except:

> Non military conduct; talking in ranks
> Delinquent at period recitation
> Irreverent conduct
> Conduct to the prejudice of good order and discipline

Rickover stood 107th in conduct among 539. His demerits for other than "minor offenses" were:

> Violation of study restriction
> Talking after taps
> On roof of Bancroft Hall
> Neglect of duty (allowing smoking in room)
> Conduct to the prejudice of good order and discipline
> Direct disobedience to orders[40]

Neither cadet starred in sports. Deak held his own for four years on the Wrestling B-Squad, where he had the reputation for being "as persevering as a starved mosquito." But for outright fun he appeared regularly at the tennis courts, where he outwitted rather than outplayed his opponents. A colleague acknowledged, "You can't beat Deak when he uses his 'mental tennis.'"[41] Rickie, however, was described in the *Lucky Bag* as "neither a star on the gridiron nor a terror in the pool." In his later acerbic years Admiral Rickover expressed his dim view of academy sports: "Abolish them as interferences to the technical studies needed by the navy." Sports were not the only targets of Rickover's later attacks upon the academy (to him, "East Coast Disneyland").[42] His vitriolic comments suggest resentments smoldering from cadet years. If so, they stand in marked contrast to the attitude toward the Yard held by Parsons, whom the *Lucky Bag* described as "convivial."[43]

By his eighteenth birthday, as Deak had predicted, his height and weight were well beyond the entrance requirement. This physical transformation did not go unnoticed by student editors of the *Lucky Bag*, who wrote, "Upon entering this land of the hereafter, no one mistook 'Deacon' for the spirit of Apollo reawakened." They then explained, "The cactus of his native haunts did not nourish him as well as the cobblestones of Crab town [Annapolis], seemingly, for 'Deacon' is now a magnificent example of auburn-covered might and power."[44]

Along with the new physique came a broader sense of acceptance and camaraderie than he had enjoyed in the limited circles of high school. He still listened more than he spoke, but when he wanted to make a point he did so, according to classmates, with "a well-oiled, double-jointed tongue." When it came to verbal sparring, whether over social issues or a controversial breech mechanism for a 12-inch gun, none enjoyed it more than Deak and his roommate, Thomas "T. B." Hill, a lanky Colorado youth who "shined in the field of argument."[45] Deak's early shyness still took over in the presence of young women, possibly as a result of the limited social life he had had during his brief time in high school. Whatever the cause, Deak's "well-oiled, double-jointed tongue" tightened up in the presence of the fairer sex. While T. B. and other friends invited young ladies to academy social events, he stood by.[46]

To the benefit of Deak Parsons and classmates, the post–World War I navy of 1921 had the advanced ships it had needed but lacked in 1917. This was the result of the historical lag between the onset of national emergencies and the response to them. Instead of taking the summer cruise of 1921 on aging ships of the Practice Squadron, the top three classes embarked on five first-class battleships of the Atlantic Fleet. Deak, now a midshipman lieutenant (jg) and member of the vaunted First Class, reported aboard the USS *Minnesota*.

Departing on 4 June, the impressive armada steamed for Christiana, Norway, via the Azores and North Scotland. Before returning that September, the battleships flew the American flag in Lisbon, Gibraltar, and Guantánamo. Deak Parsons' placement as tenth in merit out of 540 attests to superior seamanship.[47]

The battleship cruise marked the ascendancy of the class of 1922 to the elite of the Yard, the ranking regimental officers. In this final year Deak stood in the top 10 percent in ordnance, navigation, marine engineering, and language. He rated high in military character. He maintained his high position in the order of merit among the 539 midshipmen in the class of 1922 despite the fact that he spent much of his time in the last year tutoring classmates rather than concentrating on his own studies.[48]

At six feet, Deak Parsons stood tall physically as well as academically among the others in his class. Nevertheless, he could expect to be judged by his classmates as being in the bottom 10 percent of the class socially if he did not have a date for the June Ball. The pressure increased as the months passed and talk increased of graduation, visiting parents, the year-end regimental parade, and the ball—described by the *Lucky Bag* as "the sun that radiates all the joy of June Week."[49]

Deak joined academy-sponsored dance classes, and presumably he met some young ladies there, but he shied away from tendering an invitation. Just as time was running out, he received an invitation to visit relatives in Washington, D.C. There he met two sisters, distant cousins of his. "Deak," according to a family account, "was quite taken by the younger, prettier of the two sisters."[50] He asked their mother if he could invite the daughter to June Week and the ball.

Accounts vary as to how the plan went awry. One puts the blame on Deak, saying he confused the names of the girls, and even though the older sister knew better, she insisted that the invitation bearing her name gave her the right to attend. Another account accuses the mother of purposely misinterpreting Deak's invitation so that she could send the older sister. In any case, when Deak went to greet his date he was astonished to see the older sister step off the train. Yet as an officer and a gentleman he contained his disappointment and entered arm in arm with his not favorite cousin into the Rigging Loft of Luce Hall for what was to have been the big social event of his four years at the academy.

Fortunately for Deak, his father came for the graduation. Harry Parsons helped entertain the young lady, accompanying her to special services in the chapel, Presentation of Colors, graduation ceremonies, and the Regimental Dress Parade.[51]

Looking down the parade ground, Harry Parsons must have taken great pride in watching Midshipman Lt. (jg) William Parsons of the Third Battalion—tall, sturdy, posture perfect—marching at the head of his platoon. Harry knew the long road the shy boy from Chicago and Fort Sumner had traveled to reach this point. He also must have known that this was not an ending but a beginning.

Battleship Navy

*He was serious about his business [on the Idaho] but with it all
he was an excellent shipmate.*
Rear Adm. Alfred M. Granum, USN (Ret.)

The two roommates, William S. Parsons and T. B. Hill, must have rejoiced at the sight of their orders. As ensigns, not only would they be reporting to a first-rate battleship, the USS *Idaho*, they would be doing so together. The *Idaho*, then moored at Port Angeles, Washington, and due for repairs at Bremerton, had been built during World War I but, like the ensigns themselves, not commissioned until after the Armistice.

On 1 August 1922, Deak and T. B., dressed in their blues, faced the quarterdeck of the *Idaho* and saluted. They then turned and faced the officer of the deck, again saluting. Each in succession called out his name and the words "Request permission to come aboard, sir."[1]

Their earlier cruise as midshipmen on the *Minnesota* had been practice; this was real. The *Idaho* was their own "battle wagon." We can imagine the two friends quickly checking out their quarters and stowing personal gear, then rushing topside to examine firsthand the main battery with the big guns that set this and other battleships apart from all other ships of the fleet. Reaching out fifty feet beyond the massive turrets, the big guns of this particular floating fortress were twelve 14-inch Mark IVs, each capable of propelling a 1,500-pound projectile twenty miles. The remaining armaments included a secondary battery of fourteen 5-inch guns, the antiaircraft battery of four 3-inch guns, and a special section with twelve torpedoes. Capable of delivering mighty wallops, the *Idaho* was built to survive them as well. Plates of hardened steel more than a foot thick protected her waistline from torpedoes and the gun turrets from shells. With a length of 624 feet and beam of 97.5 feet, the *Idaho* accommodated a crew of 1,080—equivalent to about half the adult male population of Fort Sumner. When Deak and T. B. arrived there were fifty-three officers, of which more than half were fellow ensigns.[2]

The battleship, the heart of the postwar navy, was the product of over 150 years of evolution that started with the ship of the line in the American Revolution. Technology, periodically goaded by war, changed that simple wooden sailing ship with a hundred or so smoothbore muzzle-loaded cannon into one of the most complicated pieces of machinery ever devised. The ship of the line changed with the introduction of steam power, metal hulls, bigger and bigger guns, thicker and thicker armor, smokeless powder, explosive shells, breech loading, gun rifling, range finders, fire control, and rotating turrets. And as far as Deak, T. B., or anyone could tell, the battleship would continue to evolve.

Deak and T. B.'s excitement over the *Idaho*'s weaponry did not extend to the ship's voyaging. In their first two and a half years on the battleship, the *Idaho* ranged no further north of her home base of San Pedro, California, than Port Angeles, Washington, and no further south than Valparaíso, Chile.

In the absence of an enemy, the navy's senior officers tried to keep the fighting spirit alive through training exercises and by staging gunnery competitions among ships. As Rear Adm. Alfred Granum, then an *Idaho* ensign, recalled, "We were fighting for supremacy among ourselves." Citing his *Idaho* duty with Parsons, Granum said, "There was target practice, fleet maneuvers, ship exercises of various sorts, nothing really very exciting, nothing really strenuous either."[3]

The tedium of routine exercises could be measured in the officers' wardroom, which served at once as officers' mess, retreat, and informal communications center. Here Parsons and the other officers exchanged the latest word on pending orders, general scuttlebutt, leave plans, conflicts among the crew, and any unusual actions on the part of the ship's captain, J. R. P. Pringle.

Wardroom talk was not always idle chatter. Officers like Deak wanted knowledge beyond their own areas of expertise. They liked to know how many of the nine boilers, how much steam, and how many revolutions of the propeller shaft it took to maintain the ship's standard speed of 10 knots. How much more to go full speed at 21 knots? These were important details in the battleship navy. The rate at which 169 firemen fed coal to the fires affected not only a ship's performance in a battle exercise but also the closely watched peacetime operating costs.[4]

With no enemy on the horizon, wardroom talk turned easily from external threats to internal misdeeds—in particular, any unseamanlike conduct among the crew. The officers discussed the pros and cons of Captain Pringle's strong disciplinary actions. The arguments have been lost in time, but the ship's log documents the infractions Captain Pringle brought before the mast and the punishments rendered. A few random examples tell the story:

Concealing venereal disease: solitary confinement for twenty-four hours
Absent on leave for twenty-eight hours: solitary on bread and water for three days
Gambling: twenty-four hours extra duty
Disrespect to officer over the telephone: five days solitary on bread and water
Asleep while posted as brig sentry: twenty-four hours solitary on bread and water
Under the influence of liquor aboard ship: solitary on bread and water for five days
Theft, possession of another man's clothes: summary courts martial.[5]

All was not peaceful in the peacetime navy.

Ensign Parsons had barely gotten into the ship's routine before finding himself on a train headed for Fort Sumner, jarred by the news of his mother's death. Stepping off the train at Fort Sumner's red-roofed depot, he could as well have appeared on a navy recruitment poster: dark blue blouse neatly formed around buttoned shirt collar, black tie, sleeves carrying the gold star of a line officer and the single gold band of ensign, the white-topped garrison cap with gold band and black visor sitting squarely upon his head with the prescribed forward tilt.

If Deak's appearance in full dress uniform did not impress the cowhands herding cattle into the feedlot adjacent to the station, it more than impressed Clarissa and Critch upon meeting their brother at the train that Saturday morning of 9 December 1922. But the solemn nature of the occasion tempered the joy of reunion. Cerebrospinal meningitis had claimed Clara Parsons' life before she would ever be able to see her son return home as a tall, confident naval officer.[6]

Deak hid his sorrow beneath a shell of stoicism. He did not cry, not even for the mother whose grit had cleared away the obstacles to his early education. The same kind of emotional restraint did not, however, apply to Deak's younger brother, Critchell, now a fourteen-year-old high-school freshman. Unlike Deak at the same age, Critch was large, physically and emotionally. The mother's death appeared to stun Critchell and to turn his life into turmoil.[7]

During the funeral furlough, Deak and Clarissa rediscovered each other as young inquiring adults. They now shared philosophical observations of the world beyond the Fort Sumner bend in the Pecos. Immersed in long talks, they shared memories, ideas, and feelings. Through Clarissa's recollections of these discussions we have entrée into thoughts and feelings otherwise hidden behind Deak Parsons' reticence.

"I wonder what future there is for the armed services," he said to Clarissa. "I wonder if I should leave the service. I wonder." He spoke of becoming a banker. But then as if in argument with himself he said, "No, I'd never be happy out of uniform. Besides that, I was educated by the navy and I've had a wonderful chance and that's my life." Listening, Clarissa concluded, "He loved the sea. He was hooked by it."[8]

On learning how Deak had to buckle under to one particularly unreasonable officer, Clarissa told him, "Well I think you ought to smash your way through without regard to him." "No, that isn't the way to do it," Deak responded. "No, you have your own way of moving calmly because it is known to the highest authority always that that's a difficult person and he is simply a challenge in your path to see if you can get along under trying circumstances." He added, "You don't fight, you just go on your own way; don't make an issue of it. That hurts him more than anything else." Parsons believed that the higher authorities would recognize the junior officers who met the challenges in their paths.[9]

As an ensign, Deak Parsons knew when to bend. In the years ahead he would learn when not to.

Deak Parsons' mild, unassertive ways did not keep him from standing out among the junior officers on the *Idaho*. As reported by Granum, "Parsons was not plugging for Parsons," yet his superiors recognized him as an "outstanding young officer extremely interested in his profession."[10] They put him in charge of the number one turret of the main battery of 14-inch guns, the behemoths of the battleship.

Coordinating the complex functions necessary to load, aim, fire, and refire projectiles approaching the height of a man and weighing 1,500 pounds must have appealed to the former master builder of Erector Sets. From the turret officer's booth, Deak controlled activities going all the way from the upper deck to the powder room below the third deck. Beyond directing the hoisting and loading of shells and powder, he coordinated with the fire-control officer the training and elevating of his two monster guns. Deak's number one turret distinguished itself in competitions between gunnery teams, between turrets, between ships, and between battle groups in mock warfare. "He did," as Granum reported, "a first-class job on his duty assignment." But what distinguished Parsons, according to Granum, was that he "looked beyond normal practices to methods of improving operations."[11]

Parsons' passion for improving gunnery triggered his analysis of the 14-inch main battery's chronic dispersion problem. Projectiles fired under the same conditions and at the same elevations and azimuths created an unaccountably large dispersion pattern. In peacetime exercises the broad dispersion could mean the difference between winning and losing a pennant. In real battle it could mean the difference between victory and defeat.

Although the new skipper of the *Idaho*, Capt. W. S. Crosley, was more approachable than Pringle, it still took "a bit of nerve," as interpreted by Granum, for Parsons to "bring up a proposition to an officer of maybe thirty years' service who perhaps should have seen it himself. And here it comes from a junior officer of one year's service."[12] But none of this deterred Parsons from doing what should be done.

Parsons' approach to the problem is as revealing as his initiative in undertaking it. In his own quiet, analytical way he studied dispersal patterns recorded in the past and identified the factors that might be contributing to the disquieting results. He systematically studied every step from the measurement of powder loads to main-battery fire-control adjustments to the final command to fire. He sought ideas from officers and crew. "As a good shipmate," Granum observed, "Deak was able to work with others and avoid contention." At the same time, "he was very painstaking and patient in carrying through on the objective."[13] Quite as important, he did not hesitate to question longstanding gunnery and fire-control methods.

Time has buried Parsons' written recommendations, but legend has it that Captain Crosley adopted them and thereby improved the Idaho's gunnery scores, whereupon Parsons prepared a written analysis and drafted a letter to the Navy Department for the captain's signature recommending that the new procedures be adopted for main-battery control throughout the navy. As Granum observed, this kind of initiative was "not too common from a junior officer." The extent to which Parsons' procedures were adopted is not documented. What is clear is the mettle the soft-spoken junior officer from New Mexico showed in presenting them.[14]

Deak Parsons, now a lieutenant junior grade, welcomed the Idaho's departure in April 1925 for war games in Hawaii. War games meant action night and day for Lieutenant Parsons and his gunners. Yet for all the tactical maneuvering of friendly forces against "enemy" ships and submarines, the war games remained games. There was little in the international climate of 1925 to suggest that the guns of the Idaho would ever be fired in anger. The United States had the largest navy in the world, and its former ally, Great Britain, was a close match. By international agreement the only other major navy, that of Japan, was to remain at three-fifths the size of each of the two main sea powers. U.S. officers had no crystal ball to warn them of the consequences of Benito Mussolini's consolidation of Italian fascist power in 1925 or of Adolf Hitler's reorganization of the Nazi party that same year.

Neither Italy, Germany, nor Japan claimed Deak's attention. War games completed, the Idaho steamed to Samoa, Australia, and New

Zealand. Writing Clarissa as the *Idaho* headed back to Pearl Harbor, Deak mentioned New Zealand's beauty and fine climate, but he had more to say about the dancing of the young ladies of Auckland—"not a poor dancer in all of them." With the braggadocio of an older brother to a sister, he dropped names of young ladies to give the impression, at least, that he was something of a Casanova in the Pacific. He wrote that he looked forward to shore leave in Honolulu: "It will be fine if Veda is there, but I hear Bertie is back from Europe so California will be nice too."[15] And although we learn no more about either Veda or Bertie, we do know that Deak Parsons' early shyness around young women disappeared somewhere among the Pacific ports.

An unexpected detour interrupted the *Idaho*'s voyage home.

The battleship was dispatched to the aid of Comdr. John Rodgers and crew, whose seaplane had been forced down by engine problems during their attempted California-to-Hawaii flight. With the plane hoisted aboard the *Idaho*, Rodgers joined the ship's officers for the remaining voyage to San Francisco. We can assume that this pioneer naval aviator's presence stimulated wardroom talk on the controversy stirred up by the Army Air Service's Brig. Gen. William "Billy" Mitchell: the battleship versus the airplane. Mitchell proclaimed that the airplane would not only dominate future warfare but would make the battleship obsolete. Navy traditionalists viewed the airplane as good for observation and limited tactical use, but not a decisive weapon. Any traditionalists on the *Idaho* might well have argued that if an airplane could not make its way to a fixed location like Hawaii, it could hardly be expected to seek out and destroy a warship on the move.

Parsons, as best we can determine, represented a middle view. He saw the airplane as a growing threat to the battleship. But rather than scuttle the battleships, he wanted to give them improved defensive weapons. This was not something that could be done by shipboard tinkerers like himself. It would have to come out of the ordnance experimental establishment ashore.

To Harry Parsons, his son was not "Deak" and certainly not "the Deacon." As he confided to a friend, "It annoys Bill for me to refer to him as Lieutenant Bill but still I do it and so I say Lieutenant Bill is at San Pedro again."[16] The townfolk of Fort Sumner understood Harry's fatherly pride in Lieutenant Bill's world travels and war games, for in lauding Bill, Harry hid a falling out with Critchell.

Critchell's problems had surfaced soon after Harry, at age fifty-two, remarried during the Christmas holidays of 1924. The twenty-eight-year-old bride, Grace Hallmark, had won the hearts of her grade-school pupils and school board director Harry as well, but not that of her burly stepson. As a high-school student in revolt, Critchell was more than the newlyweds could handle. Neighbors viewed him as Deak's opposite: "a very charming, outgoing operator . . . a stinker of the first water . . . high strung and lively."[17]

Unlike Deak, who had been slow in early physical growth, Critchell at sixteen was well on his way to his eventual six feet four inches, and solid all the way. He had the same red hair and brown eyes as Deak and Clarissa and, like them, a keen mind. But as a teenager he went through a succession of difficulties. Deak's letters encouraged him to go back and finish high school. Succeeding in that, Deak, along with Clarissa, advised college. But after entering the University of New Mexico in 1924, Critchell dropped out and went into a succession of jobs as oil-well roughneck, filling-station attendant, truck driver, bridge construction laborer, and coal miner.[18]

At the same time that Critchell was trying to find his niche, Deak too was seeking a new sense of direction for his life. With the *Idaho* home-ported in San Pedro, there was a great deal of time to ponder the future. By this time he was in charge of main-battery fire control and had long since learned everything the *Idaho* had to teach. After five years on the same battleship, Deak seemed to float unguided in his career. He had not defined any particular goals of his own other than to serve the navy well and to climb the command ladder as best he could. As yet no scientific mentor had opened a vision of a special role for him in a new technologically advanced navy.

Still single at twenty-five, Deak had no steady bearing in his personal life. No young woman in his ports of call had yet sparked a desire for wife and family.

All this would change with Deak Parsons' orders of May 1927 to the Naval Postgraduate School, Annapolis.

·4·

Romance and Weapons

He could stand his ground either aboard ship or with the
scientific community in his own right as an equal.
Dr. Charles C. Bramble

By blending a little imagination with available facts, we find
Deak Parsons walking through downtown Annapolis on Monday morning, 22 May 1927, on his way to the Naval Postgraduate School. Cobbled streets, brick row houses, the sail-filled bay, and nautical shops are all familiar sights from his midshipman days. They still hold their charm for him as a full lieutenant seasoned by sea duty and now selected for ordnance postgraduate training.

Passing the sentries at the academy's north gate, he enters "the Yard" to find it much as he left it five years before. Bancroft Hall, where he had roomed, still maintains its outer solemnity, the seawall its strollers, the domed chapel its prayers for persons at sea, the statue of Tecumseh its wish makers. Yet the Yard is not the same. The tennis courts no longer ring with the laughter of T. B. Hill and others of the class of 1922. The stiffened plebes saluting Deak appear surprisingly young.

However, it is not the plebes but the morning newspaper headlines that could have made Deak deeply conscious of his age and of a new maturity in the world. They proclaim, "Lindy Lands in Paris." Only two years before, in the wardroom of the *Idaho,* Deak had heard Comdr.

John Rodgers claim that radically improved aircraft engines would soon make oceanic flights a reality. Rodgers also predicted that the airplane would transform commerce and change the character of warfare. Lindbergh's flight now dramatized Rodgers' message.

Deak, like Lindbergh, was twenty-five years old, but he had not yet fixed the compass of his life on a specific bearing. His desire for learning had prompted him to request postgraduate training, but his assignment to ordnance was probably a matter of chance. He could as easily have been assigned to advanced studies in navigation (a favorite subject), naval architecture, or, like Hyman Rickover, electrical engineering.

Ordnance is a bland name for what are mankind's most vicious products: weapons and materials for war. Deak Parsons had no illusions about that. But he was among those who believed that until mankind learned how to avert war it would be necessary to give the nation's servicemen the best weapons American ingenuity could provide. He understood that valor and tactics could be pointless if fighting men had inferior arms. He embraced the opportunity the ordnance PG school gave him to become a line officer knowledgeable in making and improving guns, ammunition, mines, torpedoes, and bombs as well as in providing countermeasures against these weapons. In the context of the time, he had no reason to believe that the weapon development process would change in the next two decades from evolutionary to revolutionary—that is, from the piecemeal improvement of existing weapons to the application of new technology to create radically advanced ones.

Deak and the other five ordnance PG students spent the lion's share of their time in the classroom of professor of mathematics C. C. Bramble, whose courses comprised the heart of the ordnance curriculum: mathematics, ordnance engineering, mechanics, and ballistics.[1] From the start, Bramble recognized that Lieutenant Parsons topped the group not only in physical height but in mental stature as well. As he later stated, "Everybody [academy professors] who had this group of officers remembers Parsons as the brilliant one in the group." As in earlier classrooms, Deak could still shine without arousing the resentment of his peers. In Bramble's opinion, Deak's classmates simply recognized that "he was out in front."[2]

Deak's interest in ballistics did not stop at the end of the school day. Fresh from the *Idaho*, he saw relationships between ballistics theory and the gunnery problems he had experienced in the fleet. When the lectures opened up fleet problems, Deak would spend his evenings working out mathematical solutions. The next day he would hand Professor Bramble a long handwritten analysis to review. Although the following extract from one of Parsons' responses conveys little about the specific technical problem involved, it does give the flavor of the continuing ballistics dialogue between graduate student and professor:

> I started on this problem when I first noticed . . . in an analysis of dispersion from near corrected ranges. . . . I had the hunch this might be explained by the assumption that p does not multiply the whole of the resistance . . . so I fitted the Sommerfield expression to the Gu tables and found a remarkably close fit. . . . Of course this throws light on the magnitude of the additional correction for temperature. . . . So now I am attempting to integrate the expression. So far I am floored by this, but you may see a way to disentangle it.[3]

Deak's immersion in ballistics and mathematics was like a baptism, but in entering this new faith he did not abandon his family ties. He maintained a regular correspondence with his father, whose letters carried a common refrain: Deak should marry. To support his case, Harry let it be known that despite the twenty-four-year age difference between himself and the former Grace Hallmark, they had a blissful, caring marriage. And they found great joy in their new son, baby "Bobs" (Harry Parsons Jr.)—Bill's younger brother by two dozen years. Harry also touted the marriage of Clarissa to Rice Fuller. They had just had their second child and were living happily at Mound City, Missouri.[4]

Harry amplified Deak's slightest mention of the fairer sex. He informed a friend, "Bill altho a haughty Naval Lieutenant, taking his P.G. at Annapolis after five years at sea, is quite like the traditional sailor with sweethearts at various ports. He makes no boast of this but every so often I hear in glowing terms of some young and beautiful and learned and charming female person at a new location." Deak's latest, according to Harry, was the "bright and beautiful red-haired Marian (a person no more familiar to Harry than today's reader)."[5]

In fact, Harry's knowledge of his son's amours was meager. When he wrote of red-haired Marian, he had not heard of Deak's involvement in the Jack Crenshaw wedding.

Deak's friendship with Jack Crenshaw went back to his second year at the academy, when Jack was one of the upperclassmen Deak tutored in Spanish. Now Jack was one of the five other ordnance postgraduate students with him at Annapolis. While Deak spent most of his weekends in study and at the Yard's tennis courts, Jack took off in pursuit of a serious romantic interest.

Deak was now a poised junior officer with only a small trace of the shyness that had inhibited him in his midshipman years. He no longer hesitated to join lady visitors in doubles' matches when the opportunity arose. Among the visitors was an attractive, vivacious young woman from Norfolk called Martha. On inquiry Deak found she was the daughter of Rear Adm. Wat Cluverius, a name that could stiffen the spine of anyone from the class of 1922, for in their day at the Yard, Admiral (then Captain) Cluverius was the commandant of midshipmen. Deak failed to follow up on his inquiries about the striking young lady from Norfolk.

In the fall of 1928, after the ordnance postgraduates had entered their second year, Jack Crenshaw informed his classmates of his plans to marry and asked Deak to be his best man. It would be no ordinary wedding. The bride was an admiral's daughter, and not just any admiral but one known for the grand style with which he performed social functions, especially those for his daughters. Jack was marrying Betty Cluverius, daughter of the commandant of the Norfolk Navy Yard, Admiral Cluverius. Betty's sister, Martha, would be maid of honor.

Martha Cluverius at twenty-four had her mother's beauty and her father's geniality. Her gracious ways had been shaped by her navy childhood, four years at a girls' boarding school, and four years of Vassar. Her familiarity with etiquette and social customs included the prescribed ritual and pomp of a military wedding. She recognized that as maid of honor she would be showcased with the best man.

When Deak and Martha were introduced at the rehearsal, he reminded her that they had met before. But what had been memorable to him had not registered with her. She later commented, "He said he played tennis with me several times, but I'd play tennis with anybody who would play tennis, you know, and I didn't know him from any other young officer."[6]

Following the military-wedding ritual of the time, Martha preceded Betty and her father down the aisle of the Norfolk navy chapel, flanked on either side by the ushers, all young officers in fresh-pressed dress uniforms.[7] As best man, Deak stood out among his fellow, not merely in height but in poise. Martha could see the natural curl in his auburn hair, the firmness of jaw, the commanding eyes. Although Deak did not have the heavy frame Martha associated with athletes, she noted that he "carried himself well."[8]

As best we can determine, the bridal chorus of Wagner's *Lohengrin* filled the chapel during the wedding procession. When Jack and Betty Crenshaw stepped forward as man and wife to lead the recessional out of the chapel, Deak and Martha moved together behind them. Unlike the bride and groom, Deak and Martha did not pass under the arch formed at the head usher's command, "Officers draw swords." Instead of vows, they exchanged approving glances. Their lives were now destined never to be the same.

Shortly before her sister's wedding, Martha Cluverius had had to face reality. For all her knowledge of the arts and her training in social amenities, she had no job skills. Charm alone was not enough; employers wanted typing. On her father's advice she enrolled in a Norfolk typing class. But after her sister's marriage, Martha found that her typing exercises could not compete with the glowing descriptions she received from Betty of Annapolis social activities. Martha joined Betty and Jack for one visit, and then another, and another, and another. Finally it became apparent that it was Deak, not sisterly companionship, that lured her to Annapolis.[9]

Martha's growing involvement with Deak concerned her mother, Nan Cluverius. Nan had nothing against the lieutenant himself, but she opposed Martha's marrying any military officer. Uniforms were fine, but enough was enough. As the daughter of Adm. William Sampson, mastermind of Spanish-American War strategy, Nan had been brought up "in the navy." She had married navy. Her son was navy. Daughter Betty was now a navy wife. Martha heard all too often Nan's refrain, "I wish somebody in this family would marry out of the navy." Martha knew that this someone was supposed to be her. But Nan's campaign was hopeless. As Martha clarified later, "I was crazy about the navy. I wouldn't even have considered anybody but a naval officer." In his own good-natured way, the admiral understood Martha's frequent visits to Crab Town. When the typing school sent him cards detailing Martha's absences and bearing the notation "Where was Martha?" he collected them and sent them all—with the question— to Lt. William Parsons.[10]

Neither the admiral's jibes nor Nan's wishes for a civilian son-in-law cooled the romance. When Harry Parsons got wind of it, he encouraged the affair from a distance. And he was overjoyed when informed that the wedding was set for November 1929. In a letter to a friend, Harry extolled the excellence of his son's choice, "daughter of Rear Admiral Cluverius, and by the way a Vassar girl"—a boast he no doubt broadcast in the social circles of Fort Sumner.[11]

Harry shared other news. Standard Oil's wildcat well outside Fort Sumner raised dreams of black gold and prosperity—not unlike his earlier visions of fruit orchards. Grandmother Doolittle celebrated her eighty-fifth birthday "in full possession of her faculties and mental activities."[12]

Dreams of oil being no substitute for money, Harry could not attend Deak and Martha's wedding. In every other way the ceremony, again in the Norfolk chapel, was flawless; even Nan agreed to that. This time Deak and Martha exchanged the vows while Jack and Betty stood by as best man and matron of honor. This time, when the head usher commanded "Officers draw swords," it was Deak and Martha who went through the steel-bladed arch. Martha had her officer, and Deak a new sense of personal direction.

As a newlywed, Martha was keenly disappointed when it appeared that she would not be able to join Deak at his next duty station, the Naval Proving Ground, Dahlgren, Virginia. The postgraduate student officers were to be housed together in the bachelor officers' quarters, in those years a male domain.

When Admiral Cluverius heard of his daughter's chagrin, he told her not to worry; he would call Capt. Herbert F. Leary, the commanding officer at Dahlgren. Herb was a longtime friend; he would find a way for the couple to be together. But while Deak desperately wanted Martha with him, he did not want his father-in-law interceding. As Martha began to recognize, Deak was "on the whole pretty 'regulation.'" He lived, she said, "pretty much by the book" and stood opposed to preferential treatment, especially for himself. Martha recognized that the difference between father and husband went beyond age and rank. Her father was very outgoing and social, whereas Deak held himself in reserve. Her father had a lot more fun out of life than did Deak, who "thought life was pretty serious and we'd better get on with it."[13] In this case, "getting on with it" meant Deak taking an advance trip in January 1930 to Dahlgren, where he met with Captain Leary. Based on Martha's account, the conversation went somewhat as follows:

Deak began, "I know this is an unusual request, but Dahlgren is an unusual place. The idea of a married couple staying in the BOQ at a regular navy base would certainly be out of the question. But Dahlgren with its experimental mission and isolation is not like any other naval base." After listening to the polite, intent lieutenant, the captain responded, "When you have married couples you have children and I absolutely will not have children running amok in the officers' quarters." Deak replied that he and Martha had no children, and in five months there could be none. After weighing regulations against the young officer's plea, Captain Leary suggested, "Perhaps your wife could take the job of running the BOQ. In that case she should live in the BOQ."[14]

Martha welcomed the solution. Like her father, she enjoyed life's ironies, and it amused her that she would be starting married life in a BOQ. The thought added to her excitement about going to Dahlgren.

Dahlgren was a big word in the life of any officer in naval ordnance. It had four meanings: officer, guns, town, and proving ground.

The officer, Rear Adm. John Dahlgren, was to nineteenth-century weaponry what Deak Parsons would become to the twentieth century, the naval ordnance leader of his time.[15] "Dahlgrens," as John Dahlgren's 9-, 10-, and 11-inch guns were known, came out of that officer's systematic study of the forces that operated within a gun barrel when fired.[16] As the best and most reliable smoothbores of their time, these bottle-shaped guns dominated naval armaments on both sides of the Civil War.

Dahlgren the town, named after Dahlgren the officer, provided housing and community services for the military and technical employees of the Naval Proving Ground. This unusual navy-built, navy-owned town on a secluded neck of the Potomac River would loom large in the family life of Deak and Martha. The name Dahlgren was also applied informally to the proving ground.[17] It was here that Deak was to report for his postgraduate research project.

While the hour's drive from Annapolis to Washington offered easy travel in 1930, the same was not true for the remaining seventy-mile drive by way of narrow, twisting Pepperhill Road. In the absence of records to the contrary, we assume that Deak and Martha chose instead to travel down the Potomac on the *Grampus,* a 1907 river steamer purchased by the navy from an excursion line.[18]

Parting the choppy waters of the Potomac, the *Grampus* provided her passengers broad vistas of winter's naked forests and the meandering shorelines of Maryland to the east and Virginia to the west. Steaming southward, she passed Alexandria, then George Washington's bluff-top mansion at Mount Vernon, and Fort Washington. The *Grampus* turned toward the Maryland shore and docked for an exchange of passengers and mail at Indian Head, Maryland, the earlier site of the Naval Proving Ground, but now occupied by the Naval Powder Factory.

Indian Head held special interest for Martha because her grandfather, William Sampson, as commodore and chief of the Bureau of Ordnance, had spurred the proving ground's move from Annapolis to this location in the 1890s.[19] One of the most forward-looking officers of his time, the commodore seems not to have questioned the assurances of officials that the firing ranges at the new site, up to ten thousands yards long, would exceed the range of the 13-inch gun of the Oregon class, "the largest gun ever likely needed for the Naval Service."[20] But Sampson was neither the first nor yet the last to misjudge the character and range of future weapons. In the case of Indian Head, it took a war and a cow to prove the inadequacy of the site. During the heavy firings of 1917 and 1918 a number of errant shells terrified those living next to the proving ground, but none caused such a stir as the one that struck out the eye of Molly Skinner's cow and so frightened the bovine that she no longer produced milk. The navy paid Molly Skinner $30 for the cow, and the search began again for a larger, more isolated area for weapon testing.[21]

The search for a new site ended with the purchase in 1918 of a 1,366-acre peninsula at what became Dahlgren. As with Annapolis and Indian Head, navy officials believed that this new site, with Blackistone Island as a target area thirty thousand yards downstream, would provide all the space needed to test-fire the navy's present and future weapons. And there was little reason to believe them wrong at the time Deak and Martha disembarked from the *Grampus* at Dahlgren.

Life at Dahlgren resembled that of a remote post in the foreign service, only with guns—lots of guns, all kinds of guns, but mainly big guns with barrels as long as seventy feet. Martha could see the steel monsters being unloaded from barges and hear their sharp blasts emanating from the main battery. These sights and sounds suited her. They were part of being navy.

Dahlgren offered Deak and Martha all the recreation they desired, including tennis courts, sailboats, and two choices for golf: Bones Cogswell's three-hole course in back of the executive officer's quarters, or the nine-hole sand greens.[22] But as the weeks passed, Deak spent more and more of his off-duty time working on his research project, an analysis of the penetrating effects of armor-piercing projectiles. Martha now had her first clue that with Deak Parsons there would always be a project. Even if she could not appreciate her husband's excitement in determining, for example, the velocity required for a 5-inch-diameter projectile to penetrate a 6-inch-thick steel plate of a given quality, she began to realize, as she said later, that "he was happiest when he had a problem."[23] Like her mother and grandmother before her, she had listened since childhood to fathers and husbands describe the unending battle between new-and-better gun projectiles against new-and-better ship's armor. Thus it was and thus, Martha had no reason to doubt, it always would be.

While ordnance officers in the 1930s took seriously the battle of armor versus projectile, the problem was not considered urgent. Despite visible signs of discord in Europe, the Dahlgren batteries fired more out of routine than necessity. "In those early days," as a member of the proving-ground staff recalled, "many believed war was never to be fought again."[24] But Deak Parsons was not so sure. He attacked his research project as if the survival of the fleet depended on it. Evenings went into reading scientific papers and test reports. He cut short weekend outings so as to analyze the results of plate range tests. The change did not go unnoticed; Martha recognized that she had a competitor. This went beyond the normal bounds of work compulsion; it was a spell, the wizardry of physics, and Martha knew the wizard by the name of Dr. Tommy.

Dr. Tommy, as L. T. E. Thompson was widely known, stood out as an aberration in the military structure of the Naval Proving Ground. With few exceptions, civilians seen at the proving ground in the 1920s and early 1930s were "range hands" or artisans, not professionals. As chief scientist—and for many years Dahlgren's only scientist—Thompson served within a hierarchy of naval officers. He reported to the proof officer, who reported to the experimental officer, who in turn reported to the commanding officer (in ordnance circles, the "inspector"), who was responsible to the chief of the Bureau of Ordnance in Washington.[25]

Many scientists regarded the military command system as an intolerable organizational straitjacket. Some were willing to serve the military under contract, but not as employees. Science, as they saw it, could not march to the drummer's beat. True science required objectivity and freedom of exploration, and these were at risk in a command structure where mission was more important than the search for the truths of the physical world.

As a ballistician—then a rarity in America—Thompson could not be so particular. If he was to study the physical forces affecting large guns, he needed to work with the people who had the guns—that is, either the army or the navy. Setting aside any concern about military bosses, Thompson in 1923 became the chief scientist at the proving ground.

By 1930, when Deak Parsons arrived, Dr. Tommy was anything but an obsequious civil servant blindly carrying out technical tasks as assigned by military masters. Through technical involvement, personal diplomacy, and unquenchable energy he had become a major force in naval ordnance.[26]

Time and strategy were on Dr. Tommy's side. While officers rotated in and out of assignments at the proving ground, Thompson, as a civilian, stayed put. He counted on the junior officers he indoctrinated on their first Dahlgren tour to return to the proving ground and to the Bureau of Ordnance in positions of authority. The only route to the top in ordnance was through Dahlgren, and no officer going through Dahlgren missed Dr. Tommy's indoctrination on the value of science in the advancement of naval weaponry. In time, he hoped, a new generation of science-oriented officers would fill the key ordnance positions. Until this occurred, he trolled for fresh minds at the bottom. When Thompson first talked with Lieutenant Parsons, he knew that this officer would be a good catch. "I realized," Thompson later reported in his characteristic governmentese, "that Parsons was going to be an important factor in the framework of the ordnance development work."[27]

As opposite poles of the same magnet, Thompson and Parsons exerted a strong, steady influence on each other: one a thirty-nine-year-old ballistician of boundless energy who understood the navy, the other a soft-spoken twenty-eight-year-old officer with uncommon scientific ability. The attraction would prove enduring. More than a decade later, after Parsons had risen to prominence, an interviewer reported in the *Los Angeles Times*, "Parsons modestly gives most of the credit [for his military-scientific achievements] to Dr. [Louis] Ten Eyck Thompson of the Dahlgren Proving Ground, who, he says, started him on the right road back in 1930."[28]

Dr. Tommy did not limit himself to technical matters in advising his prime student. He voiced concern when he learned that Deak intended to turn down an opportunity to become an engineering-duty-only officer. As an EDO, Deak would no longer have his technical assignments ashore interrupted by duty afloat. Future advancements would be based on technical performance, which Dr. Tommy saw as Deak's strongest suit. Moreover, Deak and Martha's marriage would be spared the periodic ordeal of long separations while he went to sea. In Thompson's view, the navy had hundreds of officers qualified to command its ships and fire its guns; it had precious few who could take the helm in its technological battles. Dr. Tommy said, in essence, "Deak, you are too talented to waste your time at sea."[29] Deak respected his mentor's advice but rejected it and the immediate benefits of the EDO offer. He was adamant: he was a line officer and a sailor, and that's what he would remain.

In time Dr. Tommy would acknowledge that Deak had made "a very wise decision" in remaining an officer of the line.[30] In the long run this kept him closer to the navy's mainstream, power centers, and ordnance problems. For the immediate future, it meant he would soon be heading back to sea.

·5·

Fighting for Radar

Parsons pursued [radar] as a "boy's dream," that is, with great fervor
and lack of discouragement.
Dr. Ross Gunn

On the morning of 8 June 1930 Lieutenant Parsons held the
spotlight: the mighty battleship USS *Texas,* a veteran of World
War I, awaited in Annapolis Roads at the mouth of the Severn.[1] Arriving by launch, Parsons made a conspicuous entry into his three years
of service on the *Texas.* The next day this flagship for the commander
in chief of the U.S. Fleet proceeded toward the Panama Canal and
thence to San Diego.

Deak took up his gunnery duties with the same zeal as on the *Idaho.*
But there was a difference. He now had a clear sense of personal and
professional direction. Through the postgraduate studies he had
obtained technical credentials and the inspiration of Bramble and
Thompson. He now understood the direction naval ordnance needed
to go, and how he could help it get there.

After only five months on the West Coast and a visit to Hawaii, the
Texas returned to the east through the Panama Canal. On 4 November
1930 Adm. J. V. Chase, in replacing Adm. W. V. Pratt as the fleet's commander in chief, brought with him to the *Texas* his own chief of staff,
Rear Adm. Wat Cluverius.[2]

Instead of celebrating his first wedding anniversary with Martha,

Deak found himself on 23 November voyaging back to the West Coast with his high-ranking father-in-law. "Most junior officers," according to Martha Parsons, "wouldn't have cared for this at all, believing, if I fall down [in performance] my father-in-law will be after me."[3] But for Deak the problem was to avoid any appearance of favoritism. Whatever he achieved he would do on his own, and he did not want it to be, or to appear, otherwise.

Admiral Cluverius, who too had had an admiral father-in-law, seems to have sensed Deak's concern. By unspoken agreement the admiral and the lieutenant kept to their separate orbits despite the gravitational pull of family. While aboard ship, Lieutenant Parsons and Admiral Cluverius exchanged little more than pleasant smiles when passing each other on the deck or along the gangways. Once on land, there would be time enough to be family. And, as they both knew, Nan Cluverius and Martha Parsons would precede them by land to California.

At 0918 on 2 April 1931 the *Texas* approached the channel to San Diego harbor. Shortly afterward, the commandant of the Eleventh Naval District fired a seventeen-gun salute to the commander in chief of the U.S. Fleet, whereupon the *Texas* returned a thirteen-gun salute. For Deak on the *Texas* and Martha on shore the firings had a different meaning: they would be reunited. For the rest of Deak's service, the *Texas* would remain on the West Coast. During this time Martha and Deak maintained a home at San Pedro along the Los Angeles harbor. When the *Texas* left port, Martha often "chased the fleet up and down the coast," rejoining Deak at San Francisco and the Washington ports of Port Angeles, Bellington, and Bremerton.[4]

Whether ashore or at sea, Parsons remained preoccupied with ballistics problems affecting the accuracy of the navy's guns. He kept up an active correspondence with Thompson and Bramble on a wide range of self-initiated studies—for example, the Magnus effect on spinning projectiles, cross-winds effects on range and deflection, fire-control corrections for light refraction, and, in Parsons' words, "measuring the comparative hardness numbers of the rotating bands of our 14-inch target shells." Parsons' proposed solutions included supporting equations and complete descriptions of the test firings he conducted. It was as if he had never left his graduate studies and the proving ground.[5]

While other officers swapped stories or played games in the ward-room, Parsons devoured scientific and engineering publications much as mystery-story addicts gorge themselves on the latest thrillers. When Thompson recommended he read *Reviews of Modern Physics,* Parsons subscribed to the quarterly and kept a complete file of it even though he found that "the math and the references are sometimes beyond me."[6] In effect, Parsons' doctoral studies in physics had just begun.

Deak's reclusive behavior did not go unnoticed in the wardroom, especially his refusal to join the endless bridge games. He once ex-plained to Martha, "If you play bridge on shipboard you kill an awful lot of time when you should be reading and studying." He observed that if you play at all, "you'll be pulled into the game every night."[7]

One of the mysteries of Parsons' naval duty is how he was able to withdraw from the center of officer fellowship yet be accepted for who he was. He suffered none of the derision and wardroom jokes expe-rienced a half-century earlier by Bradley Fiske, an officer-inventor similarly immersed in the physical sciences.[8] Instead, the *Texas* officers saw Deak as a ready source of technical assistance. When, for exam-ple, an ensign on the *Texas* had difficulty trying to use German opti-cal fire-control equipment whose range scale was in meters, Deak quickly came up with a conversion scale that made the equipment useful. Even then, fellow officers recognized his ability to see solutions where others saw only problems.[9]

Parsons' peers viewed him as different but not offbeat, gifted but not odd, absorbed but not unfriendly. Parsons could be decisive and firm when need be. On one occasion a hotheaded officer on the *Texas* vented his anger over a gun failure by swearing at Deak and his crew. Deak responded calmly, firmly, and immediately. He told the angry officer, even though he was senior, "Get somebody to relieve you, I want to talk to you." The two went aft and Deak said, "Don't you ever do this again. You can cuss me out all you want, but not in front of my men."[10] The officer acknowledged his mistake and agreed not to repeat it. Here was a case where Parsons could have called for higher-level intercession but chose instead to handle the matter himself. He needed no help from the ship's captain, and certainly none from his two-star father-in-law. When occasion required, he could be forceful.

Deak Parsons' three-year duty with the *Texas* gave him and Martha the closest experience they would ever have to what might be called *normal* life in a characteristic naval environment. When the *Texas* was in home port, Deak commuted between home and ship much as any husband in the workaday world. By all accounts Deak and Martha's feelings toward each other ran deep, and never deeper than early 1932 when Martha informed Deak that he was to be a father. From the day of her birth, 11 December 1934, Hannah became the center of Martha and Deak's life.[11] Martha's description of Deak as "a very gentle soul" is borne out in his tenderness with Hannah. Deak, the man who "never went overboard" in adult relationships, followed every little achievement of his firstborn daughter. Deak, the man absorbed in the nation's future, now had a deep personal investment in that future.

To Deak, the nation's future required a strong navy; and to be strong the navy needed superior ordnance. The point of assigning ordnance specialists like himself to sea duty was to acquaint them with the real problems of weaponry in the fleet so that they would know what was needed when they returned to technical assignments ashore. To this end Deak had observed significant problems in laying guns on targets twenty or more miles away despite the advances in range finders, fast-rotating turrets, fire-control systems, and devices compensating for the roll and pitch of the ship. In analyzing each possible source of error, Parsons seemed to recognize that it would take a miracle or some revolutionary new technology to make any appreciable improvement.

Deak's tour on the *Texas* also made him increasingly aware of the problems of defending ships from aircraft. Aviation had come a long way since John Rodgers' ill-fated attempt to fly a plane to Hawaii. Deak knew that the antiaircraft guns on the navy's battleships would be a poor match for the new-generation aircraft. And there was little reason to believe that traditional cut-and-try experimental methods could close the gap. Drawing on the scientific inspiration of Dr. Tommy, Deak placed his hope on new technology. It was this faith in the power of new ideas that sparked his happiness with the orders he received in the spring of 1933.

Few line officers of that era would have welcomed an assignment to the Naval Research Laboratory, Bellevue, Virginia. NRL was then a small, little-known bit of the U.S. Navy. Any officer serving there would find himself isolated from the orderliness and decisiveness of the *real* navy. He would be surrounded by civilian scientists and engineers working in strange ways on odd projects. This was just what Deak Parsons wanted.

With Hannah in a baby basket in the back seat, Deak and Martha made the trip cross-country to Bellevue by car, stopping on the way to see his father and stepmother at Fort Sumner and Clarissa's family, now at Coffeyville, Kansas.

We have Martha's recollections of the Fort Sumner visit. This was her first meeting with her father-in-law. Not having known the man in his early years, she had concluded that Deak's "real push" came from his mother. Martha must have noted that Harry Parsons' second wife was closer in age to Deak and herself than to Harry, but what she mentions is Grace Parsons' warm personality and devotion to her husband. She saw "Bobs," the seven-year-old offspring of this May–December marriage, more as a nephew than a brother to Deak.[12]

The stop at Coffeyville turned into a family reunion when Critchell joined Deak and Clarissa there. Critchell's life, always with it ups and downs, was now on an upswing. After the difficulties of his youth, he had gone back to college and graduated from the University of New Mexico with honors in politics, economics, and the arts. He excelled as well in linguistics (ultimately becoming fluent in French, Spanish, and Arabic). He now had news for Deak and Clarissa, the intellectual luminaries who had outshone him in his youth: he had been selected for a Rhodes scholarship and would be leaving soon for Oxford.[13]

The jubilation of the siblings was tempered by serious discussions of world affairs. Clarissa and her husband, Rice, had just returned from Europe. They had been, she said, "uncomfortably aware of the things we saw in Italy, Germany, and Holland." While there, they had viewed with alarm the military buildups under Hitler and Mussolini. But once back home, they lost their concern over another world war.[14]

As in the old days, Clarissa tried to lure her brothers into heated discussion. For bait she spoke of "the betrayal" of their father, revealing that he had confessed to having voted for Roosevelt. Clarissa observed that Deak withdrew from the conversation after her critical reference to the New Deal president, saying only, "He is my Commander in Chief."[15]

Deak typically avoided criticizing the president, the government, or the navy. However, he crossed that line one night after the others had gone to sleep and he and Clarissa were sitting out in her car talking. He then admitted to discouragement with the government for not keeping the navy as strong as it should be in the face of the growing clouds of war. And he felt there was not enough interest in developing new scientific techniques for the navy. But this, he said, was something he would know more about once he entered his upcoming assignment in naval research.[16]

Four years had passed since Deak Parsons and bride had steamed down the Potomac on the *Grampus* from the Washington Navy Yard to Dahlgren. Shortly after embarking on that trip, opposite Alexandria on the east bank of the river, they had passed a small cluster of buildings with weird protruding antennas. This was the Naval Research Laboratory, commonly referred to simply as NRL.

Now, in July 1933, NRL appeared much the same. Only a few minor buildings had risen around the inner core of laboratory building, machine shop, converted foundry, and power plant. The towering antennas assumed new shapes, and the surrounding farmlands had yielded, but not yet capitulated, to the encroachment of Bellevue and the adjacent Bolling Air Force Base.

As a liaison officer, Lieutenant Parsons was the technical communications link between NRL, with fewer than two hundred employees—mainly scientists and radio engineers—and the Bureau of Ordnance, the Goliath of navy bureaus. Although BuOrd was the largest of the navy bureaus, it had limited power over NRL, the navy's central scientific laboratory. The real power over the laboratory was the Bureau of Engineering. As parent organization and chief funding source, BuEng called the tunes.[17]

Parsons needed to make himself familiar with NRL's programs and capabilities so that he could advise BuOrd on research projects potentially valuable to its ordnance mission. Like a prospector, he was to look for traces of gold in NRL's research. No desert prospector ever discovered such a rich vein of high-grade ore so quickly. Within his first week at NRL, Parsons was on the trail of a technological solution to the two problems that had concerned him on the *Texas:* how to lay guns on target more accurately and how to defend the battleship against the airplane.

Parsons learned in his briefing by A. Hoyt Taylor, head of the Radio

Division, how Taylor and Leo Young had noticed by chance in 1922 that interferences they had observed between a high-frequency radio transmitter on one shore of the Potomac and a receiver on the opposite shore were caused by a passing ship. A year later, when NRL was established, this observation led to a small research effort into the use of high-frequency waves for detecting distant ships. Subsequently another accidental observation revealed that high-frequency radio waves could also be used to detect aircraft. Further experimentation showed that after the waves had been used to detect a distant aircraft, they could also provide continuous measurements of the aircraft's range and the rate at which the range changed.

Fresh from the fleet, Parsons immediately grasped the military possibilities of the experimental work described by Taylor. He later recalled, "I was tremendously enthusiastic as soon as I heard of the radio echo work."[18] A radio echo device that could detect aircraft beyond the limits of human sight could protect ships and harbors from surprise attacks, save lives, perhaps turn the tide of battles. Yet to Parsons' dismay he learned that the exploratory research on this radical concept was limping along without any priority, a part-time effort of only two professionals. Neither the navy nor the scientists seemed to share Parsons' excitement over the revolutionary potential of the discovery.[19]

This is not to say the phenomenon had not received attention as having "possible applications."[20] Notably, the secretary of the navy informed the secretary of war on 9 January 1932 of the possibilities of using "Echo Signals to Detect Moving Objects" and suggested that the system might be of more interest to the army than the navy, as it offered a means of protecting defense areas against aircraft. This lukewarm proposal had been originated by Taylor, whose original enthusiasm for the work had been blunted, it seems, by BuEng skepticism. Further, Taylor was under too much pressure from other research to exploit radio detection with anything more than part-time token support.[21] By July 1933, when Parsons arrived, the technical problems of creating a shipboard detection system remained unresolved.

The more Deak Parsons learned of the radio-echo findings, the greater was his surprise. Not only was the Bureau of Engineering uninterested in radio echoes, but NRL's scientists seemed content not to press the issue. NRL scientists appeared to be out of touch with the fleet and its needs. Parsons later wrote, "One of the senior physicists was surprised at my enthusiasm over the radio echo possibilities and remarked that he understood the navy had such fine optical range finders that radio echo could improve matters very little."[22]

Parsons was also surprised to learn that the radio-echo findings had not been reported to the Bureau of Ordnance. No one seemed to recognize what was immediately obvious to him: that the radio-echo discovery could revolutionize naval weaponry. Parsons saw that if the echoes from high-frequency radio waves could be used to detect and track distant ships and aircraft, then those of even higher frequency might be used to lay naval guns on target and to aim antiaircraft weapons. He was astonished that no one else had thought of running up the frequency of radio waves in order to produce a beam sharp enough to track projectiles in flight and to lay naval guns on target.[23]

Confident that his own ordnance bureau would be more enlightened than the engineering bureau, Parsons drafted a memorandum on the subject, "Super-High Frequency Radio: Possible Use of Reflected Waves in Airplane Detection and Fire Control." He addressed the memorandum to the chief of the Bureau of Ordnance and prepared it for the signature of NRL's director. This memo of 2 August 1933 described NRL tests in which aircraft had been detected at ranges beyond twenty miles and at altitudes above eight thousand feet. Parsons explained the method thus:

> In tests of super-high frequency radio transmission to airplanes, certain beat notes were heard in receivers located on the ground at considerable distance from the transmitting station. These beat notes were found to be caused by a combination of the transmitted and *reflected* waves which were out of phase by an amount proportional to the rate of change of distance between the reflecting object and the transmitting and receiving stations.

Parsons acknowledged that the method was not yet practical for fire control at sea but stated that the inadequacies might be "overcome as research progresses." After the understatement "The work has been going slowly," he requested $5,000 a year to hire additional personnel to work exclusively on this project (all previous work had been part-time catch-as-catch-can).[24]

The route sheet that accompanied the $5,000 proposal during its circulation in BuOrd tells us now what Parsons learned at the time:

Ordnance was no more enlightened on this subject than Engineering. One BuOrd officer scribbled, "Recommend this be followed up," but the others killed the proposal with technical and administrative quibbles: detecting airplanes was not ordnance's business, the microwaves for controlling gunfire could not be achieved with state-of-the art vacuum tubes, long-range research was better left to private industry.[25]

Rather than passively wait for a response from the chief of BuOrd, Parsons organized conferences with BuOrd fire-control officers and NRL physicists.[26] Out of these meetings came a proposal to form an NRL "Micro Ray" group, which was to build a single-beam transmitter and receiver that could detect and track an unseen ship or airplane with sufficient accuracy for fire-control purposes. Accuracy would be the same in haze, fog, or dark of night. The challenge would be in providing microwaves in the order of 10 centimeters so that the system could be small enough to be put aboard ships.[27]

By Parsons' own account, it took him several weeks to draft a second NRL memorandum to BuOrd that encompassed the proposal. Even then, it had to be changed twice on the final day (15 September) in order to get the initials of Drs. H. C. Hayes and A. Hoyt Taylor.[28] Years later Parsons would regret the "hedge" he had had to put at the end in order to satisfy Taylor's scientific conservatism. Instead of a hard-hitting clincher, the proposal ended with this bit of weaseling: "It should be emphasized that an investigation of this type offers no certainty of positive results along lines which can be outlined at present. However, if the answer is in the negative, it should be apparent in two or at most three years, and there will be a measure of return for effort and money spent in the probability that if it cannot be done by us, at least it cannot be done against us."[29]

The proposal was sent via the Bureau of Engineering, in the belief, it seems, that if BuEng was having difficulty supporting the NRL's enfeebled radio-echo detection project, it might welcome an infusion of BuOrd research dollars into the laboratory. But instead of giving the proposal a favorable endorsement, BuEng officials injected their own note of pessimism. They waffled: "The time involved to obtain either negative or positive results might well exceed two or three years. In the case of negative results it would be difficult to predict that positive results were impractical of accomplishment." In short, *this can't be accomplished on our watch, so don't do it!* Rather than take the recommendation of their own liaison officer, BuOrd officials followed the lead of their sister bureau. They declined support for the proposed microwave research for gunfire control, citing "the present stringency of funds."[30]

In his attempt to reverse the decision, Deak Parsons did more than write proposals and hold conferences. With the persistence of a door-to-door salesman, he took his arguments to all the important "desks" in the navy. In bureau parlance, the officer in charge of guns had the "Gun Desk"; similarly, there were turret, torpedo, armor, gun-director, mine, and gunpowder desks. The system was tidy: a place for everything and everything in its place. But, as Parsons recognized, the system did not provide for change. Anything new had no desk. And anything without a desk was unlikely to be funded. Typically, the officers in charge of ordnance desks sought proof that something practical would be achieved before they approved spending public moneys on a new idea. That was the catch: proof required exploratory research and development, which in turn called for funds and people. New ideas required nurturing but instead were often squelched by those at the key desks. Parsons faced an additional problem in that BuOrd's fire-control officers were insulated from the scientific work at NRL. As a result, Parsons later wrote, "fire-control officers acquired only a dim knowledge of the facts of life of what later became radar."[31]

Some of his contemporaries believed that Parsons as a junior officer put his career at risk by his relentless pursuit of radar support.[32] While some higher-ranking officers may not have appreciated this persistent lieutenant's questioning of their decisions, there is no evidence that anyone took any action against him as the result of his overzealousness. But clearly, he pressed his case to the limits; he was not an officer who could ignore his convictions. He did not rest until he had carried his message to key desks in BuOrd, BuEng, BuAer (the Bureau of Aeronautics), and the Office of the Chief of Naval Operations.[33]

When Parsons later identified his chief nemesis in the fight for radar, he did so not by name but by title. He wrote, "Due to the personality and lack of vision of the officer in the key position as head of the Radio and Sound Division of the Bureau of Engineering, radar, and particularly microwave radar, was treated as a wild dream with practically no chance of real success."[34]

The head of the Radio and Sound Desk was Comdr. Wilbur J. "Red" Ruble. One NRL scientist described Ruble as typical of a number of officers who popped up in various parts of the navy with "the disease"—that is, a communicable form of arrogance. Martha Parsons, who seldom voiced views about her husband's work associates, received the impression from Deak that Ruble was the radar "stumbling block." (It should be noted that these views of Ruble pertain to the period 1933–34 and not to his subsequent involvement in radar.)[35]

Ruble held the advantage over Parsons by virtue of position (the key desk on all matters related to radio), rank (commander over lieutenant), and age (forty-four versus thirty-one). It appears that Parsons' greatest difficulty was in penetrating Ruble's fixed views on what BuEng should or should not do. Whereas Ruble supported aggressive programs to develop conventional radio and underwater sound equipment, he balked at using radio waves for anything but communication. In the year prior to Parsons' arrival, Ruble had served as the assistant director of NRL and thus considered himself an authority on what work NRL should or should not undertake. As a navy postgraduate in radio engineering and an EDO in communications, he could claim to know more about radio waves, and what they could be used for, than did an ordnance lieutenant of the line.

Although exasperated by Ruble and other officers with "the disease," Parsons went beyond personalities in defining the problem of radar support. He summed up the core problem in one word: *cognizance*. As he used the term, cognizance established the areas of primary responsibility for the various "desks" of the bureaus. Parsons was skeptical of "neat looking organization charts and strongly coordinated programs," which he believed froze organizations in place and blocked the flow of new ideas and technology. Freezing an organizational structure assumed that someone "could see around the problem [at hand]" before the exploratory research had been done. "No one," he said, "argues about cognizance of marlinspikes or saddles. But in important partially exploited fields, cognizance can be synonymous with 'paralysis' or 'stranglehold.'"[36]

Parsons in his later years pointed back to the radar experience as the prime example of a stranglehold on new technology:

In the Fall of 1933 certain parts of the navy (including desks in CNO, BuAer, BuOrd, and BuEng) were aware of the possibility that radar could be developed for search and fire control . . . yet for nearly three years radar had to proceed at NRL on a bootleg, "redheaded stepchild" basis because the radio and sound division of the Bureau of Engineering, which jealously insisted on *cognizance,* was dominated by an officer [Ruble] and a tradition which could not conceive that radio waves were not primarily useful to *send messages.* The result was that the navy, which had the initiative in its grasp, lost something like two years getting radar into the fleet.[37]

While Parsons failed to awaken the navy to its unique opportunity, he was more successful in rekindling the enthusiasm of NRL scientists and engineers for their own discovery. He surprised them right off with his grasp of the technical details of the project. He talked their language. He understood both the science behind radio echoes and the military ramifications. He assured the scientists that what they were doing was important—was needed by the navy now and could be absolutely critical in war.[38]

Deak Parsons' office at NRL adjoined that of Ross Gunn, a physicist who properly characterized himself "a fighter."[39] The two soon became an imposing team—an officer and a scientist similarly committed to a better navy through technology. They were also alike in age and, except for Deak's uniform, physical appearance. Both stood tall and straight and emanated confidence, but the most striking similarity was their high foreheads. Phrenologists of old might have explained these as signs of extra braininess—not implausible in the case of these two.

At the time Parsons moved next door, Gunn's responsibilities had just been expanded. In addition to heading the Heat and Light Division he was also technical assistant to the director—that is, a chief link between civilian researchers and NRL's director. Gunn's ties to the director's office help explain the readiness with which Capt. H. R. Greenlee and Assistant Director Comdr. J. B. Wills signed proposals drafted by Parsons for radio wave research.[40]

Gunn saw Parsons as an enthusiastic officer who "pursued the promise of radar for gun laying as a 'boy's dream,' that is, with great fervor and lack of discouragement." His enthusiasm gave the NRL professionals increased confidence in the importance of their work. "He added impetus," Gunn stated, "by showing if you can get this or that kind of frequency, the fleet needs it."[41]

Gunn described Parsons as "one of the brightest minds that ever came through NRL in military uniform"—a rare compliment from this physicist ordinarily critical of military officers in the laboratory environment. "Often," he said, "early officers didn't know what they didn't know . . . and they automatically thought everyone in science would be a screwball." Parsons, however, was the epitome of what an officer who works with civilian researchers should be. He had, Gunn said, "the intrinsic qualities needed to be a great creative scientist, yet he chose to exert his own expertise as an ordnance officer familiar with fleet."[42] Even as a junior officer fighting a losing battle with the bureaucracy, Deak Parsons was proving to be a new kind of naval officer.[43]

Parsons' assignment to NRL occurred at the beginning of the end of NRL's lean years. During his time the fortunes of the laboratory began to change as part of the Roosevelt administration's response to the resurrection of the German military in Europe and the Japanese renunciation of the disarmament treaties of 1922 and 1930. By early 1943 the new political and economic environment had opened the way for greater technological progress within the navy. NRL, in the reawakening to which Parsons contributed, made itself ready to rise with the tide. When Taylor and the scientists learned early in 1934 that members of a Naval Appropriations Subcommittee would be visiting the laboratory, they decided to showcase the radio-detection project. To prepare the equipment for demonstration, they hired Robert M. Page. For the first time the project had a full-time person. Page opened the way for dramatic technical progress by shifting from a system of continuous waves to short pulses of radio energy, thereby making it possible to co-locate a radar transmitter and receiver—the solution to the basic navy requirement that the system should fit on the deck of a ship.[44]

Also in 1934, Parsons saw microwave research begun under a pretext quite different from the fire-control application he had proposed. The extent to which he participated in the manipulation that went into the project for an "altidrift meter" is not known, but the modus operandi is characteristic of his later creative financing. For some time, according to Parsons, NRL had been working on a Bureau of Aeronautics project to develop a device to measure airplane altitude and drift. After the original plan to use supersonic sound pulses failed, it was decided, with BuAer approval, to use microwaves as the means for providing continuous measurement of aircraft altitude. "This was put over," Parsons wrote later, "in spite of BuEng objection that the instrument would certainly be too heavy and clumsy to carry in an airplane." To Parsons' delight, BuAer, then under Rear Adm. Ernest J. King, replied that the system would be useful even if it could only be carried in the airship *Macon*.[45]

King—a key player in Parsons' later career—understood, as did Parsons, that the best interests of the navy were not in cramming an experimental altidrift meter into a plane but in conducting research into the characteristics of microwaves. Neither officer was averse to bending the rules for a worthwhile objective. Nor did either one expect the results of this research to pay off on their watch. Their faith in the long-term benefits was not misplaced. By the end of World War II the SCR-718 radar based on this research would be carried by most U.S. military aircraft.[46] And NRL's microwave research would provide the foundation for the industrial development of the first shipboard fire-control system.

Just as NRL's radar investigations for both detection and fire control (via altidrift meter) took on a new life, the Naval Postgraduate School needed an ordnance instructor. In the summer of 1934 Dr. Bramble informed the selection committee that he could recommend none better than his former student, Lieutenant Parsons.

Martha welcomed the move to a house on Porter Row in Annapolis. Here, she thought, Deak would be able to spend more time at home with her and Hannah. She soon learned that this was not to happen. By agreement with the Bureau of Ordnance he was to divide his time between teaching and following up on liaison tasks begun at NRL. Once again, the navy and Deak's conscientious attention to duty controlled Martha's life as well as his. As a mother she felt the constraints more than before. Looking out across the Severn, Martha could see where she and Deak had walked along the seawall during courtship. She could look back on their first years together when Deak was attached to the *Texas* and she joined him at various ports up and down the coast. All that was now changed. No ships to follow. No trips. And again pregnant.[47]

Martha missed her father's gaiety. However, she understood Deak's serious disposition and respected his dedication to whatever he undertook. She later commented, "You get indoctrinated in this kind of life and you may fuss about it, but I could understand his preoccupation with his job."[48]

And there was a lot Martha could say in Deak's behalf as a husband: "He was not stiff; not the spit and polish kind at all which some military people are who want everything shined up and looking perfect." By Martha's account, the orderliness that Deak brought to his work and his thinking was not always present in his personal life. "He didn't care," she said, "if the curtains didn't match or how the house was. He wouldn't care unless it got so bad dogs were eating off the table." Nor was Deak—the officer who would later complete the assembly of the atomic bomb on the *Enola Gay*—a Mister Fix-It at home. "He wasn't interested in fixing things or gardening," Martha said. "He used to let me do an awful lot of things."[49]

More important to Martha than these minor flaws, Deak was a loving, faithful husband. He was completely devoted to her, who like his own mother was a take-charge person. This he seemed to admire in her, just as his father had appreciated the grit of Clara Doolittle Parsons. Deak did not delegate command of the home to Martha; she just naturally took over. He did share the burdens and pleasures of parenthood, however, spending countless hours with Hannah and looking forward, as did Martha, to the arrival of the new baby.

Margaret Parsons, to be known familiarly as Peggy, was born in 1934 on Hannah's birthday, December 11. The birth doubled the joy that Hannah had brought. The parents enjoyed the miracles of growth and the interactions of Hannah and her baby sister. But then one morning in May, Hannah became disturbingly quiet. Her temperature rose suddenly. Deak and Martha took her to the doctor, who dismissed her symptoms as "a little sore throat." When they returned home, her temperature rose higher and her condition worsened. As recounted by Clarissa Fuller, "They grabbed her up and rushed her into Washington. As Deak carried Hannah into the hospital, she died in his arms."[50]

The death of their firstborn child by polio devastated Deak and Martha. Nothing so penetrated the inner self that Deak had barricaded against the world. Hugging Martha in the quiet of their home, he wept.[51] But Hannah's death went deeper than tears. Beyond the immediate anguish and pain, the shadow of the lost child cast a permanent pall over Deak and Martha. Those in the Parsons and Cluverius families recognized it as "the secret sorrow"—one never discussed, but always there. As she grew up, Peggy would be the one most affected by "the secret sorrow." In years to come she would feel the presence of a beautiful, perfect older sister who could not be seen nor played with but was yet the person she herself was somehow expected to be, the one whose birthday she shared.[52]

In his year at NRL, Deak Parsons had made the scientists and radio engineers more aware of the tremendous military potential of their radio wave discoveries. He breathed new hope and energy into the work. Vannevar Bush, the World War II leader of American science, would later credit Parsons with being the first military officer to recognize the full military potential of this new technology.[53] Parsons fought for his vision with unusual boldness for a junior officer. But the future master at hot-wiring the bureaucracy failed to spark the Bureaus of Engineering and Ordnance into action.

During Parsons' short time at NRL he was the first to foresee the use of microwaves for fire control.[54] It was an idea ahead of its time. The proposal Parsons drafted in September 1933 to use radio reflections for search and fire control came seventeen months before Sir Robert Watson-Watt documented the experiments that would lead the British to aggressively develop radar. Parsons later observed, "I am all for giving the British scientists credit for the major job they did in developing radar and other devices. They certainly went after radar with more top-level support and more talent than we did between 1935 and 1940."[55] One major result of the parallel program by the British was their magnetron, which produced the high frequencies essential to the development of the shipboard fire-control systems Parsons had envisioned.

Although Parsons hailed the magnetron and other later radar successes, he harbored deep regrets over the navy's early failure to recognize its unique opportunity. He wrote: "The Navy had a magnificent opportunity to capitalize on its major discovery at NRL." He believed that it had failed twice: once because of the "personality and lack of vision" of the head of BuEng's Radio and Sound Division, and next, at the start of World War II, because of an NRL director Parsons described as "churlish, selfish, credit-grabbing."[56] He was referring to Vice Adm. Harold Bowen, who in his view had kept NRL out of the mainstream of radar development in World War II by failing to cooperate with the Radiation Laboratory established at the Massachusetts Institute of Technology.[57] But that puts us ahead of our story.

Parsons' contributions to radar continued after his move to Annapolis. Commuting to Washington, he carried the message of radar's revolutionary potential to fellow ordnance officers, including Comdr. F. I. Entwistle at the Antiaircraft Fire Control Desk. Entwistle later recalled Parsons' missionary zeal: "By gosh he informed everybody; he kept everybody informed! He was at it all the time."[58]

By "keeping at it," Parsons helped open the way for eventual BuOrd support. His converts picked up the cause and amplified it. As a retired rear admiral, Entwistle credited Parsons for the navy's having operational radars by the start of World War II.[59] But this arguable claim must be tempered by Parsons' own criticisms of the early radars. At the end of the war he wrote, "It really pained me when I looked over the electronic gear in our ships in the Pacific in early 1943 to see the massive radio communication transmitters, sealed for the duration of the war [as unwieldy], and to think how much two years of fleet experience with radar *before 1941* could have saved us in lives, planes, ships and battles lost during the initial phases of the Pacific war."[60]

As significant as his radar contributions were, the importance of this experience was not just in what Parsons did for radar but also in what radar did for Parsons. The radar experience became for him the grand exemplar of the need for the military to work closely with the nation's scientists. Dr. Tommy of Dahlgren had preached this philosophy; NRL radar proved it. The radar experience revealed to Parsons the weakness of the existing bureaucracy in recognizing and nurturing important new ideas. It demonstrated the importance of placing fleet-knowledgeable officers in the laboratory environment—or, conversely, exposing technically gifted officers to the fleet environment. What Parsons learned at NRL he later applied in the creation of the proximity fuze, the atomic bomb, and postwar weapons for the nuclear navy.

But first came renewal of his fleet credentials. Still shunning engineering-duty-only status, Deak Parsons in June 1936 again answered the call of the sea.

·**6**·

Breaking Storm

**Everything [on the *Aylwin*] flowed so naturally that you never thought
whether he was going by the book or just the way things ought to be.**
Capt. Ward F. Hardman, USN (Ret.)

On 22 June 1936 Lieutenant Parsons reported aboard the
destroyer USS *Aylwin* in the dual role of executive officer and
navigator.[1] Half the length of a battleship, the *Aylwin* brought Deak
Parsons into a new and closer relationship with the sea. Less than
steady underfoot, the destroyer's deck shifted constantly in a constant
struggle among sea, ship, and man. Storms became personal adventures. Tight living quarters created close bonds among the ship's nine
officers. In letters home, Parsons described the *Aylwin* as a "taut" ship
where everyone knew his job and discipline prevailed. A fellow officer described her as "a happy ship."[2] Here for the first time Parsons put
his natural skills as a navigator to work. As executive officer he stood
responsible to the captain for actions throughout the ship. In this role
he displayed another of his strong suits, the ability to handle detail
without losing sight of major objectives.

For all its importance to Parsons' naval career, this routine assignment to the *Aylwin* revealed an attitude of business-as-usual within the
navy even as world crises thickened. In 1936 Emperor Haile Selassie of
Ethiopia fled before the Italian army. Full-scale civil war raged in Spain,
with no sign of any major power standing up against fascist aggression.

Even so, Parsons and other officers with proven technical skills were still being groomed for command at sea. While military leaders recognized the growing threat of war, few if any foresaw the degree to which the outcome of such a war would depend on advanced weapons and officers equipped to deal with new technology.

And no one, within or outside the military, anticipated that the war ahead would trigger an unprecedented weapons revolution. Through Parsons we will see how the United States led that revolution through creation of the smart fuze and the atomic bomb. At the same time, his career opens a window on the nation's near-catastrophic failure to beat the enemy in the development of jet propulsion for modern military rockets.

In the summer of 1936, when Parsons was going to sea, the German armed forces were purchasing a remote site known as Peenemunde on the Baltic coast for the use of rocket scientists, including Wernher von Braun, to enlarge their research. As von Braun later acknowledged, much of this early work exploited the findings of Robert H. Goddard, the American rocket pioneer. With the establishment of Peenemunde, the race for the first of the secret superweapons was on. But only the Germans knew it.

For Parsons and others on the *Aylwin*, military rockets were still Buck Rogers comic-strip weapons. Their immediate concerns in July 1936 were the hazards of leading the destroyer squadron through the inland passage to Kodiak, Alaska. As described by a ship's officer, "[It] was pretty hairy in those days going through the narrows . . . like going down an avenue where the trees were growing over the road."[3]

On the return trip through Admiralty Bay, Parsons put his technical skills to use in the sonar tracking of submarines. After returning to home port at San Diego, the *Aylwin* operated in Southern California waters until April 1937, at which time she participated in fleet training operations in the waters off Hawaii. As a fighting ship of White Force she "bombarded" Hilo and covered a simulated landing of marines. Although "damaged" in action, she subsequently opened fire on three "enemy" ships. Within three minutes of action, she was proclaimed *hors de combat* by the umpires. In May 1937 Deak became Lieutenant Commander Parsons. For the rest of that year and early

1938, the *Aylwin* alternated between stays in home port and training exercises along the Southern California coast.[4]

From conversations with Capt. Ward F. Hardman we learn that Parsons was well liked and admired by his fellow officers. "He led by example," Hardman said, "and in a way that you could not fail but admire. . . . Everything flowed so naturally that you never thought whether he was going by the book or just the way things ought to be." Parsons spent hours studying and working on the ship's antiaircraft director, a troublesome piece of equipment. This tinkering resulted in improvements but did little to relieve Parsons' growing concerns over the whole problem of antiaircraft defense. It did result in a triangulation method for using aircraft observations to control surface gunfire. Parsons had no difficulty implementing his solutions because, as Hardman said, "he was very influential on all things ordnance-wise."[5]

Recollections of Vice Adm. R. T. S. Keith reveal that Parsons applied his analytical skills to operational as well as technical problems. As ship's executive officer he developed what became known among destroyer officers as the "*Aylwin* line" for night searches to locate the assault force on which a torpedo attack was to be launched. For this the squadron's destroyers were positioned at intervals equal to twice the night visibility. When contact was made, according to Keith, "you joined up at 25 knots and went boiling in to make your attack." If nothing else, the tactic yielded excitement. Keith describes it: "You had no radar, you couldn't see, but you were sitting high in the air with the wind rushing by. And it was a wonderful sensation."[6] It is little wonder that Deak Parsons relished his twenty-one months in the destroyer squadron.

The *Aylwin* assignment provided Deak and Martha a chance to savor life in the idyllic seaside setting of Coronado. Although the Great Depression was still strangling the nation's economy, life on Coronado remained unchanged, as if the problems of the world had been left behind on the San Diego side of the ferry. There was less room for worries on the navy side, with Coronado's beaches, parks, small shops, and flower-adorned cottages, including the Parsons' rental.

At Coronado, Deak was drawn into the busy social calendar of Wat Cluverius, who placed people above books and, in effect, collected them and read them from cover to cover. He believed, it seems, that his son-in-law could profit from some people-browsing. At Cluverius social gatherings, Deak found himself surrounded by admirals who had known Martha from childhood. Deak rose to the challenge. As Martha tells us, "He was able to hold his head up with any of them, which a lot of young officers would have been scared to death to do."[7] As a Gun Club member he understood the ordnance issues of the dominant clique of flag officers, but he could speak equally well on broad issues of world and military affairs. By nature, however, Deak was a listener, and he enjoyed the tales of these older men who had a wide range of naval experience. He listened as attentively to the old mossbacks as to the forward-thinking officers. The insights he gained from these associations would prove useful to him in the weapons revolution ahead.

One of Deak's attributes that must have impressed the senior officers was his commitment, not just to the navy but to peacetime training, particularly training cruises. "If the ship was going," Martha tells us, "he was going to be there!"[8] This readiness did not yield to family emergencies. On Saturday, 13 November 1937, Martha gave birth to their daughter Clara, whom we will come to know familiarly as Clare. The delivery had been exceptionally difficult, and on Monday morning, when the *Aylwin* was scheduled to sail, Martha was still ill, with the burden of caring for the new baby and three-year-old Peggy at the same time. Nonetheless, Deak reported back to the ship—duty was duty. No matter how much he wanted to remain at home with Martha, he saw the ship as his first responsibility.

Comdr. E. E. Stone saw peacetime duty in a different light. When Parsons insisted on remaining on board, Stone ordered him off the ship, saying, "Your wife needs you. Go home!" According to Martha, "Deak didn't get over that for a long time. He thought this was really not the right thing to do—he felt in another case he might never have done that."[9]

Parsons' performance on the *Aylwin* and his ordnance background caught the attention of Rear Adm. William R. Sexton, commander of destroyers of a Pacific battle force. It appears that the gunnery scores for the destroyers had been abysmal. The admiral needed a take-charge, savvy ordnance officer to analyze the problems and correct them. In peacetime, gunnery scores could be more important than a lieutenant commander's career aspirations. Parsons responded to the transfer with, in essence, an "Aye, aye, sir."[10]

In March 1938 he was transferred to Admiral Sexton's flagship, the USS *Detroit*. One documented incident of this period occurred when the *Detroit* shared the same port with the USS *New York*. When Parsons spied the huge "bedspring" antenna on the *New York*'s conning tower, he knew that the ship was equipped to undergo sea trials with the first NRL radar (the CXAM P-band air-search radar). As soon as possible, he set off for the *New York* to find out how the radar tests were going. He was ill prepared for his reception. As he later recalled, "I was 'invited' to leave the *New York* immediately." When he tried to explain his interest in the equipment, he was ordered off the ship and threatened with a court martial. In Parsons' view, this was "unimaginative compliance" with the navy directive limiting information on the new "super-secret apparatus" to senior officers.[11]

In June 1939, shortly after the *New York* incident, Deak Parsons completed his sixteen months on the *Detroit*. All he could claim for this time was improved gunnery scores for the admiral.

As she had in her youth, Martha spent the summer of 1939 at the "old Cluverius place" at Hancock Point, Maine. This rambling seven-room house, built by a lighthouse keeper who added rooms as needed for an ever expanding family, had been purchased by Admiral Sampson in the 1890s. Since then it had served generations of Sampsons, Cluveriuses, and assorted kin. Whoever could come would come. Whoever was present shared the cooking in a large kitchen dominated by a cast-iron coal-burning kitchen stove and a wooden icebox for which fifty-pound blocks of ice were delivered by horse-drawn wagon.[12]

Martha learned to her delight that Deak would be joining her and the girls for several weeks. Not every navy wife would have been thrilled with the rest of the news: Deak's next duty would return them to the Naval Proving Ground, Dahlgren. While some officers' wives equated Dahlgren with Foreign Legion outposts, Martha thought of it as an oasis on the wooded banks of the Potomac.

Deak first reported to the proving ground and then joined the family for what would become his last vacation for seven years. Once the embroiling storm of world war struck, there would be precious little time for recreation. Perhaps Deak and Martha sensed this, for they made the most of this time together in Maine: clambakes, tennis, square-dancing, and, if family legend is correct, frequent episodes of sneaking off alone together for "beer in the bushes."[13]

At the end of Deak's leave, the reunited Parsons family loaded their V8 Ford sedan with luggage. Martha's feisty fox terrier, Racket, jumped into the back seat with Peggy and Clare. In the 1930s it was still common when traveling to stay overnight with friends, and one advantage of "being navy" was knowing people in many places. The family broke their journey to Dahlgren by staying overnight in the home of Rear Adm. John Townsend at the Philadelphia Navy Yard.[14]

They arrived at the Townsends' in early September 1939. Presently, a radio news bulletin interrupted the relaxed conversation of the navy families: the German army had invaded Poland. Deak and the admiral correctly concluded that England would now declare war on Germany. As far as Deak was concerned, it would only be a question of time before the United States would be brought into the war. With the storm breaking, he did not anticipate being at Dahlgren very long; as a lieutenant commander of the line, he expected to be called to sea duty in a fighting role soon.

By the time the Parsons family drove through the main gate of the Naval Proving Ground, Britain had declared war on Nazi Germany. But Deak's other prediction would not materialize: the international emergency would not bring him orders to sea. Instead, through his new position as Dahlgren's experimental officer he would be drawn into a different kind of warfare: the battles of science against time.

The *Who's Who* of a military base is its housing list. At Dahlgren, three two-story Southern-style homes with large porches stood out above all others. All three provided views on Machodec Creek, a scenic tributary of the Potomac, and their spacious elegance went well beyond the norm for military housing. Indeed, when they were built in 1921, the design and cost of the largest of the three, intended for the commanding officer, had spurred a congressional inquiry.[15]

Capt. J. S. "Dad" Dowell, the amiable commanding officer at the time of Parsons' arrival, now occupied the controversial mansion. The other two houses, while less sumptuous, were nonetheless imposing and superior to the rest of the married-officers' quarters, which looked like carbon-copy two-story boxes uniformly spaced like so many seamen in parade formation. The proof and executive officer occupied the second of the select homes. The other was assigned to Parsons as experimental officer and third in the proving-ground hierarchy.[16]

The street behind the Parsons home was the line of demarcation between management and the managed. Consistent with his position, in the context of the times, chief physicist L. T. E. "Dr. Tommy" Thompson occupied one of the boxlike houses normally reserved for officers. He and Deak quickly wore a path between their two homes. The stark whiteness of the houses gleamed against the rich green of unfenced well-groomed lawns. However, the serenity that met the eye did not extend to the ear. The pounding of guns and the shrill shriek of projectiles penetrated the community. As in Parsons' student-officer days, there was no forgetting that the proving ground's main business was testing guns, lots of guns: battleship guns ranging all the way from 12-inch to 18-inch bores; small 3-inch/70-caliber guns; rapid-fire antiaircraft guns; American, British, Swedish, and Swiss guns—any gun that might be useful to the U.S. Navy. As Martha Parsons well remembered, the biggest blasts of all occurred by chance on the day she and Deak arrived: the firing of the triple-mount 18-inch gun, which, according to Martha, "caused the whole place to nearly fall to pieces."[17]

However, most of the firing was routine: proof-testing new guns before fleet acceptance; firings to calibrate the effects of experimental gunpowders, or different powder loads, on projectile velocities; penetration tests of armor plate of varying thickness and composition. Parsons' technical staff consisted at the time of Dr. Tommy and six civilian technicians. As experimental officer, Parsons took charge of any pioneering work. As one contemporary put it, "Anything crazy that came to Dahlgren went to 'Experimental'"—for example, the "rubber duck project," for which they shot rubber balls out of a 5-inch gun against aircraft windshields to evaluate the effects of planes having, in experimental terms, "high-impact encounters" with wild ducks.[18]

The investigations conducted by the Armor and Projectile Laboratory, which went into operation soon after Parsons' arrival, provide the clearest example of research under his aegis. Small-scale models were used in the A&P Laboratory to test penetration of projectiles against armor of different thickness and quality. Through analogy and mathematics the results could reveal the effects that would have been achieved in full-scale testing. The difference was in the low cost of the scale models. Dr. Tommy took great pride in showing Deak the A&P Laboratory. It was, after all, a product of Thompson's persistence over the objections of the Naval Research Laboratory (which contested the idea of the Naval Proving Ground doing research) and of the steel companies (which believed that they themselves should test the armor they produced).[19]

Besides the new laboratory, Dr. Tommy pointed out to Deak the advances in ballistic measurement devices that had been achieved since 1929, when he and Deak had last worked together. Then, the relationship had been one of Lieutenant Parsons conducting a student project under Dr. Thompson; now, the official roles were reversed, with the civilian scientist reporting to the officer. But in practice it was a partnership. After sixteen years at Dahlgren, Dr. Tommy had grown accustomed to seeing former student officers rise above him. He applauded their advances. As one of the few civilian scientific professionals working for the navy, he accepted the realities of the time: full officer control of the navy's experimental work, and a short ladder of advancement for civilian professionals.

An experimenter at heart, Parsons often favored direct, practical experimental action over Thompson's more sophisticated scientific approach. As part of his managerial style, Parsons liked to involve himself in enough hands-on experimentation to gain a close understanding of the problem. Besides, he did not want the civilians to have all the fun.

Deak's personal involvement in projects sometimes went beyond "hands-on." One morning Martha heard her husband groaning as he got out of bed. "What in the world is the matter with you?" she asked. "Well," Deak said, "we've been putting armor on airplane seats so pilots won't be killed so often. I gave this big burly chief out there a sledge hammer. Then I'd sit on the seat and he'd hit it. Wherever it really hurt, we put on more armor."[20]

While involving himself in the experimental work of the moment, Parsons remained alert to future trends. From his office he could hear the continuing cacophony of bangs, booms, and rat-a-tat-tats from the gun line—a kind of music to ordnance officers. He could distinguish a 5-inch Mark 42 gun fired at the main battery from a 5-inch Mark 45 at the plate battery. The discord of a misfire would jar his well-tuned ear.

As the months went by, Parsons sensed that something was wrong in the firing-line ensemble. The big guns, the bass drums of the Dahlgren orchestra, were overwhelming the other instruments. Instinct and his radar experience told him that too much emphasis was going into the refinement of guns and other conventional weapons and not enough into new technology. What he was hearing was an old familiar song, the polishing of the cannonball. He believed that the navy needed some new orchestrations.

Deak shared his concerns with Dr. Tommy during their frequent evening strolls. At the office they addressed specific tasks, but on the evening walks, as Thompson reports, "Deak and I spent many, many hours discussing the navy's program of experimental work and what was needed to make it more effective." A contemporary recalled the common sight of the officer and scientist strolling together: "They did what men who had things in common would be doing. I had the feeling they were not visiting socially but working on problems. And enjoying it."[21]

From Thompson interviews we learn that he and Parsons discussed the historical rift between science and the navy. Observing the typical aloofness of scientists to military problems, they saw a corresponding indifference of officers to science. They discussed the problems of cognizance (bureau desks protecting their turf) and of compartmentalization (parts of problems walled off from the whole). They talked about the inflexibility of navy bureaus and the government as a whole, resistance to new ideas, and the limited incentives for scientists to work in government, as well as the reluctance of most American scientists to be involved in military research at all.

While focusing on needed changes, Thompson and Parsons must have recognized the accomplishments and strengths of the navy's ordnance program.[22] The steel breech-loaded guns of the U.S. Navy were second to none, whether measured by accuracy, fire control, rapidity of fire, or reliability. The navy planes making instrumented bombing runs at the proving ground should have reminded the officer and scientist of Carl Norden's revolutionary bombsight—a product of individual ingenuity, industrial cooperation, and the navy. Tests on the gun line testified to advances made in smokeless gunpowder. The two men recognized that gyroscopes and analog devices had greatly improved fire-control directors. Technical reports from other ordnance facilities told them of advances in mines and mine counterwarfare. From Parsons' NRL experience they would have been aware of the technical advances in sonar. Yet despite these advances, they sensed an underlying stagnation. Both Thompson and Parsons had seen firsthand how administrative barriers could block revolutionary new ideas. For Parsons, the grand exemplar was radar; for Thompson, it was the military rockets of his early scientific colleague, Robert Goddard.

In 1914, at the start of World War I in Europe, Thompson and Goddard had both taught in the Clark University Physics Department of Arthur Gordon Webster, a ballistics pioneer in the United States.[23] At that time Goddard was making his first proposal to the navy for a "rocket apparatus." Although the navy's Bureau of Ordnance found the idea interesting, it raised the pet bureaucratic stall of the time: government funds could not be expended until the inventor could demonstrate the device—an impossible task for Goddard on his university salary.[24]

Goddard's next disappointment was with the army. After the United States entered World War I, scientists of the Smithsonian Institution and the National Research Council persuaded the Army Signal Corps to develop artillery rockets. But the project had a late start, and it was not until 6 November 1918 that Goddard and his assistant, Clarence Hickman, successfully demonstrated their artillery rockets to army and navy observers. Everyone was enthusiastic, but five days later the Armistice was signed, and interest died.[25]

Unlike other scientists, who were quick to drop their wartime research with the end of conflict, Goddard continued to seek military support. In July 1920 he received a navy contract to develop a rocket device to propel a depth charge away from the firing ship and out to the expected location of the enemy submarine. But this part-time research was shelved when tests showed his rocket projector to be only minimally better than the existing gun system. Little account was taken of improvements possible through future research.

Although Goddard failed in peacetime to obtain sustained military support, he was able through the assistance of Harry Guggenheim to develop a site near Carlsbad, New Mexico, for his rocket research and testing. Working with only a few assistants, he laid the foundation for the technology that would eventually take man to the moon and beyond. In the process Goddard had all but given up on receiving military support.

The ultimate irony of the American prewar rocket effort is now apparent. In 1940, while the mastermind of modern rocketry was all but pleading for military assistance, the German military was supporting its rocket scientists by building the elaborate rocket research and test station of Peenemunde on the Baltic Sea coast.

Goddard was not entirely alone in his quest for military rocket research. Among his supporters was his old friend from Clark University, Thompson. Early in 1940 Thompson wrote Goddard assuring him that it was time to give the navy another try. He himself had proposed a rocket project to the navy Bomb Board that Goddard could undertake at his New Mexico research site. The contract would cover the development of a rocket device to give an armor-piercing bomb enough additional velocity to penetrate five inches or more of a battleship's deck armor.[26] If the navy accepted the proposal, Thompson hoped Goddard would take on the project not only on its own merits but also as a step in opening up a broader navy rocket program.

Parsons backed the idea of rocket work for Goddard from the beginning, although he did not pursue it with the evangelistic zeal that characterized his fight for radar support. Parsons' advocacy of the rocket grew out his belief that it was reasonable to gamble on new ideas that could bring large payoffs. By late May 1940, when Goddard agreed to come to Dahlgren to explore the matter, Parsons was as deeply involved in the scheme to get the navy into rocket research as Thompson was.[27] What is noteworthy in hindsight is the trouble, as well as the scheming, the officer and scientist had to go through in their attempt to create a small unconventional rocket project in 1940, on the eve of the weapons revolution.

Few, if any, creative persons ever fought longer and harder to obtain military support for his new ideas than the mild-mannered, unobtrusive visitor Dr. Tommy met at the train in Fredericksburg on Saturday afternoon, 25 May 1940. The visitor, Robert Goddard, would in time be recognized as the father of modern rocketry. But back then, outside of scientific circles he was often seen as a loony physicist who made bizarre predictions of travel beyond the earth.

During the short drive to Dahlgren, Thompson informed Goddard and his wife, Esther, of a cocktail party being given for them that evening by Commander Parsons and his wife, Martha. Goddard no doubt recognized the evening's hidden agenda, since the other guests included Rear Adm. William Furlong, the chief of the Bureau of Ordnance, and his wife, and Capt. J. S. Dowell, proving-ground commanding officer and also senior member of the navy's Bomb Board.[28]

Cocktail parties had evolved to a high state of art at Dahlgren. The tradition of extraordinary hospitality began in the early days, when the snakelike road from Washington or the slow boat cruise down the Potomac called for special treatment of those who made the journey. Although the new Potomac Bridge to Maryland had now cut the journey to an hour, the tradition remained. And as of old, cocktail parties often set the stage for later office decisions. Since Deak and Martha, with live-in cook Charlotte, were master cocktail-party hosts, we can assume that the reception for the Goddards was done in style. Although Deak preferred beer himself, he mixed a good Manhattan and a tasty Old Fashioned.

As we can imagine, Martha's usual attempts to encourage pleasant social banter instead of talk of war and work were doomed that particular Saturday evening. The war news from Europe distressed scientists and officers alike: A German blitzkrieg had pulverized the French army. British forces were retreating. Nor could Martha compete with her husband's and Dr. Tommy's unstated agenda. On one hand they were trying to impress Admiral Furlong and Captain Dowell with Goddard as the potential developer of a rocket device for armor-piercing projectiles. On the other, they wanted to overcome Goddard's almost paranoid suspicion of the military.

The extent to which the party modified anyone's attitude is open to speculation. When Deak and Dr. Tommy had a chance to meet with the admiral and Dad Dowell, they found them in agreement on the potential benefits of the proposed project. The big question was Goddard. He had not been his own best salesman. On the one hand he wanted to put his expertise and his New Mexico facility to work for the government because of the national emergency; on the other, he kept bringing up conditions to be met if he was to take on the navy project. The final impasse arose over whether the rocket devices should be powered with liquid or solid propellants. Goddard insisted on the former. Furlong knew the hazards of storing and handling liquid propellants on ships and insisted on solid propellants.[29] Parsons and Thompson tried to allay Furlong's concerns over Goddard's seeming lack of openness and his insistence on doing the work in his own way and at his own pace without outside interference. The matter would not be settled until after Goddard returned to New Mexico. But for Parsons and Thompson it had become a losing battle: Goddard's rigidity matched that of the bureaucracy.

Goddard left on Monday for Washington, where he was joined by Harry Guggenheim in another attempt to obtain military support for a rocket program. The scientist described numerous military possibilities for rockets to officers of the Army Air Corps, army ordnance, and the navy's Bureau of Aeronautics. Of these, the only officers to see any useful application for rockets were those from the navy's Bureau of Aeronautics. Their interest was limited to a rocket device to give added thrust to airplanes on takeoff and climb.

Soon after his return to New Mexico, Goddard summarized the results of his trip. He was disgusted. He had obtained no support for a large-scale rocket program; nor were there any guarantees that navy contracts would come through for the BuAer rocket-assist device for airplanes or, even with the help of Thompson and Parsons, for a rocket booster for armor-piercing bombs. The scientist expressed his frustration in a letter to Thompson: "I am therefore wondering if this is a case of slow motion of large bodies."[30] In the meantime, the German rocket scientists at Peenemunde, who had solid military support, moved forward on a 21-foot 12-ton artillery rocket—then a revolutionary size—that could deliver a 1-ton warhead 160 miles.

Following Goddard's departure, Parsons and Thompson continued their attempts to overcome BuOrd's resistance. Their chief opponent in BuOrd, Capt. Garret "Mike" Schuyler, later acknowledged, "I'll say honestly that in those Goddard early days, I didn't see the rocket shooting around the moon."[31] Nor did he foresee rockets replacing the navy's big guns.

During the impasse, Goddard's assistant in the World War I rocket project, Clarence Hickman, wrote his old boss declaring that every effort should be made to make the government aware of the importance of developing military rockets. He offered his services in bringing the work to the attention of the proper government officials. Goddard promptly told him to go ahead.[32]

On the eve of the weapons revolution, the best hope for American military rockets appeared to lie with Hickman. There was nothing on the horizon to indicate that in time Parsons would be urging Thompson to become technical director of an "American Peenemunde," a navy laboratory and test range devoted mainly to rocket development.[33]

·7·

Sparking a Weapons Revolution

**"Deak" was a commanding presence. . . . Wherever he appeared he was
a leader. Even though he may have been a junior, he was a leader.**
Dr. Leonard Loeb

In World War I, the sinking of the luxury liner *Lusitania* on 7 May
1915 by a German submarine stirred scientists to converge on
Washington seeking ways to prepare for war. In World War II, it was
the evacuation of the British Expeditionary Forces at Dunkirk in late
May 1940 that alarmed American scientists and sent them packing
to Washington.[1]

In 1915 the scientists—contemptuously referred to by military con-
servatives as the "Damn Professors"—failed to launch any significant
programs affecting the war's outcome. By contrast, the scientists of
1940 not only exerted a strong impact on World War II's outcome but
have had a profound effect on American defense, science, and technology throughout the remainder of the twentieth century.

The new post-Dunkirk voices in Washington were mainly those of
university scientists who spoke not only for themselves but for their
institutions. They advocated aggressive military research and aired
deep concerns as to whether American armed forces were equipped
to fight the kind of war the nation was being drawn into. These, as we
know, were also Parsons' concerns, but he was then a field-grade officer with little influence on the Washington scene. The leaders of the

scientists had national stature as well as insight into the cause of the World War I failure to mobilize science fast enough to be effective. No one understood that failure better than the popular Cape Cod Yankee in charge of the Carnegie Institution of Washington, Vannevar Bush—the scientific leader who would later snare Deak Parsons for key roles in the development of the two most remarkable weapons of World War II, the proximity fuze and the atomic bomb.[2]

As the energetic leader of the scientists, V. Bush (as he signed his memos) formulated a plan not likely to be welcomed by the military. He wanted to reverse custom. Instead of officers stipulating what they wanted from scientists and engineers doing contract work for the navy, Bush wanted the civilians to be free of rigid specifications after being briefed on the military objectives. He wanted enough independent funding to allow the scientists to perform exploratory research without having to go through stringent budgetary approvals. He wanted full partnership.

In June 1940 Bush took his recommendations to President Franklin D. Roosevelt. In the wake of Dunkirk, he did not have to cite urgency. After only ten minutes he left the White House with the essential "OK—FDR" above four brief paragraphs on one sheet of paper.[3] That sheet of paper established the National Defense Research Committee (NDRC), with Vannevar Bush as chairman, and provided a precedent-breaking charter for American science. Unlike George Ellery Hale, the civilian scientific leader in World War I, Bush had an open door to the president. Vice Adm. Harold G. Bowen, the navy representative on the new committee, stated—with some bitterness—that the NDRC had a "private pipeline to the President of the United States and the U.S. Treasury."[4]

Word of NDRC spread down the halls of Main Navy, a sprawling wood building on Washington's Constitution Avenue left over from World War I. From there it quickly spread to Dahlgren and the navy's ordnance facilities. The hidebound saw the NDRC scientists as a new wave of Damned Professors. Not Parsons, who saw the NDRC as an opportunity for the military services to have direct access to the nation's scientists.

One of Parsons' first NDRC contacts occurred on 11 July 1940, when Richard Tolman, dean of graduate studies at the California Institute of Technology (CalTech), visited Dahlgren. In meeting with Parsons and Thompson, Tolman used his new title, head of Division A of NDRC, which was the armor and ordnance component of the civilian organization. As for military experience, Tolman claimed none. But he could assure Parsons and Thompson that if the military could define the problems, he had a lot of physicists in university laboratories who could go to work on the solutions. After discussing a host of conventional ordnance items where advances would be useful—gun directors, turrets, aiming devices, range finders—the three men turned to the subject of unconventional weapons. Quite casually Tolman asked, "Do you have any rocket work that you would like to have us take up?"[5]

The question itself raised Parsons and Thompson's estimation of NDRC and Tolman. For months they had tried to get funding for Goddard to pursue a simple, yet pioneering, rocket task. And here was a university professor seeking just such unproved, high-risk projects. Here was a man who understood that it would take more than conventional weapons to win the war then looming on the horizon. As Thompson later recalled, he just happened to have the rocket correspondence clipped together on his desk: "I pulled it out and handed it to Tolman, and I said, 'we need a jet assist for AP bombs.'"[6]

In contrast to the preceding months of indecision, Tolman received V. Bush's approval the next day for rocket investigations including that for the AP bomb.[7] Immediately thereafter NDRC formed the first, but not the last, rocket program of World II. Located at Indian Head, Maryland, this program was placed under the direction of Clarence Hickman. The weapons revolution was under way.

In offering their services to the government, the NDRC scientists provided two essential elements to this revolution. The other element needed was a more enlightened military leadership. Fortunately, the crises that opened the way for scientific participation in weapon developments also cleared the way for the cream of the military to rise to the top. Nowhere was this clearer than in naval ordnance, where the officer on the way up was Capt. W. H. P. "Spike" Blandy.

In the summer of 1940 Blandy, as head of BuOrd's Research Desk, was among the first in the navy to fully appreciate the opportunity that NDRC opened up for major advances in weaponry. In particular he encouraged applied research that might lead to improved antiaircraft weapons.[8] As a rising ordnance star, Blandy joined other progressive BuOrd officers in involving the NDRC scientists in navy problems.

Years later Parsons wrote, "By June 1940 things began happening fast in many places and Dahlgren was no exception." Parsons identified the harbingers of the new enlightenment as "first-ranking scientists" alarmed by the fall of France. He reported, "In a short time we at the Proving Ground began to receive enthusiastic [scientific] groups first with ideas to discuss, then with gadgets to test."[9] In September 1940 the scientific visitor of note was Merle Tuve, head of the newly established Section T (for Tuve) of Tolman's division.

Parsons knew in advance of Tuve's scientific brilliance from his and Gregory Breit's 1925 pioneering use of radio pulses to measure the height of the ionosphere. But it took the direct meeting for Parsons to experience the scientist's dynamic personality. Like Parsons, Tuve did not acknowledge any wall separating scientific and military learning. Just as Parsons devoured scientific treatises, Tuve immersed himself in ordnance studies.[10] Just as Parsons consulted with Thompson, Ross Gunn, and other people of science, so did Tuve tap the minds of Blandy, Schuyler, and other officers in the Bureau of Ordnance. With Parsons, Tuve continued his questioning. It was an intense discussion, both men being aware that while they talked people were dying in the war in Europe. The airplane had increased war's viciousness and taken it from conventional battle lines to industrial centers and cities as well.

Both Tuve and Parsons understood that Britain's defense was America's defense. They recognized the alarming ease with which German bombers penetrated English antiaircraft fire. The best gunners had little chance of making a direct hit on an invading airplane, yet this was what was required when using shells with contact fuzes. "Clock" fuzes improved the odds slightly by making the shell burst at a preset time after firing. But there was no way to determine the precise distance between the aircraft and the gun or of measuring all the variables affecting a projectile in flight. By some estimates it would take twenty-four hundred shells to destroy a plane; others believed one hundred thousand a more likely number.[11] Yet the security of nations depended upon defense against aircraft.

The problem transcended traditional approaches. Refinements in gunsights and fire control, improvements in range finders, and more rigorous training of gun crews would not resolve it. Parsons agreed with his visitor that marginal improvements would not be enough; the problem demanded a radically new system with the brains in the ammunition itself. And this is the change Tuve intended to make.

Tuve explained that he and his colleagues in Section T were exploring a wide range of fuzes using infrared, magnetic, optical, and radio phenomena as the sensory power to trigger the bombs, rockets, or gun projectiles at the opportune moment. He said Section T was not alone in this quest. British scientists already had a research program under way, and an exchange of information was anticipated. He stated that Section T had some exploratory work under way on proximity fuzes for projectiles but said the better prospect for the initial research seemed to be a photoelectric fuze for bombs. A bomb offered more space for the fuze and was not subject to the intense jolt of a gun firing. A rocket offered similar advantages, but the American military had as yet no artillery rockets.

If the rationale for developing a proximity fuze for bombs met the test of logic, the same seems questionable today for the proposed tactical use of the bombs. If Parsons questioned the prescribed use, he never let the scientists know it. To him, judgments of bizarre ideas with potentially large payoffs should not be made until after the basic premise and technology had been tested. It is doubtful that he even blinked when Tuve described the fuze that would allow bombers to bomb bombers.

In Tuve's scenario—formulated in league with BuOrd officers—a plane would drop a bomb armed with a photoelectric fuze into the center of a formation of attacking enemy bombers. As the bomb fell through the formation, the optical fuze would sense either a glint of light or a shadow from one of the bombers. "Seeing" that it was close enough to damage the enemy plane, the fuze would trigger the bomb's explosives.[12]

Parsons listened to the scientists, examined the literature, read their papers. By the time he had completed the test plan, he understood both the theories and the practical gamble involved. For the first tests he had a navy airplane fly over a working model of an optical fuze— mounted in a coffee can. As the shadow of the plane crossed over the coffee can, the experimenters observed a definite fuze reaction on an attached oscilloscope. The Section T civilians on this test had not met

Parsons before. They reacted with dismay when this naval officer joined them during test preparations, raising incisive technical questions they had failed to ask themselves, yet doing so in their own scientific vernacular—half-waves, cosines, oscillations, and modulations. And he did so not like a military steward but as a member of the team.[13]

After satisfactory results from the flyover tests, Parsons arranged a complex test with four bombers at Cape May, New Jersey. The first plane, a TBD bomber flying at eight thousand feet, towed the target— a twenty-five-foot black cloth sleeve. The second plane, flying at ten thousand feet, was to drop a 100-pound inert bomb equipped with an experimental optical fuze. Two additional planes carried observers and cameramen.[14]

In this period of unsophisticated ground-to-air communications, merely coordinating the flight paths of four airplanes challenged Parsons' experimental skills. And there was always the additional task of scanning the river to make certain that some boat had not wandered into the impact area, an inherent problem with over-water ranges. After a series of failures, Charles Lauritsen, deputy chief of NDRC's Armor Division, pleaded for one more try. He told Parsons, "This time if it doesn't work, I'll jump in the river." The result was another failure, whereupon Lauritsen gamely said, "All right, let's go down to the river."

"Don't worry," Parsons replied, "when the photographic planes came in, we found that a cameraman on one of them had forgotten to take the cap off the lens. On the other plane, we didn't have the right plugs to get power to the cameras. We've been taking pictures for a hundred years, and we still can't do it right. You have nothing to worry about."

"That," Lauritsen later reported, "made me feel good!" He added, "Parsons was always very understanding, very patient."[15]

Another test revealed Parsons to be quick-witted as well as loyal. On this occasion a delay occurred in the release of the bomb. Even without a warhead, a 100-pound bomb falling from the sky is no small hazard to those below. Instead of the bomb following its intended path, it nearly hit the Cape May Bridge. Afterward the project leaders met with Parsons in his office to discuss what went wrong. During the gathering the phone rang. Parsons was heard to answer, "Yes, yes,

yes." Then in a firm voice he said, "Now let me tell you something. The navy has the best bomb sights in the world. If we wanted to hit that bridge, we would have hit it!" He then hung up and dialed another number, saying, "Bill, for God's sake, never drop another one within a mile of that bridge!"[16]

Deak enjoyed the orderliness and calmness of Dahlgren but, as elsewhere, limited his social activities. He went to Officers' Club receptions, community events, and dinner parties more as a matter of duty than enjoyment.[17]

As at sea, Deak avoided bridge, but he could not avoid Dahlgren's ubiquitous poker games. The social pattern as described by Martha was "You had dinner. Then everybody played poker. We were drawn into it, but he didn't really like it." Nor, it seems, did he like Martha's introduction to the game. Following her first evening of poker, Deak let her know she had embarrassed him. Here is her account: "Well, I lost about $3; well, $3 was $3 and I said after it was all over, 'Now tell me this, did everybody lose money like this?' And he said, 'The way you reacted, I thought you lost $40 or $50.'"[18]

If Deak winced over Martha's poker, he had nothing but admiration for her golf and tennis. Unlike her, he was not a natural athlete, and any advantage he gained was through strategy and the application of physics to control small spheres in motion. In any case, sports were not central to his life.[19]

Martha presided over the recreation agenda and the Parsons household as well. To her, successful household management meant spending as little time as possible on household chores and cooking. These duties fell to Charlotte, the maid who lived with the Parsons. In the summer, Martha would have Marjorie Clark (Ackerman) come from Maine as a nanny for Clare. On Charlotte's nights out, Martha would serve the same thing every time: steak, potato chips, and salad.[20]

Deak and Martha had one common concern that competed with his work and her sports: their daughters. In November 1941 Clare—the younger, more aggressive, and naughtier of the two—celebrated her fourth birthday. Even at four, Clare's capers had become legend, to wit: on the floor with Toby the cocker spaniel lapping up the remains from the eggnog bowl; finding and eating all of her mother's cache of Hershey bars; jumping against orders from the backyard shed and breaking her arm. In December 1941 the birthday party was for Peggy, who like her father at age seven was exceptionally quiet and well behaved.[21] Deak spent less time with the girls than Martha did and sometimes injected too much science and seriousness into family games, yet he was the more nurturing of the parents. Clare's antics exasperated and inflamed her mother, whereas, as Clare recounted later, "Father had almost 100% tolerance for all my shenanigans. They bothered him almost not at all."[22]

During this time Dr. Tommy, then divorced and not yet remarried, became part of the Parsons family. When there was a family outing or a holiday dinner he was there. A "Yo ho" at the back door meant that Dr. Tommy was there. He was the girls' surrogate grandfather. Most important, he was Deak's confidante on the evening strolls through the grass-covered yards of Dahlgren.

By early 1941 the evening talks of Deak and Dr. Tommy had progressed from merely identifying naval ordnance flaws to "a kind of dreaming." They dreamed of a navy laboratory where scientists would work closely with officers familiar with the fleet's ordnance requirements yet would have the freedom they needed for effective research. The laboratory's broad technological base would allow it not only to respond to the immediate needs of the fleet but also to explore new technologies—such as Goddard's rocket investigations—with long-range military potential. Scientists would be able to follow their innovations from idea through research, development, test, and in some cases through pilot production and introduction into the fleet. In formulating the concept, they talked of the "close couplings" needed between civilians and the military, scientists and engineers, research labs and test ranges. In the model laboratory, no one would be able to claim a monopoly on good ideas, or have sole *cognizance*—Parsons' pet word—of any areas of research. Yet neither man expected their dream lab to become a reality or their principles of operation to become embodied in a network of naval research centers.[23]

Parsons and Thompson devised their dream laboratory largely in answer to their negative experiences of the past, not realizing that another lesson on the ills of the system lay directly ahead. The first clue lay hidden in Dad Dowell's suggestion that they should push through any important requisitions they might have pertaining to the proving ground's scientific work. Dowell made it clear that he would sign these immediately. In his own sly way, the amiable commander of the proving ground was forecasting a storm that could threaten local research.[24]

A month or so after Dowell's suggestion, April 1941, the storm hit Dahlgren with the arrival of Capt. David I. Hedrick, Dad Dowell's replacement. With an outpouring of autocratic power, as reported by an officer of the time, Hedrick proclaimed himself "the boss of everything that had to do with the Proving Ground, everything in the community, everybody who lived on the station—civilian, military, anything else."[25] Like the captain of a ship, he did not need the advice of boards or committees. After thirty-six years in the navy he knew enough to be his own committee. As to mission, he asserted that the proving ground was purely a proof and test station. Its purpose was to test ammunition, projectiles, and armor, not to do research. Ordnance research was the business of industry.[26]

For views of Hedrick and Parsons we have the recollections of Capt. Leonard Loeb, one of a growing number of scientists with reserve commissions brought to Dahlgren in the post-Dunkirk military buildup. Loeb found his own relationship with the station commander paradoxical. Hedrick would belittle Loeb's research in front of the scientist's peers yet end the day drinking whiskey with him. In Loeb's view, Hedrick was "a regular Queeg," but amiable.[27]

As the new officer in charge of the A&P Laboratory, Loeb saw himself as the target of Hedrick's efforts to undermine Thompson and proving-ground research. It did not help that Loeb was a reservist, which in Hedrick's book made him "neither fish [nor] fowl." When Hedrick crippled the A&P Laboratory by cutting its staff and reassigning its most experienced people, Loeb decided it was time to fight back. To build a case, he kept a little black book in which he documented, among other things, what he saw as Hedrick's illegal interference with congressional appropriations for the A&P Laboratory. With the little black book in hand, Loeb called on Parsons and Thompson, offering to put Hedrick "on the rack." He asked, "Do you want me to do that? If not, I am getting out. . . . I'm finished."[28]

Parsons and Thompson were fighters, but not wild sluggers. Although they agreed with the merits of Loeb's case, their style was to go around obstructionists rather than stiffen the opposition through confrontation. By August 1941 Loeb had returned to his civilian position in the Physics Department of the University of California, Berkeley. To Parsons and Thompson the experience was another example of the difficulty in that era of building and retaining a competent civilian technical staff within a military organization. It demonstrated the kind of autocratic military control that would have to be guarded against in their dream laboratory. You could not, they believed, run a laboratory like a ship.

Technical support of NDRC projects lay beyond Captain Hedrick's control. Taking local initiative for this work, Parsons was one among those in the navy who encouraged Tuve to shift the Section T work from the optical fuze for the bomber-versus-bomber tactic to another seemingly wild idea, a radio proximity fuze for gun projectiles.[29]

Since Tuve's first visit to Dahlgren, Parsons had pressed the view that the big military payoff for a proximity fuze would be in artillery projectiles. Parsons recognized the immense tactical value of a gun projectile with a fuze that could sense when it was close enough to an airplane to destroy it.[30] He did so even though he understood the immense difficulties of designing and mass-producing such a fuze. In essence the scientists would have to create a miniature radar that could fit into the nose cone of a projectile—a space no larger than a pint milk bottle. Such a device would contain at least four glass vacuum tubes that, along with the intricate circuitry, would have to withstand firing from a gun with forces twenty thousand times that of gravity and the centrifugal pull of five hundred rotations per second during flight. All the while, the fuze would have to be transmitting radio waves in search of its target aircraft. When the target reflected the signals back to the projectile, a receiver would have to convert this information into an electronic command that would trigger the explosion.

From his first meeting with Tuve, Parsons had known of the scientist's early experimental work on the radio fuze. As an ordnance officer accustomed to systematic proving-ground procedures, Parsons may well have been amazed at both the resourcefulness and the foolhardiness of the Section T scientists in their early testing for the radio fuze. To determine the vulnerability of glass vacuum tubes to the shock of being fired from a gun, they had mounted hearing-aid tubes in wax and dropped them onto the concrete out of their three-story laboratory. Needing a harsher test, they sawed off a section of gas-line pipe and used it as a smoothbore howitzer. They bought gunpowder—from a florist with a side line of explosives—and arranged for some igniters from the navy. They potted vacuum tubes in wax and took them to a nearby farm where they fired them, as well as batteries, electronic circuits, and other fuze components, into the air. The scientists held boards over their heads to give them a feeling of protection in the event that what they shot straight up came straight down and hit them. All the while they watched for splashes in the dirt that told them where to go with their posthole digger to recover the fallen test items for inspection.[31]

Later the scientists obtained guns from the navy and conducted their tests in an open field near Stump Neck, Maryland. Here a Chesapeake Bay retriever named Curly volunteered. Attentively watching the loading of the vertically aimed guns, Curly was off in a run at the bang of the gun looking for the inevitable splash of dirt. Always among the first to discover the landing spot, he would dig away until the next firing sent him off to another splash.[32]

As rudimentary as they were, these early tests proved the feasibility of a radio fuze. Through this progress Tuve obtained greater access to Dahlgren's instrumented ranges and to Parsons. One crucial test Parsons set up at Dahlgren was to demonstrate the ability of the fuze to transmit radio signals after being fired downrange from a 5-inch naval gun. Anticipating a milestone, scientists Tolman, Lauritsen, and Tuve insisted on being present along with Parsons and the fuze designer, Richard Roberts.

On 8 May 1941 Parsons located himself and the four scientists in a boat directly under the anticipated flight path of seven projectiles. Had they not had on headphones the men could have heard the screeches of the projectiles whizzing past overhead. But with the headphones pressed close to their ears they heard a sweeter sound, that of radio emissions from at least two of the projectiles as they passed over. The miniature radar inside the projectile, despite the shock of being blasted out of a gun and spun like a top, dutifully transmitted signals. To the men in the boat, this was a case of one hearing being worth more than ten thousand words.[33]

On their return to Washington the scientists poured their enthusiasm out on Capt. S. R. "Sam" Shumaker, the project's BuOrd coordinator. However, before agreeing to a still higher priority on the fuze, Captain Sam called Parsons and asked him to provide justification for greater effort. After some study, Parsons came back with the answer: "Delays in getting the fuze into action are equivalent to the loss of a battleship every three months, a cruiser a month, and one hundred fifty men a day."[34]

Following the 8 May firings, Dick Roberts and two other Section T scientists came to the proving ground with ten handmade fuzes. They wanted Parsons to test these with full powder loads and simulated explosive heads in order to show whether or not the proximity fuzes would work at the end of a long flight. After setting up the test, Parsons and the civilians took a range boat halfway down the fourteen-thousand-yard impact range.

One advantage of firing the fuzes over the sea range was that when a fuze came within a set distance from the water, it would react in the same way as if it had detected an airplane. Scientists monitoring the tests expected to hear a rippling sound through their radio headsets when transmitted and reflected waves met. This rippling would trigger smoke puffs to simulate an explosion in the final device.

Through radio contact with the firing battery, Roberts and Parsons could hear the countdown for the firing of each of the ten handmade fuzes. The scientists grimaced as the first nine rounds, one after another, fired prematurely or splashed in as duds. Parsons revealed not the slightest trace of disappointment. Nor did he show any elation when the tenth round rippled perfectly and triggered the smoke puff fifty feet above water. This was the first demonstration that a proximity fuze in a fully loaded shell would work, yet Parsons showed not so much as a smile. Just as he had given no sign of discouragement over the failures, he was not going overboard with the success.

With continuing good news from the test ranges, Shumaker formally requested that Section T place radio fuzes for gun projectiles at the top of its priorities. The fuzes worked. Concept and design were sound. But as Parsons and the scientists knew, the fuzes used in these tests had been made in the laboratory. To be effective instruments of war, fuzes had to be produced not by the dozens but in the millions, not by scientists in a laboratory but by laborers on factory production lines. They had to be fired not by professional range engineers under controlled conditions but by common sailors and soldiers under the rigors of war.

•

Throughout 1941, fuze testing had taken more and more of Parsons' time away from his experimental-officer duties. Under normal circumstances this would have stirred objections from Captain Hedrick. The difference in this case was the new chief of the Bureau of Ordnance, Rear Admiral Blandy, who brought to the office a deep concern over the navy's vulnerability to aircraft. Through Blandy it was understood that Parsons was to support the fuze work when needed, but for Merle Tuve, that was not enough. He argued, "The main reason for wanting experienced officers now is to give us foresight. It is absurd to expect civilians with no experience whatever to anticipate every difficulty and every requirement for such a new weapon as the Radio Fuze. . . . The Services should share this responsibility with us, instead of being simply 'available on call.'"[35]

Tuve wanted nothing less than Parsons full-time. So too did Captain Hedrick. And while this issue was being resolved, the gods of war were preparing to release their fury on the United States.

Peggy Parsons as a seven-year-old was a sensitive child whose parents were always there for her when she needed them, but she felt herself abandoned on the morning of 7 December 1941. That Sunday morning Peggy and a neighbor boy had been left at an Episcopal Sunday school in rural Virginia where her father was to pick them up on his way back from golf. The classes ended and the other children went home, but Peggy's father did not arrive. Peggy and the boy played in the graveyard. But with time the play turned to worry, then bewilderment. Still her father did not come.[36]

Peggy lost track of time, but finally her father arrived. He seemed different, as if in pain. She did not understand the meaning of what he said: Japanese airplanes had attacked Pearl Harbor. He promised that when they arrived home he would show her Pearl Harbor on the map. President Roosevelt was certain to declare war on Japan, and this in time would mean war with Germany and Italy as well. Peggy asked how long the war would last. She misunderstood the answer and thought her father said that five people would die. Later when she heard that a lot of people had been killed she thought the war should be over. But she learned that war was not that simple. In fact millions of deaths would occur worldwide, over three and a half years, before that war would end, and then only after Peggy's father helped create two deadly new weapons and took them both to war.

The news of Pearl Harbor struck Deak like a two-edged sword. In one fell swoop over three hundred Japanese aircraft had pierced the heart of the American fleet. The sunk and damaged ships included those Deak had known; among the dead were former classmates. Deak's knowledge that this catastrophe need not have happened intensified his pain. While others sought inquiries into the failures of the officers in charge of Pearl Harbor's defense, Deak bemoaned the navy's failure to recognize the potential of radar in the early 1930s. Had the navy responded with reasonable support then, he believed, a tested and reliable early-warning detection, communication, and command system would have been in place to alert the Pearl Harbor naval forces in time to man their defenses and get ships under way.[37] (In fact an SCR-270 army radar had picked up the invading airplanes 130 miles away, but the warnings of the inexperienced radar operators were ignored because a responsive command system had not been developed to take advantage of radar technology.)[38]

In recalling the early resistance to radar research, Parsons concluded that "the Navy, which had the initiative in its grasp, lost something like two years in getting radar into the fleet." This was the lost time Parsons decried. "It really pained me," he said, "to think how much two years of fleet experience with radar *before 1941* could have saved us in lives, planes, ships, and battles lost during the initial phases of the Pacific War."[39]

·8·

Into Battle with the Smart Fuze

**[Parsons' presence] gave us confidence that this wasn't just a
silly exercise invented by some civilian.**
Dr. Merle Tuve

The United States' entry into World War II raised the stakes on
the smart-fuze gamble. The navy responded immediately by let-
ting four high-priority contracts for the pilot production of completed
fuzes. These contracts for tens of thousands of the secret device were
anything but ordinary. Only the heads of the contracting firms knew
what the device was designed to do. Stranger yet, 90 percent of the
completed devices were hauled away and crunched into waste by
huge presses. The other 10 percent went to firing ranges for testing,
after which they underwent postmortem exams in the laboratory
before themselves being crunched.

The nation was at war, and this was the price of building an industrial base so that immediate mass production could begin just as soon
as the design and engineering problems were resolved. Perhaps the
largest manufacturing gamble in history, this was a battle against time.
As Parsons and the bureau leaders understood, the certain way to
identify production problems was to produce; hence, they considered
these early contracts as "educational orders."[1]

But even education can come at too high a price. As the crunching continued, only 10 percent of the fuzes fired on the test ranges

functioned properly. All attempts to identify the problem eluded the experimenters. Section T morale was down. The team needed to be fired up about its military mission. For this, Tuve and his deputy, Lawrence "Larry" Hafstad, turned to Parsons, whose role had by now expanded well beyond proving-ground tests. Hafstad explains Parsons' broad influence: "He had earned our confidence, and was just one of us. I think one of the things that made him so effective was that he could talk to scientists in their own language. He understood what they were saying, and yet he was enough of a line officer so that he had a lot of influence in the navy."[2]

Parsons impressed on the laboratory staff the military importance of what they were doing, the reality of the final objective: a device that could shorten the war and save thousands of American lives. To fight the gloom, Parsons talked informally with the researchers, eliciting and addressing their concerns. He would take a pencil and fill a sheet of paper with black circles. "Look at this," he would say to those within earshot. "You have seen firing exercises where antiaircraft bursts fill the whole sky with black puffs. You think, how can a plane survive that?" He then rubbed his eraser through the black circles. "Those puffs are harmless, any airplane can fly through the puffs. It's only a fraction of a second that each is dangerous. So every time you see a puff, you ought to erase it."[3]

Parsons reminded the scientists that the existing time fuzes for projectiles were effective only one-tenth of 1 percent of the time. Section T's 10 percent success rate represented progress. The fuzes did not have to be perfect to be extraordinarily useful in battle. The odds were against the enemy if only half the fuzes worked among all the projectiles fired against an attacking plane. The difference could determine whether a battle was lost or won. His message: raise the rate from 10 percent to 50 percent, and the proximity fuze would be far ahead of time fuzes. This 50 percent goal, informally prescribed by Parsons, provided the basis for the position soon taken by Shumaker. Captain Sam announced that BuOrd intended to go into mass production as soon as the fuzes functioned properly 50 percent of the time or more.[4]

While Parsons improved morale, his assurances of eventual success did not change the test results. No matter what was done, 90 percent or more of the pilot production fuzes failed. Laboratory postmortems only intensified the mystery. Disheartened, Tuve called his group together. "There are some things that just can't be done," he told them. "We are going to try another two weeks. If at the end of that time we haven't hit a fifty percent score, we're going to just call it off."[5]

In the next two weeks everything that could be fired was fired—including one batch of questionable fuzes. Doubt had existed whether this batch should be tested at all because of small cracks in the plastic around an insert. More from whim than logic, a scientist dipped these in a rubberlike mixture of cerise wax and Visanex to seal the cracks. He then set this questionable batch aside. They might not have been tested had the range engineers not been temporarily out of rounds to fire because of a delayed train. To the amazement of the range engineers, not 10 or 15 percent but a whopping 65 percent of these operated as designed.[6]

Whether science or magic, no one cared. Cerise wax and Visanex became the elixir for the ailing fuze assemblies. Wilbur Goss of Section T tells the story: "Every round we could get our hands on, we dipped into cerise wax and Visanex. Those rounds also averaged greater than 50 percent, almost regardless of prescription. Well, we didn't understand it at the time, and nobody gave a damn."[7] Goss and others later determined that the magic mixture absorbed heat that otherwise, more often than not, melted a critical solder joint.

On 29 January 1942 Parsons telephoned Admiral Blandy. Fifty fuzes from the pilot assembly line had just been fired down the bay from 5-inch guns at Dahlgren; twenty-six functioned properly. The long-sought 50 percent goal had been surpassed. On the strength of Parsons' message, Blandy and Shumaker called in some of the leading scientists and congratulated them. Shumaker said, "This proves you know what you are doing. From now on the sky's the limit. We're going into full production as fast as we can."[8]

The fuze crunching stopped. But far-reaching administrative changes were needed before the fuzes, each with its miniature radar, could be produced by the millions. To open the flow, BuOrd took over program direction and production contracting. But in doing so, Blandy wanted Vannevar Bush to retain overall technical direction of the fuze program, including Tuve's research and development. By this time Bush had been made head of the newly created Office of Scientific Research and Development, which replaced the National Defense Research Committee as the central operating organization of the scientists. At the same time, the NDRC became the chief advisory committee to the OSRD.[9] "I agreed," Bush later recalled, "to keep the affair [the Section T fuze project] in OSRD provided they would attach one damn good officer to my office for liaison." To this he added, "They certainly did."[10]

The damn good officer assigned was Parsons, and the position went far beyond liaison. Bush clarified Parsons' unusual role in a letter to Tolman: "I am accepting your recommendation that the present activities of Section T be transferred . . . to a Section in my office under the supervision of Commander W. S. Parsons." Bush added, "The immediate direction of the work of the Section will remain under Dr. M. A. Tuve as Chairman, reporting through Commander Parsons to me."[11]

For clarification we have the words of Edward Moreland, executive officer, OSRD: "Commander W. S. Parsons . . . is in charge of Section T and has final authority as to the control of the project." According to two project leaders, Bush said to Parsons and Tuve, in essence, "Get the job done; I've got a lot of other things to worry about. You let me know when there is a big problem." Hafstad describes the change: "This was at the point when the navy moved in with Deak Parsons running it [the fuze program] and took responsibility for greatly expanding this whole business."[12]

Placing Parsons between himself and Tuve solved several problems for Bush, including what he saw as Tuve's personality problem. On one hand, Bush recognized Tuve's high energy and resourcefulness. These had, Bush wrote, "undoubtedly brought [the fuze work] to its present state where the navy is spending some seventy million dollars on the subject." On the other hand, he saw Tuve as being resentful of controls over his expenditures and inclined to spend funds freely. "More serious," according to Bush, "Tuve is inclined to write unwise letters, and he may send them almost anywhere." Bush feared that one such "violent letter" to the wrong place could damage important OSRD relationships. Moreover, according to Bush, Tuve did not "take guidance from any source readily."[13]

Under most circumstances, the worst way to provide guidance to a scientific prima donna is to have it come from a military officer. But Bush knew that Tuve regarded Parsons highly. And there was no forgetting Tuve's early pleas to have a top-caliber naval officer assigned permanently to Section T. As "special assistant," Parsons would be speaking for Bush administratively without stepping on Tuve's scientific prerogatives. Nonetheless, despite the cosmetics, Parsons, an officer, reported directly to civilian V. Bush, and Tuve's Section T, now numbering about one hundred civilians, was under Parsons. But that was the paper organization. With Bush as figurehead, Tuve and Parsons formed the core of an extraordinarily effective military-scientific management team. Joining them in the day-to-day program management were Larry Hafstad and D. Luke Hopkins, a university trustee. In his classic *Scientists against Time,* Baxter describes the foursome as "one of the ablest and smoothest working teams which ever sought to translate new scientific ideas into mass-produced devices for combat use."[14]

By placing Parsons between himself and Section T, Bush solved a major fiscal concern. He did not want to be personally responsible for the large sums that would be spent as the fuze moved from pilot to full production. Any postwar congressional inquiry might look askance at Bush as president of the Carnegie Institution, Washington (on loan to OSRD for the duration of the national emergency), approving funds for Tuve's Section T, which was in fact the Carnegie Institution's Department of Terrestrial Magnetism (also on loan to OSRD).[15]

In the new organization, the fuze project was moved from the Carnegie Institution to Johns Hopkins University, where it formed the Applied Physics Laboratory (APL). Besides being Bush's voice in this new civilian laboratory, Parsons also spoke as the navy's project manager. Wearing a second hat, he was BuOrd's representative on the proximity fuze program, carrying responsibility directly for $2 million of fuze-research, and indirectly for $80 million of fuze-manufacturing, funds.

Neither Parsons nor Tuve assumed the traditional role of boss. As managers of this military-scientific project they became a team that did more stimulating and clearing of roadblocks than directing. Parsons' effectiveness as the military man in this partnership went beyond his control of the purse strings and his knowledge of ordnance and military applications. He had, as Tuve recognized, "a direct connection to the best technical people in the navy."[16] Beyond this, Parsons' distinct management style fit the applied-research environment.

"One of his techniques," according to Hafstad, "was to always ask for just a little bit more and not ask too much." Not until the fuzes scored over 50 percent did Parsons come out and say, "Now we have to make sure these things will stand the salt spray test." Knowing that the thought of salt water in circuits was the worst kind of image to an electroniker like Hafstad, Parsons had not mentioned that problem earlier; it would have been too discouraging. And after the salt-spray problem was resolved, Parsons brought up his next concerns, one at a time: safe handling, safety of firing crews, storage life, rough handling at sea. When, for example, the technical team had made the fuze operable in the tropics, Parsons would say, "Now let's see what we need to do to make it work in the Arctic."[17]

Like Tuve, Parsons believed that in research no single person had all the answers: advances came through the collective mind and the scientific process. And just as Tuve's dynamic personality and restless drive inspired the team, so too did Parsons' steadiness give it confidence. Most of Tuve's "running orders" posted in the laboratory reflected Parsons' managerial philosophy as well. But the style and color were distinctly Tuve's:

I don't want any damn fool in this laboratory to save money. I only want him to save time.

Run your bets in parallel, not in series. This is a war program, not a scientific program.

We can't afford perfection. . . . Don't forget the best job in the world is a total failure if it is too late.

Our moral responsibility goes all the way to the final battle use of this unit; its failure there is our failure.[18]

Deak Parsons took on the stewardship of the fuze program in April 1942 with the understanding that he would stay with APL only through the initial development and fleet use of the fuze. Then he was to be released—or so he believed—for the sea duty for which he was overdue. He also asked that he and his family be allowed to keep their quarters in Dahlgren even though this would mean an hour-and-a-half drive each way between Dahlgren and the APL laboratory at Silver Spring, Maryland, near Washington.

Why Captain Hedrick agreed to this is open to speculation. The captain was being asked to give up Parsons' services even though Parsons, for security cover, would still appear on the proving ground's organizational charts as experimental officer. Moreover, the proving ground would be providing a navy car and gas (in a time of war rationing) for Parsons to shuttle back and forth to Washington. Most precious of all, Parsons would retain one of Dahlgren's choicest quarters. Logic suggests that Blandy simply told Hedrick, This is the way it will be.

As for Parsons' characteristic disdain for any special treatment, that did not apply when it came to housing for his family. What he would not do for himself, he would do for Martha and daughters.

The Dahlgren residence was more a way of life than a house to Deak and Martha. The creek view, the neighborhood tennis court, and the lawn surrounding all the senior officers' quarters were all amenities they could not hope to find in wartime Washington. Neither could they afford a live-in maid or summer help to care for the children in Washington.

While the APL assignment limited Deak's time with his own family, it opened opportunities to be with his brother Critchell. After leaving Oxford, Critchell had become a manager in Alexandria, Egypt, for Socony-Vacuum Oil Company. He had married Helen Ferris, an American touring abroad, and the two lived in Egypt until World War II when the oil company brought them back to the United States. Critchell, multilingual and a world-oil specialist, went to work for the Foreign Economics Administration of the federal government. Critchell and Helen had a home in Silver Spring, and this made it convenient for Deak to stay over frequently instead of making the long drive back to Dahlgren every day. Long evening chats with Critchell were among the few relaxing activities Deak allowed himself during this time of national peril.[19]

Not long after Deak began commuting to APL, Martha had narrowed the subject of his secret work down to "some kind of shell." She could correlate, she thought, the days he remained at Dahlgren with the kind of sounds she heard from the gun range as she worked in her vegetable garden. One evening as he entered the house she said, "Gee, that really works better!"

Deak answered, "What are you talking about?"

"Well, whatever you're working on. I could hear it. It used to go bang—bang—bang——bang—bang———bang, and now it goes bang-bang-bang-bang-bang-bang. It sounds better to me."

"You're not supposed to know this," Deak replied crisply.

Martha said, "How can anyone stay here day after day and not know?"[20]

In fact, Martha did not know what the mysterious item was, but that she even speculated disturbed Deak.

Leonard Loeb, back at his university position and unaware that Parsons had become a phantom figure at the proving ground, wrote Thompson in February 1942:

> My dear Tommy:
>
> It was quite a shock to me to learn of your leaving the Proving Ground. . . . I feel that your leaving will now place the Proving Ground completely at the mercy of Captain Schuyler [in BuOrd], Captain Hedrick, and the powers of darkness and technical ignorance. Parsons, of course, is a valiant disciple, an able politician, and a thoroughly competent officer. He will do a great deal to keep alive the tradition that you started as long as he is left at the Proving Ground. . . . What will happen when Parsons and Hoffman [proof officer] go, God knows![21]

After nearly two decades, Dr. Tommy was abandoning his campaign for ordnance research at the Naval Proving Ground. He had accepted a managerial position with the Carl L. Norden Company, makers of the Norden bombsight.[22]

Despite Loeb's prediction, the sky did not fall with Thompson's departure and with Parsons' absence in all but name. Lt. Comdr. Ralph Sawyer, a physicist in uniform, became the chief scientist, and through him the A&P Laboratory made significant contributions to the war effort. Like Thompson, Sawyer had to work his way around Captain Hedrick, who held fast to his views that the Naval Proving Ground should be purely a test and proof facility.[23] More important to this account than military-scientific issues at Dahlgren is whether the dream Thompson and Parsons fashioned there for a new kind of ordnance laboratory could ever become a reality. With the partners going their separate ways, this now seemed highly unlikely.

•

Beginning in the spring of 1942, Commander Parsons and the Section T scientists converged inconspicuously each morning in an old garage building in the quiet Washington suburb of Silver Spring, Maryland. The old garage provided a ready-made security cover for the unusual undertaking of the newly formed Applied Physics Laboratory. Not even the nearest residential neighbors suspected that the garage housed top-priority, top-secret military research.

Time would prove the radio proximity fuze to be the navy's best-kept secret of the war. Much of this success is attributable to the security practices established by the military-civilian partnership of Tuve and Parsons. When Parsons joined the Section T management team, he introduced an interviewing technique designed to impress applicants with the concern for secrecy. At the end of the meeting he would reach for an ashtray, and while both parties looked on he would burn the written equations and rough sketches made during the discussion. Double-talk also played a security role. Each fuze component had an innocuous or misleading name. When it became necessary to order nose cones, Johns Hopkins University, having a medical reputation, placed orders for millions of "rectal expanders."[24]

During the first weeks in his new position, while administering million-dollar contracts, Parsons designed a unique way to demonstrate the capability of the fuze to detect an aircraft within lethal range. He covered a Taylor Cub airplane with aluminum gauze and had it suspended from a navy balloon. The small plane was attached so that it could swing with the wind through an arc of about one hundred feet. On 13 April 1942 a gun crew fired 182 projectiles with proximity fuzes against this target. As the shells sped by the airplane, 20 percent sensed the target and rippled when they were within kill distance. While not a high score, it convinced Parsons that the time had come for the big test: firings from standard navy guns by regular gun crews from a real ship against attacking aircraft. No ordinary navy commander would have had the power to commandeer a new light cruiser fresh from sea trials for an ordnance test. But by now Parsons was no ordinary field-grade officer. Because of a unique combination of personality, reputation (military and scientific), and circumstance, he had the backing of the biggest guns of the uniformed navy—Admirals Ernest King and Spike Blandy—as well as the president's science czar, Vannevar Bush. Thus, the crew of the USS *Cleveland*, about one thousand all told, found themselves in the summer of 1942 off of Norfolk, Virginia, preparing their 5-inch antiaircraft batteries for secret tests.

Obtaining a cruiser was one thing; acquiring six radio-controlled aircraft to serve as pilotless drone targets was another. Priority or not, air-facility officers refused to provide more than four. The airmen were accustomed to overoptimism on the part of the gunnery officers they usually served. They told Parsons they were not afraid of his destroying any of their drones, but they did not like to patch shrapnel holes in any more than necessary. In fact, with the ammunition of the time, target drones were seldom damaged beyond repair.[25]

On the morning of 13 August 1942, with all hands at battle stations, Parsons ordered the first drone launched. It crashed ignominiously from defects of its own. Prospects for the day did not look promising.

Parsons calmly ordered the next drone to make its simulated torpedo attack on the *Cleveland*. With one burst of projectiles tipped with the new fuze, the drone crashed into the sea. Parsons called for the next drone. Before ten rounds were fired, the drone burst into flames. Just as rapidly, the last available drone made its run at the ship. It too splashed down to a watery grave.

Vannevar Bush wired his colleague, James Conant: "Three runs, three hits, and no errors."[26] The smart fuze was ready for trial in combat.

The efficiency with which the proximity fuze was introduced into the fleet and rushed into battle is attributable largely to Parsons: first, in that he had kept the development focused on a fleet-usable weapon, and second, in that he personally took the weapon into combat and introduced it into the fleet. Parsons' first role was later described by Larry Hafstad: "He really knew the fleet and knew how it operated. He coached us in making sure that the things we did [from development through production] would fit in."[27] Parsons took on the second role by convincing V. Bush and Spike Blandy that someone familiar with both the fleet and the new weapon should take it into combat, namely himself.

Parsons began arrangements for his trip to the Pacific immediately after the *Cleveland* test. But even in the haste to bring the weapon into battle, he did not relax experimental procedures. During October 1942 he had five hundred fuzes from the production lines flown to the ammunition depot at Mare Island, where they were inserted into the noses of 5-inch antiaircraft shells. Four hundred and fifty of these shells were then set aside in a special stockpile under his name. The other fifty shells, complete with fuzes, were flown back to Dahlgren, where they were tested to assure Parsons that no new problems had crept into the process. He followed the same procedure on all the succeeding shipments.

When the special stockpile approached five thousand, Parsons flew to Mare Island to arrange ship transportation to the Pacific. Three navy lieutenants, all in brand-new uniforms, joined Parsons at Mare Island. The three officers had good reason to be ill at ease and none too smooth on navy protocol: only a few days earlier they had been scientists in civilian dress at the garage-front laboratory, with no thought of becoming commissioned officers. But Parsons needed assistance in introducing the fuze into the fleet, and he wanted to avoid the resistance of war-hardened sailors to civilians explaining naval weaponry. At the same time, he wanted fuze-knowledgeable assistants who could help him devise technical solutions to any problems that might occur overseas. As testimony to Commander Parsons' new powers, Neil Dilley, Robert Peterson, and James Van Allen (whose later research on cosmic radiation led to the discovery of the Van Allen belts) received reserve commissions and orders overseas virtually overnight.[28]

Still stunned by their metamorphosis, the new officers accompanied five thousand shells with special fuzes—officially designated VT (variable-time) fuzes—on a ship headed to the naval base at Noumea, New Caledonia. Parsons flew on ahead, ready to go to war, if not in his own ship, at least with weapons he had helped create.

On arrival in Noumea, Parsons reported to Adm. William Halsey, the naval commander of the South Pacific. After Halsey saw films of the rapid-fire demise of the three drones that had made mock attacks on the *Cleveland,* he gave Parsons the equivalent of a hunting license to find commanders of combat units willing to use their ships for the ultimate test of the new weapon against enemy aircraft.[29]

From Adm. Arleigh Burke we have a description of what may have been the first tactical use of the new fuzes. By this account, Parsons, bringing crates of the new ammunition, boarded a destroyer under Burke's command during the Solomons campaign. But as Burke observed, when you go looking for action, "that is the time the enemy never cooperates." The only Japanese aircraft that came in range were nighttime reconnaissance planes. After two or three nights out, Parsons concluded that "snoopers are better than nothing" and authorized the first combat use of the new fuzes. To the surprise of the crew, who expected little more than to harass enemy aircraft at night, a reconnaissance plane was brought down right away. They were delighted, but Parsons apparently found this a shallow victory. In any case, he did not report it. He wanted to use the fuzes against a full-scale enemy attack. After a few days of test-firing against rocks as simulated surface ships, Parsons left the destroyer group in search of action.[30]

From inquiries in Noumea, Parsons learned that if he was looking for trouble from the "Japs," he should join the light cruiser *Helena,* which had a fighting reputation. Parsons promptly sought the help of the commander of the six-cruiser task force that included the *Helena.* By chance the chief staff officer of the task force was Comdr. (later Rear Adm.) Levering Smith, a former shipmate of Parsons on the USS *Texas.* Smith later recalled, "Parsons came to see if he could get these things battle tested. . . . And we weren't really anxious to go looking for trouble. But he came out there, 'Come, let's go; let's go get into a fight.'"[31]

Parsons, with fuzed shells to follow, boarded the *Helena,* reporting to Capt. C. P. Cecil, the commanding officer. Cecil proved extraordinarily supportive of this added mission. As the *Helena* entered hostile waters on her next mission, Cecil and Parsons kept their eyes to the sky, not with apprehension but with hope of being attacked by Japanese planes.

During this time the *Helena* bombarded Japanese shore entrenchments and airfields in order to disrupt Japanese attempts to reinforce their troops at Guadalcanal. Parsons would receive the first of his three battle stars for participating in this engagement for the capture and defense of Guadalcanal.[32] He split his time between indoctrinating the gunnery batteries on the use of the new fuzes and making himself useful through his ordnance and gunnery background. All the while, he watched, waiting for enemy aircraft to take the bait.

On the morning of 5 January 1943, the task force recovered its observation aircraft at a position eighteen miles south of Cape Hunter.

But, as Parsons and others aboard the *Helena* could see, there were still aircraft overhead. Four planes—later identified as Aichi dive bombers—could be seen circling eleven thousand feet above like hawks seeking prey. Then four more aircraft appeared from out of the clouds. Parsons watched as both groups of Japanese aircraft joined in a screaming dive upon the task force. Defying hundreds of shells with conventional fuzes, the attackers scored a devastating hit on one cruiser and two near misses, yet remained unscathed. Captain Cecil later reported, "The attack was a surprise and gunfire was not opened until the dives had been completed and the attacking planes were withdrawing from the rear of our formation."[33]

As two departing Aichis streaked by the *Helena,* the 40-mm and 20-mm antiaircraft batteries with standard munitions opened fire with no discernible success. It was now up to the 5-inch after battery under Lt. "Red" Cochrane. The lieutenant fired two (some say three) rounds of proximity-fuzed shells.[34] A "very close" burst, characteristic of the new fuze, sent the plane crashing into the sea.[35] The new weapon had made its first kill. By one account Parsons exclaimed, "Oh boy, this beats target practice all to Hell!" By another account, "This is the best test we could have arranged for this thing."[36]

A second plane also crashed into the sea during the 5 January assault, but its demise came from accumulated damage from various task force projectiles, conventionally fuzed as well as proximity-fuzed. However, for Parsons and Cecil, the important hit was the one completely attributable to the proximity fuze. Captain Cecil reported to navy headquarters, "The value of the Mark 32 fuzed projectile cannot be too highly stressed."[37]

Cecil later told a senior APL scientist what happened when a cruiser in the task force found one of the Japanese planes still afloat. The search team found a dead enlisted man and the injured pilot, both of them riddled with shell fragments. After the search team brought the pilot aboard the cruiser, he pulled out a pistol and shot himself.[38] This kind of fanatical devotion to duty convinced Parsons and other fighting men in the Pacific war that they faced an enemy of extraordinary resolve—an enemy prepared to die rather than accept defeat.

If Parsons had had his choice, he would have relieved the *Helena*'s executive officer, then due for shore duty, but that was but a dream-like wish expressed later to Martha. Parsons still had his own mission to complete. And the *Helena*—in Parsons' view, the "tightest" and the "battlingist ship in the navy"—had her own date with destiny.[39]

The months of work that went into the creation of the proximity fuze had come to a climax in just a few moments in combat. The gunner on the after deck of the *Helena* tracked the ill-fated Aichi forty-five seconds before opening fire. The hit occurred within the next fifteen seconds. The time from the first to the last shot was two minutes.[40] In that brief time, the history of warfare changed; the first mass-produced smart weapon had proved itself in battle.

Parsons, with the help of his three officer-scientists, now needed to accomplish for the entire Pacific Fleet what he had done on the *Helena*—that is, indoctrinate crews in the use of the weapon and imbue them with confidence in it. Even for a former gunnery officer like Parsons it was a formidable task. Some veteran gunners distrusted anything new and were reluctant to leave the thinking to a few radio tubes in a fast-flying, spinning projectile. The antidote for this skepticism lay in Parsons' impressive knowledge of guns and his contagious confidence in the new creation.

After successfully launching the indoctrination program, Parsons went to sea with at least one more task force. On 18 February 1943 he reported aboard the USS *Cleveland*. He needed no introduction, certainly not to Capt. E. W. Burrough and the gunnery crews. Six months earlier Parsons and the fuze had made themselves a legend on the *Cleveland* by destroying three drones in succession during mock attacks. Little did the crew know that what they witnessed that day had caused them to be sent directly to the Pacific war without any final liberty in the States lest some slip of the tongue reveal the navy's biggest secret.

As on the *Helena,* Parsons involved himself in the *Cleveland*'s mission, helping wherever his expertise might be useful, but always keeping an eye to the sky. The ship was in action almost constantly during Parsons' three weeks aboard. She bombarded Japanese shore installations and took part in at least one major night action in support of troop landings. For his service on the *Cleveland* Parsons received the second of his three battle stars.[41] We know none of the details except that the captain commended Parsons for "his great assistance" and noted the value of his outstanding "experience in ordnance and gunnery details." And from Captain Burrough we learn what we might expect—that even in combat Parsons' fellow officers were struck by "his unfailing courtesy."[42]

By the end of March tens of thousands of the proximity fuzes were being produced daily and shipped to the Pacific Fleet. Much work still remained for the three officer-scientists from APL, but Parsons' foundation for the task was now complete. He could now, he believed, return home, wrap up his work at APL, and await orders that would take him back into the war in command of a ship of his own. He did not know that the smart fuze would have a bigger brother or that the same weapons revolution that gave birth to the fuze had also spawned plans for an atomic bomb.

Ultimately, the fuze's big brother, the atomic bomb of the Manhattan Project, would so stun the world that the immense success of the smart fuze would be obscured. Part of the lost history of the fuze is the role it played as pathfinder for the atomic bomb. The fuze project demonstrated that aggressive use of applied science toward military objectives could pay enormous dividends in battle. It set the precedent for military-scientific-industrial collaboration, thereby pointing the way to the atomic bomb and Big Science. To understand the fuze, the granddaddy of today's smart weapons, we must not look back at it through the nuclear haze but see it, rather, by the light of its own time upon the stage.

This joint accomplishment of the navy and the Applied Physics Laboratory went beyond the technical ingenuity of the radio fuze. The organizational achievement transcended anything of the time. Never before had such an effective alliance been established among the military, science, and industry. By the last year of the war, eighty-seven companies were producing ninety different types of proximity fuzes. Nearly one million people were in some way involved. Fuzes came off the assembly lines at the rate of seventy thousand a day. All told, 22 million fuzes and 150 million rugged tubes were produced.[43]

The smart fuze was not only effective, *it was on time*. The history of warfare is filled with weapon advances that did not become operational until after the end of the war that had provoked their development: the submarine, sea mines, sonar, modern rockets. The radio proximity fuze was ready in time to give the naval forces in the Pacific the antiaircraft protection needed to pursue the enemy aggressively into his home waters.

"Had it not been for those fuzes," Adm. Arleigh Burke said, "our ship losses and casualties in the last half of the war would have been enormously larger than they were."[44] Moreover, the fuze made it possible for ships of the Pacific Fleet to operate much more aggressively than would have been otherwise possible.

The fuze was ready in time to help counter attacks by Japanese kamikaze pilots who threw normal tactics aside and dove headlong into American ships. And three months before the first V-1 missile—the "buzz bomb"—fell on London in June 1944, a large supply of proximity fuzes had been shipped to England in anticipation of this "secret" weapon of Hitler's. In combination with two other OSRD developments—the M9 gun director and SCR-584 radar—the proximity fuze blunted the massive buzz-bomb attacks on London and Antwerp. From the start, Parsons was among those who warned against allowing the fuze's technical secrets to fall into the hand of the enemy, lest it be employed against Allied aircraft. For this reason the fuze was restricted at first to use over water, where there was little chance of a round being recovered by the enemy. Despite this concern, Parsons was also among those who approved the navy's making the fuze technology available to the army in order to produce fuzes for army antiaircraft batteries and for controlled airbursts by ground artillery.[45] To maintain the secret as long as possible, it was agreed that these smart fuzes would not be used over land until they were available in massive numbers and could be used decisively. The opportunity came sooner than expected.

On 16 December 1944 Field Marshal Rudolf von Rundstedt led Hitler's last desperate offensive, soon known as the Battle of the Bulge. He achieved initial success through surprise and through a massive concentration of tanks and crack troops against the thinnest section of the Allied line. If ever a time existed for an army to come forth with a revolutionary secret weapon, this was it. On 18 December the fuze made its entry into ground warfare.

In the days that followed, thousands upon thousands of the new weapons rained shrapnel over bridges, road junctions, and advancing German troops. For the first time in history an army was able to maintain sustained aerial bursts over both stationary and moving targets. German prisoners of war characterized American artillery in this battle as "the most demoralizing and destructive ever encountered."[46] One group of American infantrymen and combat engineers, having never heard of a smart fuze, credited divine intervention.[47]

What the troops witnessed was not a miracle but the result of a four-year race against time. In this instance, scientists and officers, along with American industry, had won the race. The fuzes were available early enough to become a major factor in this decisive battle, as acknowledged by Lt. Gen. George Patton's high praise of the "funny fuze."[48]

No weapon concept in modern history went from development to production, and on into battle, so smoothly, timely, secretly, and effectively. No officer did more to make this happen than Comdr. Deak Parsons, a sailor who knew how to talk the language of scientists.

·9·

Into the Secret World of "Y"

My candidate for the UNSUNG HERO of Los Alamos is Admiral Deak Parsons.
Dr. Joseph Hirschfelder

No brass band greeted Deak Parsons in late March 1943 when he stepped off the plane onto the tarmac at Bolling Air Force Base in Washington, D.C. He was a new kind of warrior returning from a different kind of war. Then as now, leaders in the secret battles of military technology seldom received recognition. Naval heroes are not often made in laboratories.

Before returning to Dahlgren, Parsons, who characteristically put mission before family, called on Vannevar Bush to report firsthand on the successful introduction of the proximity fuze in the Pacific and to plan the wrap-up of his work with the Applied Physics Laboratory. Even though Deak Parsons had been V. Bush's chief conduit for the proximity fuze program, then the exemplar of a successful secret weapon, he did not have access to his civilian boss's even bigger secret: the high-priority work then under way to build an atomic bomb.[1]

If Bush had intentions of shanghaiing Parsons into this atomic bomb program, it is unlikely Parsons would have known of them. When it came to the game of management, V. Bush was a poker player who never tipped his hand. As observed by historian Stanley Goldberg, Bush kept a low profile and regularly accomplished his ends without revealing his intentions.[2] If Bush intended to break his pledge not to interfere with Parsons' plans to go to sea, it was not something to be revealed.

Back in June 1940, when the president scribbled "OK—FDR" on Bush's plan to mobilize science, Roosevelt also put his Advisory Committee on Uranium under Bush. This committee had been established in October 1939 at the instigation of Albert Einstein and other concerned scientists to investigate the possible applications of uranium fission. The work had moved at a snail's pace, largely because the leading nuclear scientists could not agree on the direction the work should take and because the committee's chairman, Lyman Briggs, gave it little sense of urgency.[3]

Upon taking over the uranium committee, V. Bush himself had doubts whether or not a large effort to develop an atomic bomb was merited. However, he changed his position in April 1941 when he received reports that German scientists were working intensely on the development of a nuclear bomb. When British intelligence confirmed the German activity, Bush committed himself to building an American atomic bomb. As it turned out, the Germans, who did have the scientific talent and the resources to make an atomic bomb, did not employ them in a large-scale effort early in 1940 when they had the initial advantage. Had they done so, according to Thomas Powers in *Heisenberg's War,* they might have had a nuclear bomb in 1943 before the Allied bomber offensive began taking its toll on German industry.[4] Bush understood the threat, but neither American nor British intelligence gave him a clear picture of the reality. The only prudent defense against this new superweapon was to have it first.

Once committed, Bush spent the next months building a consensus among nuclear scientists for a high-priority bomb program.[5] Having achieved that, he visited the president on 9 October 1941 in the company of Vice President Henry Wallace. At that meeting Roosevelt approved an expanded program. Five months later, Bush was able to report to the president:

> The technical aspects are in the hands of notable physicists, chemists, and engineers. . . . The work is underway at full speed.
>
> Recent developments indicate, briefly, that the subject is more important than I believed when I last spoke to you. . . . The stuff will

apparently be more powerful than we then thought, the amount necessary appears to be less, the possibilities of actual production more certain.

The endeavor, Bush reported, was rapidly approaching the pilot-production stage where limited amounts of fissionable uranium and plutonium would be produced. At that point the most promising methods for full production could be selected.[6]

Bush recognized that production of the fissionable materials, uranium-235 and plutonium, would require a huge industrial effort, and he considered the U.S. Army Corps of Engineers to be best equipped for constructing and operating the plants.[7] To this end, in the fall of 1942 the War Department formed the Manhattan Engineering District (MED). At the same time, Bush formed the Military Policy Committee (MPC) to formulate policy and provide overall direction for the project. By this arrangement, he, as MPC chairman, reported directly to the president. With himself as chairman and James Conant as alternate, Bush thus safeguarded the interests of the scientific community in the bomb project. In the arrangement finally approved by the president, Brig. Gen. Wilhelm Styer represented the army and Rear Adm. William R. Purnell the navy. Under normal circumstances the directors of the MPC would have had a hand in the selection of the project's chief executive. However, the army jumped the gun and, to V. Bush's consternation, promoted Col. Leslie Groves to brigadier general and made him director of the Manhattan Engineering District—and de facto chief executive of the atomic bomb project. A shocked V. Bush, after only one meeting with the general, doubted whether Groves "had sufficient tact for such a job." He wrote a colleague, "I fear we are in the soup."[8]

In March 1943 Deak Parsons knew nothing of the chain of nuclear events in Vannevar Bush's life that were now about to encircle him as well. Not knowing left Deak free to fully enjoy his welcome back to his Dahlgren home on the banks of Machodec Creek.

Having been in the war zone and expecting to return again soon, Deak had extra reason to enjoy the welcoming embraces of Martha, Peggy, and Clare. Although Deak spoke only in general terms of having been on ships in the Pacific, Martha could sense the inner glow of a warrior, albeit one of a different kind, one fresh from victory in battle.

As was their custom, Martha welcomed Deak home with one of Charlotte's fried-chicken dinners served savory brown and crisp, surrounded by stuffing, mashed potatoes, and gravy, as well as peas and squash fresh from the Virginia countryside. Amid the filling of plates, the girls' demands for drumsticks, and the pulling of the wishbone, Martha held her silence about where the chicken had come from. This was one of Martha's little secrets. She knew Deak disapproved of her buying chickens from, of all persons, Captain Hedrick.[9]

Deak believed that the commanding officer of a military base should not be selling chickens or anything else to those under his command. Despite the reluctant support Hedrick had given Parsons during the fuze assignment, Parsons recognized that Hedrick begrudged bureau use of *his* experimental officer—that is, Parsons—for *their* secret assignments.[10] Parsons understood Hedrick's feeling and gave him all the respect his position and rank required, but that did not mean buying his chickens.

In the weeks that followed his homecoming Deak continued commuting to Silver Spring and Washington as he completed his fuze reports and aided his successor, Capt. Carroll Tyler, to meet the increasing demand for the smart fuzes. However, he also allowed more time than usual for rekindling family life with river walks, home games, and picnics. He took advantage of the interval to reach out more to his daughters. One means he chose was to improve their tennis; however, as with most things, he approached tennis more as science and strategy than as a game. Peggy complained, "Oh, mother, he makes me count one, two, three, four and I get so tired of this. Why can't we just play?"[11]

Nonetheless, these were pleasant family days. There were prospects of a family vacation in Maine. But even as Martha and Deak spoke of this, Vannevar Bush in Washington was planning a meeting of the Military Policy Committee that would change their plans for years to come.

V. Bush's concerns over General Groves as the Manhattan Project director would eventually diminish, but not before the 4 May meeting of the Military Policy Committee. At that time, it appears, the science chief was still looking for ways to counterbalance army domination of the project and to offset Groves' insensitivity to scientists and their ways.

After calling the meeting to order, V. Bush asked General Groves to report on Project Y, the secret weapon site being built on a remote New Mexico mesa for the nuclear research and engineering leading toward an atomic bomb. The general had much to report: laboratories, offices, homes, security fences going up. A whole new community was emerging at the hamlet named Los Alamos. Robert Oppenheimer, the newly appointed director of Y, now had commitments from 150 persons for his professional staff, and a few of these were already at the secret site. The weapons laboratory was being built on Oppenheimer's premise that scientists working together in a remote area free of distractions would stimulate each other in the search to release the power of the atom. But that was not enough for Groves. Whatever some scientists might think, there was much more to building a bomb than physics.

Groves did not have to dredge up past history to make his point. Everyone on the committee knew that past plans for combining the military and scientific elements of the program had failed. At one point Groves had convinced Oppenheimer that the project should be entirely military, with all the scientists commissioned as officers. Oppenheimer had had no problems personally with this, believing as he did that what a man wore need not affect the quality or objectivity of his thinking. The physicist even went so far as to order his army uniform, complete with the insignia of lieutenant colonel.[12] But he encountered unyielding opposition from key nuclear physicists he was trying to bring into the project. To mollify this opposition, Oppenheimer in conjunction with Groves and Conant came up with a two-phase plan. In the first phase the laboratory was to operate on a strictly civilian basis as it performed "certain experimental studies in science, engineering, and ordnance." At a later date the project would enter the military phase covering "large-scale experiments involving difficult ordnance procedures and the handling of dangerous materials."[13] Any scientist agreeing to stay with the project after the first phase would be commissioned. This plan satisfied the immediate concerns of the scientists. It ended the debate and allowed the project to get under way. With time and with Parsons' entry into the project, the moment never came to begin the second phase.

Just as the two-phase plan reveals the early failure to comprehend the magnitude of the weapon aspects of the problem, so did another of Oppenheimer's early plans to give the project the needed weapons expertise. He proposed sending several Los Alamos scientists to army or navy proving grounds to gain the ordnance experience needed to come back to Los Alamos and build the bomb.[14] This also proved to be simplistic, as it failed to recognize the magnitude of the weapon problem. In a final effort to get out from under the ordnance problems himself, Oppenheimer turned to Richard Tolman, CalTech scientist and OSRD official. By the time of the MPC's May meeting, Tolman was penciled in on Oppenheimer's organizational chart as head of ordnance, but in fact with Tolman in Washington busy with other OSRD affairs, Oppenheimer still had no ordnance expertise at Los Alamos, and that was where such a person was needed.[15]

Groves saw a better way to provide weapon leadership. At the May meeting, the general told the president's policy committee that it was essential to begin designing and engineering an operational bomb without delay. To do that, he said, "I need an ordnance officer, particularly in the development of the bomb itself, so that we will have service equipment instead of some dream child."[16]

Groves knew what kind of man he wanted. This person should be well versed in theoretical and practical ordnance, including high explosives, guns, and fuzing. He should be someone with a high reputation among ordnance people, as he would need the support of the army and navy proving grounds, gunmakers, and ballisticians. And he should have a broad background in scientific development, as he would have to gain and hold the respect of scientists.[17]

Groves recognized that some scientists at Y questioned whether an Ordnance Division was needed at all. If needed, why shouldn't it be under a civilian scientist like the other divisions? To counter such notions, Groves argued, "This person would have to set up ballistic tests of experimental bombs, plan for the combat use of the weapon and quite possibly be the one to use the bomb in actual battle." These tasks, he believed, called for a regular military officer.[18]

"I went through the list of army ordnance officers," Groves told the directors, "and I just can't find anyone that I think could do the job."

"Would you have any objections," V. Bush asked, "to a naval officer?"

"Not at all," Groves responded, "if he is good."

Bush played his card: he recommended Deak Parsons. Purnell spoke up, "We can't get a better man."[19]

•

On Thursday morning, 5 May, Admiral Purnell telephoned Commander Parsons: report without delay to Adm. Ernest King.[20] Parsons must have recognized that something unusual was afoot. Admiral King filled the two top positions in the navy: chief of naval operations (CNO) and commander in chief of the U.S. Fleet (ComInCh). Officers less than captain were not called into King's rarefied world of admirals and top planners without strong reason.

When Parsons presented himself, the trim, stern admiral went directly to the point. The services of an ordnance officer were needed, he said, "to supervise the actual production of an atomic bomb."[21] Because of the ultra-secrecy, the admiral emphasized, he and Purnell were the only officers in the navy who then had knowledge that such a bomb was in the works. He wanted to assign Parsons to this "important and urgent wartime duty."[22] As the admiral spoke, Parsons saw his hopes for a wartime sea command dashed against a reef.

King assured Parsons that if he accepted the assignment he would have the complete support of himself and Admiral Purnell. This army program could end the war, and he strongly backed it. An army general named Groves would provide the details. King recognized that Parsons was due for sea duty and that the MED assignment would deprive him of an opportunity "to make a war record for himself at sea."[23] He pledged to make the reason for this clear in Parsons' postwar records. However, as Parsons knew only too well, even the navy's commander in chief had limited control over ageless customs governing promotions. He also knew that when the admiral requests, when the demands of war intercede, when duty calls, an officer of the U.S. Navy salutes and says, "Aye, aye, sir!"

Parsons later described the meeting: "I was plunged into the Manhattan District with a set of verbal orders and a discussion with Admiral King lasting less than ten minutes."[24] Those brief minutes completely altered Deak Parsons' career. For the foreseeable future his target would no longer be a career at sea but the making and delivery of a bomb that could end the war.

Parsons called immediately on General Groves. In introducing himself, he reminded the general that they had met before when both were junior officers involved in related experimental projects.[25] A few minutes into the conversation, Groves knew that Parsons was his man. Parsons impressed him then, as he had earlier in their careers, with his "understanding of the interplay between military forces and advanced scientific theory."[26]

Groves briefed Parsons on Project Y and the role he envisioned for its ordnance chief. The general later reported, "Parsons was very much interested. Of course he pointed out that he wanted to get to sea—that he had been sidetracked on the proximity fuze." Groves understood; he too had wanted combat duty. But this mission went beyond personal considerations. He told Parsons, "You are the man for the job." Even so, he said, "to smooth things out in advance," he did not want to send Parsons to Los Alamos until Oppenheimer met him and felt "simpatico."[27]

Events moved rapidly. Groves presented Parsons to Oppenheimer the next morning and Parsons, by his own report, immediately assumed the role of chief engineer in charge of Project Y ordnance.[28] Meetings were quickly set up in Tolman's office and in the board room of the National Academy of Sciences to provide Parsons a review of the project in relation to ordnance requirements, weapon design, and plans for Los Alamos test ranges and instruments. Three of the civilians present were designated to help Parsons in the design of the special gun then seen as the heart of the nuclear weapon. The three included "Dr. Tommy" Thompson; Dr. Charles Critchfield, then at the Geophysics Laboratory of the Carnegie Institution, Washington, but soon to go to the Los Alamos scientific staff; and Edwin Rose, chief gun designer for the Jones and Lamson Machine Company, who through Tolman had been involved in the initial attempts to get an ordnance program under way.[29]

Soon after the meeting at the National Academy, Parsons left for a brief visit to Los Alamos accompanied by Oppenheimer. As the train rattled westward, the lanky slouched physicist and the square-shouldered officer spent two days in uninterrupted conversation. A better management retreat could not have been arranged. The officer and the scientist engaged each other, as Parsons said, "in a highly satisfactory exchange of philosophies."[30] Parsons' views reflected the openness and organizational flexibility he had experienced with Tuve on the fuze program. Oppenheimer's views at that time are less clear. He was then emerging from a metamorphosis: from idealistic researcher to scientific manager, from self-immersion to openness with colleagues, from the naive belief that a few physicists could build an atomic bomb to the realization that a large multidisciplinary team was needed. But there was no ambiguity on one point: Oppenheimer wanted to divest himself of the ordnance engineering and the problems of actual bomb making.

At the heart of the discussion was the relationship between the nuclear physics and weapon engineering. When the possibility arose of having two independent organizations for the scientific and military objectives, Parsons told Oppenheimer that "the uncertainties and research nature of the problem demanded overall integration by a physicist."[31] As the train sped westward the two men concluded, as Parsons recalled, that the scientists would "produce the nuclear guts of the gadget," which Parsons' division would then "engineer into a totally reliable service weapon."[32]

Besides discussing the split in responsibilities and the Ordnance Division's organization and staffing, the physicist and officer laid out the division's laboratories, machine shops, and firing ranges—all this before Parsons had even seen the site.[33]

Each click of the rails brought Deak and Oppy, as they now knew each other, into closer understanding. Each whistle brought them nearer to a place each loved, New Mexico. This "land of enchantment" encompassed the ranch of Oppy's summers near Los Alamos as well as Deak's hometown on the plains. But a world of difference separated Fort Sumner, cursed by the shifting sandbars of the Pecos River, and Los Alamos, a jewel hidden among the pines and junipers of the Jemez Mountains.

At the time of Parsons' arrival, the Los Alamos charm was obscured by a cacophony of saws, hammers, and bulldozers. But an end to the construction seemed in sight. Oppenheimer's plan then called for a work force of about three hundred people, well beyond his original dream of a half-dozen scientists and staff, yet still small enough for close intellectual ties.[34] But again Oppenheimer's plan was shattered. By the end of Parsons' visit, Oppenheimer found it necessary to more than double the planned work force, with most of that increase going into ordnance engineering functions slated for Parsons. Whereas the planned number had crept upward in the past and would do so in the future—to twenty-five hundred full-time employees at the end of the war—the abrupt increase in May 1943 was in some ways the most significant. It destroyed Oppenheimer's original concept of a small laboratory.[35] Just as the proximity fuze had taken on a life of its own, so too did the atomic bomb; henceforth Los Alamos would be whatever the bomb demanded.

While Parsons contributed to the dramatic expansion of plans in May 1943, he was adding to forces already in motion.[36] His visit happened to coincide with the release of a report by a committee Groves had selected to review the Los Alamos program and organization. Chaired by Warren Lewis of the Massachusetts Institute of Technology, the committee endorsed Groves' views on the need for balancing the scientific research with more aggressive ordnance engineering. It also recommended that Los Alamos take responsibility for the purification of uranium.[37]

Oppenheimer's response to the Lewis report might have been different had he not been joined by Parsons at the time. As it was, he and Parsons used the Lewis report as leverage for more ordnance facilities. In a memo to Groves they requested (in addition to an ordnance laboratory and warehouse already under construction) an administrative and office building, a second ordnance laboratory, an engineering and shop building, a bomb-proof control center on the explosives range, and a chemistry and metallurgy laboratory (the one addition not slated for Parsons). And they requested housing for an additional 175 married and 130 single people. By having the memo come with the heading "From: W. S. Parsons and J. R. Oppenheimer," the officer and scientist made the first use of what would become a standard tactic in obtaining approvals on critical issues from Groves: their combined signatures or initials as evidence of military-scientific concurrence.[38] The combination worked from the start. In this case it assured that the sounds of saws, hammers, and bulldozers would continue to reverberate among the pines of the Jemez Mountains for months to come.

After four days at Los Alamos, Parsons returned to the East Coast confident that Oppenheimer and the physicists could unlock the power of the atom and that with his own help a bomb could be built.

At home in Dahlgren, Martha Parsons faced the age-old difficulties of a navy wife maintaining a family in a world dictated by military orders and missions. In mid-May, when Deak had left suddenly on his trip to she knew not where, Martha prepared herself for another change. In times like these she liked to remember the composure with which her mother had responded to military disruptions of family life. When Admiral Cluverius suddenly announced, "Nan, we're going to China tomorrow," her mother had replied, "All right. What time?"[39]

Martha may have found this recollection comforting at the coming-home dinner for Deak in late May. At the end of the meal, Deak announced that he had a new and important assignment. The trip to Maine was out; the family would be moving. Like her mother and grandmother, Martha did little more than ask, "When?"

Martha sensed that Deak had lost the elation that had marked his return from the Pacific anticipating sea duty. In its place she sensed preoccupation, an inner excitement, a deep bewitchment. She knew this mood. Deak was happiest when he had big problems to solve.[40]

Back in Washington, Parsons called on General Groves in his plain and inconspicuous office in Washington's Foggy Bottom. Parsons began by identifying their common objective, "a perfectly delivered, perfectly functioning atomic bomb that could end the war." This result could be assured, Parsons argued, if he as chief engineer also served as weaponeer on the first combat mission with an atomic bomb. He buttressed his argument by citing his success in taking the proximity fuze into battle. Parsons assured the general that, by his knowing during the making of the atomic bomb that he would accompany it on its war mission, he most certainly would take a deep personal interest in getting every detail exactly right.[41] It was a convincing argument and, according to Parsons, Groves agreed.[42]

Believing that the issue was settled, Parsons called next on the two men who had been the source of his power in the fuze program: V. Bush on the civilian side and Rear Adm. "Spike" Blandy on the navy side. Each had reason to welcome the selection of Parsons as Los Alamos ordnance chief. In him they would have someone at the heart of the nuclear work they knew and trusted. Parsons left their offices knowing that their doors were still open to him.

Rear Admiral Purnell, the navy representative on the president's nuclear policy committee, provided Parsons a third route to the top of Washington's wartime power structure. This senior officer, who had commanded naval forces early in the war, knew the navy from stem to stern. Now as an assistant chief of staff to Admiral King, Purnell embraced the idea of having a naval officer inside the management team of Project Y. If Purnell was to be committing major naval resources to a project hidden from most navy eyes, he would like to do so in response to a naval officer. And to Purnell there was no one more to be trusted than Parsons.

On 1 June 1943 Purnell had Parsons detached from the Naval Proving Ground and assigned to Admiral King's ComInCh staff. Parsons' promotion came through at the same time, giving him the captain's eagles. Purnell originally put Parsons on King's staff as an expedient while awaiting his formal transfer to the atomic project on 16 June. However, Purnell and Parsons quickly recognized that there could be long-range advantages in keeping Parsons' name on the rolls of Admiral King's staff. For one thing, it provided security cover for Parsons, a plausible explanation of his whereabouts. When well-meaning friends saw him in Washington and wanted to know what he was doing, the answer was simple: "I'm on Admiral King's staff."[43] More important, the phantom position gave him the authority to originate high-priority requests and purchases out of King's office without disclosing the Los Alamos connection. The ComInCh position and the backing of Admiral Purnell added to Parsons' unique powers within Project Y. In short, Parsons went into the bomb project with a direct line to the summit of the U.S. Navy. He wore this power, as well as his influence with Vannevar Bush of the scientific community and Spike Blandy of BuOrd, much like a concealed weapon. He knew it was there. Groves and Oppenheimer knew it was there. Project leaders at Los Alamos sensed its presence. Yet possessing the weapon, Parsons brandished or used it only when essential.[44]

Much of Parsons' effectiveness in his new position would depend on more than his unusual connections to the summit, however. By the time he joined Project Y he had a host of loyal contacts. As advocate and pioneer in radical military-scientific innovations, he had gained the respect of many forward-looking scientists and officers. Fellow officers saw him as being their man on the cutting edge of technology; scientists viewed him as an officer who understood them and what it took to do good science. Characteristically, Parsons used his influence only on important issues. But involving as it did a project that could end the war and save countless lives, his new assignment would present many occasions for him to draw heavily on a virtual *Who's Who* in science and ordnance.

On Tuesday, 1 June 1943, Captain Parsons resumed his battle against time from his ComInCh Washington office. He set his first goal: by Friday he would have design specifications for a gun capable of bringing together the critical mass of plutonium needed for a nuclear explosion. He set Saturday, his last day in Washington, as the deadline for locating sources of critical equipment and instruments for Y. By then he would also have, according to his predetermined plan, recommendations of eastern colleagues as to engineers, technicians, draftsmen, and machinists for his first round of Project Y recruitment.[45] Every phone call, every moment, had to count.

Parsons called a meeting of his ad hoc weapon design group for 4 June. In addition to Thompson, Rose, and Critchfield, who had been selected at the 15 May meeting, Parsons brought in George Chadwick, former chief gun designer for the Bureau of Ordnance and now with private industry in Detroit, and Robert Brode, a physicist and colleague of Parsons on the proximity fuze project.

This pragmatic group of scientists and ordnance specialists began with the already established premise that the simplest and most direct way to bring together a critical mass of fissionable material would be with a gun. Their task was to design this gun for the inside of the atomic bomb. Unlike conventional artillery, this gun would be fired but once, so durability was not an issue. Absolute reliability and safety were. The target would be feet, not miles, away. The gun would be fired not from the deck of a ship but from inside the housing of the bomb as it plummeted to a prescribed altitude above the enemy. As if these requirements were not enough, both the projectile and its target would be made of uranium-235 or plutonium, strange new metals whose mysteries were only then being explored by nuclear physicists. As yet the physicists could not tell them what quantity of plutonium, in the combined assembly of projectile and target, would cause a nuclear explosion. To get the experimental program under way, Parsons' ad hoc group would have to design the experimental gun using best guesses as to size of the projectile and target.

By the end of the meeting, Parsons had a program under way. Its key features are revealed in a secret memo he dictated before leaving Tolman's office. In it he informed Oppenheimer, "Mr. Chadwick will obtain design of a smooth bore gun of 5 inch caliber to give 3,000 ft/sec to a 60 pound projectile. Dr. Critchfield will obtain several powder pressure curves . . . and furnish these to Chadwick. . . . Mr. Rose in consultation with Dr. Thompson to design gun tubes."[46]

Parsons created a schedule certain to maintain the pace. Knowing he was to arrive at Los Alamos on 15 June, he informed Oppenheimer that his group would meet there the following day and produce "fairly smooth sketches covering the 5-inch gun and the gun test tubes."[47] In the style of another Fort Sumner notable, Billy the Kid, Deak Parsons planned to return to New Mexico with both guns blazing.

·10·

In a Nest of Scientists

Parsons had a unique position in the laboratory with respect to over-all control of this whole show. . . . He could ask for almost anybody and . . . almost any material and have priority.
Dr. Kenneth Bainbridge

In 1939 it had been the feisty terrier Racket who jumped into the back seat of the Parsons Ford for the move to Dahlgren. On Sunday morning, 6 June 1943, Toby, a timid cocker spaniel with downcast eyes, crawled warily in beside Peggy and Clare in the back seat of a sporty maroon Mercury convertible whose flash belied the personality of its owner.[1] For Peggy, now eight, and Clare, six, life had centered around the big white house on Machodec Creek that they now left behind. Their mother advised them to regard moving as an adventure, but Peggy in her quiet, shy way was not all that keen about leaving her garden and familiar surroundings. Clare, on the other hand, was stoked, fired, and ready to go. Her only problem was in leaving Momma Cat. But Martha stuck with her longstanding rule on moving: dogs go, cats stay.[2]

New Mexico stood high among familiar names in the sisters' vocabularies. All their lives they had heard about the old days when their father was a boy there. Now they would be part of this fabled land.

But Peggy and Clare had little idea anything could be so far away. The road moved endlessly out behind the Mercury, past Burma Shave jingles and countless Highway 66 signs. There were overnight stops at tourist cabins clustered like little playhouses alongside the highway. Nothing the girls saw on the trip west matched Granddaddy's Parsons' place with its assemblage of outbuildings, including workshop, barn, and granny house. The Eclipse windmill with its creaking rods added background music. What intrigued them most was their grandfather's cow and knowing that the milk they drank and the butter they ate came from her.[3] The girls did not notice that the house needed repair or that Harry's 287 acres supported no crop, and scarcely any life beyond horned toads and rattlesnakes.

The girls did note with wonder the mealtime prayers and religious art throughout the house. Granddaddy Parsons' piety gave the two sisters a view of religion that they never received from their parents, who were Christians in belief but not, as Peggy would later observe, "big churchgoers." Awareness of her grandfather's righteousness intensified Peggy's embarrassment when he caught her trying to remove the fig leaf from the front of a male religious figure. But Harry was less concerned over his granddaughter's curiosity than her fear of chickens. To correct this, he assigned Peggy the daily chore of feeding the fowls.[4]

Beyond the daughters' distant memories, little is known of Deak's first wartime visit home. But from one of Harry Parsons' neighbors we learn that the town itself barely noted his brief visit. By contrast, when navy commander Ken Wilkinson, Deak's closest boyhood chum, returned on furlough, everyone in town was aware of it. With Deak it was different.[5] Now heading into another secret mission, he was only too happy to go unnoticed. Before leaving town he told his father not to mention his New Mexico presence in letters to friends. Harry knew better than to ask why.

Martha drove the last leg of the journey, the forty miles from Santa Fe to Los Alamos. In the final climb to the secret site, she had to concentrate on the dirt road as it wound its way up the mountain. As Clare tells it, "Switchbacks, ravines, dirt roads—nothing daunted mother, she just drove to Los Alamos like she belonged there."[6]

On Tuesday afternoon, 15 June, Martha Parsons pulled the maroon Mercury to a stop in front of the Military Police at the Los Alamos main gate. She expected a quick salute to Deak and a wave of the hand to proceed. But even after Deak showed his orders, the guards refused to let them pass. Deak disappeared into the guard shack with the MPs, leaving Martha and the girls with nothing to do but wait.

We learn from General Groves what happened. Parsons was the first naval officer to arrive at Los Alamos, and the army MP on guard became suspicious when Parsons' papers identified him as a captain, which in the army called for the insignia of two silver bars and not Parsons' eagles, which were equivalent to an army full colonel. The excited MP telephoned the sergeant of the guard. "Sergeant," he said, "We've really caught a spy! A guy down here is trying to get in, and his uniform is as phony as a three dollar bill. He's wearing the eagles of a colonel and claims that he is a captain."[7]

Parsons and the sergeant resolved the issue, much to the relief of Martha—and to the later amusement of Groves. Just as the incident at the gate ran contrary to Martha's long experience of military bases, so too did the drive from the gate to their new home. Never before had she seen such frenzied activity—block after block of offices, apartments, laboratories, and shops in various stages of construction, from newly poured foundations to framed skeletons ready for roofing and siding. Men with saws and hammers moved like ants in and out of the rising structures. Open ditches scarred the shoulder of the road, and bulldozers ate at hillsides. Dump trucks added to the hazards and excitement of the two-mile drive from the main gate to the new Parsons home.

Passing through this hubbub, Martha must have found some comfort in knowing they would not be moving into the temporary housing she saw being built. As at Dahlgren, the housing list was a virtual *Who's Who* of the base. The difference here was that there was no distinction between civilians and military in the hierarchy. If there was ever any doubt as to Groves' view of Parsons' importance to Project Y, it was clarified in the assignment of the two most desirable houses to Oppenheimer and Parsons. These two neighboring houses were the finest of a half-dozen on what was known as Bathtub Row—that is, the Los Alamos quarters having the luxury, and status, of bathtubs. Of the two houses, the larger not only had bathrooms downstairs and upstairs but had bathtubs in both. This went to Deak and Martha Parsons because they had two children and the Oppenheimers only one. This three-bedroom log house, previously occupied by a Los Alamos Boys School professor, stood among a cluster of pines and looked out over wooded, often snow-capped, mountains.[8]

Beyond ensuring the comfort of the Oppenheimer and Parsons families, General Groves wanted the number one civilian and the number one officer living adjacent to each other for security reasons. In his view, these two men—one working on the physics of the bomb and the other on its engineering—would have in their two heads all the important details of the project. Groves therefore saw to it that the two lived close enough that their homes could be patrolled around the clock by a single cadre of armed guards—an extraordinary precaution, considering that the homes were already within a fenced and gated military community.[9]

Parsons had no secretary to greet him upon his arrival the first morning in his temporary office. But the large freestanding safe he had ordered provided a kind of welcome, a sign that he was expected. With all the bearing and heft of a Sherman tank, the safe made an imposing centerpiece in an otherwise drab room. Only a blackboard with chalk competed for visual attention. Four standard-issue blah green government desks with nondescript chairs swallowed up most of the space. One desk belonged to Parsons, the others to the first three heads of ordnance groups.[10]

The plain and crowded office belied the enormity of the task ahead. In tackling that job, Parsons' main asset was his own indomitable confidence in himself. Unlike the scientists, who were strangers to the world of weapon making, Parsons was uniquely qualified by past experience for his assigned position. His ordnance knowledge gave him a better understanding than most of the magnitude of the task ahead. He knew that the main battle would be against time. To win that battle he would have to proceed at full speed with the technical tasks while simultaneously building his staff.

Parsons did not have time enough even to outline his organizational chart on the blackboard before Thompson, Critchfield, and Chadwick arrived for the follow-up three-day conference on gun design. Ed McMillan was among those already at Los Alamos who joined the meeting. Rose, the gun designer originally brought in by Tolman, could not make the meeting, but in excusing himself he set forth in a memorandum, as did others, the principles he felt should govern gun design.

The details of the design meeting are less important to us today than the insights they provide into Parsons' managerial style. Many of these are reflected in a letter Parsons provided Rose on what transpired. After defining the core problems, Parsons cast a wide net for ideas, which were then narrowed down to alternative approaches that could be weighed and tested against each other. When there was a choice, as in the case of the primer to fire the gun, Parsons favored the navy Mark 25 electric primer because it had proved itself simple and safe—two of the most sought-after criteria in his vocabulary. But for Parsons, it was not enough to know that an item had been reliable in the past; it had to be tested under the new conditions of use. Prescribing tests to this end with the Mark 25, he then went on, as was characteristic, to design extraordinary infallibility into the gun by providing backup systems to the backups. In the case of the primers, he wrote Rose, "If the gun design proves satisfactory, the next step, I believe, is a similar design with four primers; one axial, percussion only, and three off-axis electric primers. I realize this greatly complicates the breech plug and cartridge case design, but it is my idea of a system to give 10^5:1 certainty of operation."[11]

Today we do not know anything about Monsanto Propellant #218 except that Parsons rejected it as the gunpowder for the "high-pressure job" of propelling the plutonium projectile at the very high velocity required. Instead, from his long ordnance experience, he identified M1 powder "as the best prospect at present."[12]

Sandwiched in among the technical details of Parsons' correspondence with Rose is one item quite unlike the rest: Parsons needed a good secretary! And Rose assured him that he knew exactly the person needed: Hazel Greenbacker, Rose's own secretary in former years. At Parsons' behest, Rose wrote Miss Greenbacker about the possibility of her working for a naval officer on a western assignment. But even as Rose wrote the letter, General Groves in Washington had all but concluded that Parsons' secretary should be a WAC—that is, she would come out of the administrative pool of the Women's Army Corps contingent soon to arrive at Los Alamos. Giving Parsons the freedom to select his own scientific and engineering staff was one thing, a secretary quite another.

As Project Y's head of ordnance, Deak Parsons was an anomaly: an officer in a nest of scientists. Unlike other division heads, he reported not only to Oppenheimer but also to General Groves. According to

Groves' biographer, William Lauren, the general had made it clear from the start that Parsons would operate virtually as Oppenheimer's co-equal. As one scientist observed, "Parsons ran his own show."[13]

Groves considered Parsons his own military insider within Project Y. The general had an army colonel as the base commander, but it was Parsons to whom he turned for the military perspective on the technical activities of Project Y. Groves himself lacked close rapport with the scientists and thought they "tended to look upon themselves as superior beings." Worse, in his book, many of them "had the idea the military couldn't contribute anything." By Groves' account, Parsons did a great deal to alleviate civilian-military friction because the scientists "didn't think about his uniform very much and of course when they did they thought, 'well, he's Navy and not Army.'" Groves said, "Parsons was able to do certain things for me without being disloyal to Oppenheimer. He was able to keep me posted on potential difficulties and to use his influence to smooth things down."[14]

Oppenheimer understood and accepted Parsons' unusual position with respect to Groves as well as his direct support from Admirals Purnell and Blandy. Indeed, Oppenheimer capitalized on Parsons' ability to get things done through his powerful connections.[15] Other scientists at Y did not always see Parsons' independence in the same favorable light. The congenial military-scientific environment that Parsons had enjoyed in the proximity fuze work did not exist at Los Alamos in the summer of 1943. During the proximity fuze work at the Applied Physics Laboratory, there had been one scientific prima donna, Merle Tuve; at Los Alamos there were many. Whereas Tuve had fought to bring an ordnance officer into the project, the Los Alamos scientists, Oppenheimer and Ordnance Division scientists excepted, were not certain any such person was needed.

To avoid delays in getting his program under way, Parsons had little choice but to start his division with some group heads already hired by Oppenheimer—that is, physicists. Of the Ordnance Division's first three group heads, Edwin McMillan had the longest association with the project. This mild-mannered physicist from Berkeley, a close personal friend of Oppenheimer, knew a great deal about nuclear physics but little about guns, explosives, and weapon testing. As if by reverse logic, he was named head of the Proving Ground Group. McMillan had one of the four desks in Parsons' original office but spent most of his time making Anchor Ranch, a former homestead farm, into a test site for the gun device.

The next group head was Charles Critchfield of the Carnegie Institution's Geophysics Laboratory, who had been virtually ordered to Project Y by Richard Tolman.[16] Critchfield managed to stay on in the Washington area until June, when, like Parsons, he made the permanent move to Los Alamos. He had tested experimental devices at the army's Aberdeen Proving Ground and was familiar with the sabot method of firing scale-model projectiles from guns, but he was far from being an old hand at ordnance. Parsons named him head of the Projectile, Target, and Source Group—a rather colorless name until one realizes that the projectile and target would be made of scarce, strange plutonium and uranium metals, and "source" meant the supply of neutrons for initiating an atomic explosion.

The occupant of the fourth desk in Parsons' office was Seth Neddermeyer, reputedly the most stubborn physicist on Parsons' team—and the most controversial.[17] Neddermeyer, like Critchfield, had been transferred to Y at Tolman's behest. He was already at the site by April 1943. During conferences held before Parsons' arrival, Neddermeyer had argued for implosion as an alternative method to the gun for bringing together a critical mass of neutron-active material. The idea of implosion was not new. Richard Tolman, an early advocate, described the original concept as the use of ordinary explosives to create a nuclear explosion by blowing a shell of fissionable material together in the center of a sphere.[18] But it was Neddermeyer's championing of the method that led Oppenheimer to open up this area of research. By the time Parsons arrived, Neddermeyer had become a persistent implosion advocate—hence, the natural choice as head of the Implosion Experimentation Group.

Other groups that Parsons identified for the new division included the Instrumentation Group, which Kenneth Bainbridge, a physicist from MIT's Radiation (radar) Laboratory, would fill in August, and the Fuze Development Group, for which Parsons would bring in physicist Robert Brode from the proximity fuze program at APL. For the Engineering Group Parsons had high hopes of obtaining George Chadwick, a mainstay of the gun design team. Parsons' plan from the start called for a Delivery Group to be formed under Norman Ramsey as soon as this civilian physicist could be released from Army Air Forces duties.

On the Los Alamos organizational chart, Parsons was surrounded by physicists—above and below and from side to side. This was fine by him, except that in June 1943 his division desperately needed ordnance and engineering talent as well.

As a step in remedying the ordnance deficiency, Parsons called Thomas Olmstead, an old hand with navy guns at the Naval Proving Ground. Parsons supposedly told the technician, "I'm stuck out in the wilderness with a bunch of eggheads and I want someone who knows what he is doing. I want you to join me." Those "eggheads," as Critchfield later acknowledged, "were Ed McMillan, Seth Neddermeyer, and myself—the three of us with whom Deak occupied one 12 by 12 office."[19] Tommy Olmstead, described by one physicist as a member of the Black Powder Society and "a regular guy in an irregular way," accepted the position of ordnance specialist in McMillan's Proving Ground Group at Anchor Ranch. In the early range firings he could be identified, as Critchfield recalled, as the only one with sense enough to plug his ears prior to the shot. In the months ahead Parsons would rely on Olmstead to keep the guns in working order and the firing program on schedule.[20]

The engineering problems were not as easily remedied; indeed, they would plague the wartime atomic bomb project to the end. As Deak Parsons soon learned, the very thing that gave Los Alamos its creative strength—that is, its superb staff of the scientific elite—contributed to its engineering weakness. While the chance to work with the nation's leading nuclear physicists appealed to bright young physicists, the same attraction did not exist for engineers. Parsons was caught between two philosophies of how to turn ideas into hardware: the academic and the industrial. Before the war most of the Los Alamos scientists had been in research positions at universities. When they wanted to try out a new idea, they just made a rough sketch of whatever they wanted built on the nearest notepad or cafeteria napkin and took it down to the shop foreman. From the sketch and a little explanation, the foreman would have the item made and ready for testing before the idea cooled off in the scientist's head.[21] The university scientists were unaccustomed to the practices of industry, where chief engineers required that uniform and specific instructions accompany job requests because they did not know which of their many machinists might finally complete the job.[22] George Chadwick, Parsons' prime candidate to head the Engineering Design Group, came from the industrial mold.

From his first visit to Los Alamos, Chadwick seems to have foreseen that he would have problems fitting in with the scientists—except at a distance. Because of Parsons, Chadwick toyed with the idea of coming to Y but finally rejected it, suggesting instead that he would be more valuable working out of Detroit with its industrial resources and engineering talent. Lacking a better solution, Parsons agreed to an arrangement whereby Chadwick would coordinate industry contracts in the East for the production of the scale and full-size models of the bomb as well as casings and other non-nuclear components for the final bombs. Creating the "Detroit Office" of Y allowed Chadwick to be kept on the team, but not as a group leader. The arrangement still left Parsons without a chief engineer to set up and supervise the laboratory's drafting room and machine shops at Los Alamos.[23]

Likewise, Parsons needed a secretary now, not the promise of a WAC assistant later. Physicists and engineers were critical, but so too was a good secretary. Groves relented, and Hazel Greenbacker agreed to take the job.

Parsons did not slow his pace while awaiting Greenbacker's arrival. Doing his own typing and filing in an overcrowded office, he pushed forward aggressively on concerns large and small. A few examples of the latter reveal his indefatigable drive. First we see him pushing to improve the road from Espanola to Los Alamos. He wrote Oppenheimer, "As a sample of the loss of effectiveness caused by our 'improved' road, yesterday I drove Dr. Thompson to make his train. A scraper had piled several rocks in the middle of the road. One of these hit the pan causing an oil leak and forcing me to have the car repaired in Santa Fe. This cost Dr. Thompson a twenty-five dollar taxi ride to Albuquerque [since he had missed his train connection near Santa Fe], and cost me seven dollars in repair."[24]

Parsons' concerns included the need for more schools and teachers for the expanded community. He successfully urged Oppenheimer to define what was needed for first-class schools and to transmit a request to General Groves for "early, favorable, and positive action." Parsons' community concerns also extended to the cramped quarters of single and childless scientists and engineers. Better housing, he argued, would increase professional effectiveness.[25] There can be no doubt but that Parsons' needling, which could be irritating, put extra starch in Oppenheimer's demands on an otherwise intimidating general.

If we accepted the common interpretation of Parsons' early priorities, we would find Seth Neddermeyer's work on the implosion method of bomb assembly somewhere after gun design, range development, recruitment, better roads, and improved housing.

Some accounts of Project Y give the impression that Parsons doubted Neddermeyer's seriousness, openly belittled him, and observed his failures with gleeful contempt. One account has Parsons scoffing at Neddermeyer in the April meeting at which the scientist first proposed implosion research, when in fact this meeting occurred a month before Parsons' first visit to Los Alamos. Some of these accounts stereotype Neddermeyer as a flaky, withdrawn scientist who liked to infuriate his military boss. At the same time they portray Captain Parsons as a conservative nuts-and-bolts technocrat so wedded to the "good old gun" that he was blind to any other method of creating a nuclear bomb. Such accounts run counter to what we know of Parsons' management style, his openness to new ideas, and his inborn courtesy.

At the outset of the ordnance program, relations between Parsons and all his group leaders were harmonious.[26] But in time, as we will see, tensions did develop between Parsons and Neddermeyer. These, however, are often overstated. Just because Parsons, like most of the scientists, favored the gun method did not mean that he opposed implosion research. On the contrary, he went to great lengths to provide Neddermeyer the resources and materials he needed. At the same time, Parsons sought the best advice available to him on implosion prospects. He turned to the scientist whose judgment he trusted most: Dr. Tommy, the leading naval ballistician of the time. Following the June gun design meeting, Parsons arranged for Thompson to meet with Neddermeyer to review the scientific assumptions behind implosion.

After returning east, Thompson gave his appraisal in a letter to Neddermeyer. He confined his remarks to Neddermeyer's planned experiments with spheres, which were at the heart of his proposed bomb—that is, a spherical shell of plutonium that would be imploded inward by high explosives upon a smaller spherical shell of plutonium at the center. Thompson came to the point in his first paragraph: "It seems to me there is a fundamental difficulty with the system that makes it quite certain not to be satisfactory." This was more diplomatic than the earlier reaction of scientist Richard Feynman, who simply said, "It stinks."[27]

Thompson provided a three-page scientific explanation for his conclusion. It would be impossible, in his view, to obtain sufficiently symmetrical ignition in the external spherical shell to avoid a collapse of the central sphere. The result was likely to be "a shredded and twisted plate-like piece, or a general disintegration."[28]

While Thompson questioned the method, he did not doubt Neddermeyer's professional capabilities. He saw him as a "first-class experimentalist" whose talents could be better used elsewhere in the project. Parsons rejected that idea and continued implosion research under Neddermeyer, even though the early tests showed little promise.

The first of the implosion tests took place on the Fourth of July, 1943, which fell on a Sunday. With an air of confidence, Neddermeyer invited Parsons, McMillan, Critchfield, and others to the show. Neddermeyer had an array of explosives—TNT, Primacord, tetryl pellets, and blasting caps—as well as numerous lengths of kitchen stovepipe and two-inch sewer pipe. While the others watched more or less silently, Neddermeyer and his assistants packed explosives around the sewer pipe, put in four detonation points, and encased all this within the stovepipe. Neddermeyer waved an arm directing everyone to crouch behind boulders sixty yards and more away. Then he detonated his creation.[29]

"The explosion made that pipe like a rock," Critchfield later commented, "and that was Seth's idea of implosion."[30] This was not the same as the later approach to implosion, in which the nuclear material would be compressed, not merely blown together. While a stovepipe laden with TNT satisfied the test purposes, it did not fulfill youthful scientists wishing for more robust Fourth of July fireworks, particularly in view of the array of unused explosives still on hand.

Parsons, wishing neither to condone nor to halt what lay ahead, left the test site for the town of Pecos to buy a horse for Martha. With the boss away, the young scientists combined their creative talent to make a gigantic firecracker. They packed a long length of stovepipe with TNT and other leftover explosives and wrapped this in turn with prima cord. The result was, in festive terms, a blast.

•

For Deak Parsons there would be no waiting for the completed bomb design before taking on the problems of actual use of the combat weapon against the enemy. Within his first week at Los Alamos, Parsons formed plans for a Delivery Group and began his campaign to obtain Norman Ramsey as the unit's leader. But Parsons was not the only one to recognize the unique talents of Ramsey, a modest young string bean of a man who had not only a background in nuclear physics and radar but also air force experience with the latest bombers and bombing procedures. The determination with which Parsons went after Ramsey, a civilian employee of the Army Air Forces working in the Office of the Secretary of War, tells us a lot about Parsons' and Oppenheimer's tenacious recruiting tactics.

On 21 June, Oppenheimer forwarded to General Groves an urgent request from Parsons for help getting Ramsey released. There was no equivocating: "There is not another man in the country whose experience covers so adequately the wide range necessary to doing this job so well."[31] Later Oppenheimer and Tolman quoted Parsons as saying, "If we do not get Ramsey it will be necessary for us to have a group of four or five men from the Army and Navy, and they will be key men; and they will not do the job as well."[32] These arguments did not impress Edward Bowles in the Office of the Secretary of War. Bowles seemed to see the attempts to snatch Ramsey as an affront to his powers. He stiffened his opposition.

Facing failure, Parsons brought in the big guns: Groves, Tolman, Conant, and Bush himself. They all interceded in behalf of the transfer. Like a pack of dogs, they would not let up once they had the scent. In late September, Bowles capitulated but with the face-saving, meaningless provision, "Dr. Ramsey will remain attached to my office and will thus be on loan to General Groves."[33]

During this high-level chase, the unassuming young man in question quietly kept working full-time for Parsons on Project Y. Through his own manipulation, Ramsey began the study of factors involved in the aerial delivery of an atomic bomb. These included the size and kind of aircraft, bomb carriage and suspension system, and delivery tactics. Except for a week at Los Alamos during vacation leave, Ramsey's initial work for Project Y was done in Washington and at Dahlgren.

As part of the organizational shell game orchestrated by Parsons,

Ramsey—while officially with the Army Air Forces—appeared on the staff of Section T at the Applied Physics Laboratory. There, with Merle Tuve's agreement and Parsons' connivance, he directed the construction of $^{14}/_{23}$ scale models of the first version of the atomic bomb. The design then called for a seventeen-foot gun within the bomb casing. This length was needed to achieve the 3,000-feet-per-second velocity for the fast assembly of the critical mass of plutonium required for an atomic explosion. Because none of the available aircraft at Dahlgren could accommodate a bomb of such great length, Parsons directed that the preliminary aerodynamic tests be conducted with scaled-down models. The $^{14}/_{23}$ scale was determined by the ready availability of fourteen-inch sewer pipe. The completed models were produced at APL under Ramsey's direction by welding a long length of the sewer pipe into the middle of a split 500-pound bomb.[34]

On 13 August 1943 the first drop test of the prototype took place at the Dahlgren Naval Proving Ground to determine flight stability. Although the skinny creation officially designated the "Sewer Pipe Bomb" arrived at Dahlgren as a routine test item from APL, it soon laid claim to proving-ground notoriety. The bomb dropped from eight thousand feet, as described by Ramsey, "in a flat spin the like of which had rarely been seen before." He declared the first test of an atomic bomb model "an ominous and spectacular failure."[35]

The day after the sewer-bomb failure, Ramsey learned that Parsons was in Washington. Still distraught, the young scientist broke into a Saturday morning meeting the captain was holding in Tolman's office. As if he still could not believe what he had seen, Ramsey described what seemed to him an utter failure. But Parsons viewed the results as progress; they now knew more than they had before.[36] Later in the day Parsons inspected sewer-pipe bombs under construction at APL and suggested moving the center of gravity closer to the nose. Cut-and-try experimenting would continue, but wind-tunnel tests were also made part of the plan. After thus tweaking the test program, Parsons returned to the important business of team building.

In the same way Parsons had locked onto Ramsey as *the* person to head the Delivery Group, he narrowed his candidates for heading interior ballistics down to Joseph Hirschfelder. Hirschfelder's situation was complicated by the fact that the army wanted him in a headquarters position and was in the process of giving him a reserve commission. When Critchfield, a close colleague, approached Hirschfelder in late July about coming to Project Y, he reacted negatively. Before having the question raised again, Parsons sent a telegram to Groves requesting that he give Hirschfelder "the fight talk."[37] This talk varied with the presenter—usually Groves, Parsons, or Thompson—and was a hard-hitting appeal to patriotism and the demands of war, combined with the professional challenge of participating in the greatest scientific experiment of the millennium. After treating Hirschfelder to the fight talk, General Groves reported that the prospective head of interior ballistics had reversed course and was seriously considering giving up his commission and coming to Y. To help clinch the deal, the Los Alamos housing rules were bent to secure family housing for the young bachelor and his mother.[38] The bigger problem, however, would be in releasing him from other defense commitments. "There was," as Parsons later wrote, "quite an involved situation for a day or so, but Groves and Tolman carried enough weight to decide the issue in our favor."[39] Hirschfelder began his work for Y immediately in the Washington area and made plans to report to Los Alamos in September.

With Hirschfelder locked in, Parsons turned to his next important target: John R. von Neumann. In the afternoon of the same day and again in Tolman's office, Parsons met with von Neumann, an acknowledged mathematical wizard and a theorist with uncommon ability to apply his knowledge to practical ends. He had, for example, put the tank-busting punch in the army bazooka through his design of its shaped-charge warhead. Oppenheimer and Parsons realized that if anyone could make a workable design for nuclear implosion it should be Johnny von Neumann. A "Dear Johnny" letter from Oppenheimer set the stage. Referring obliquely to Los Alamos, Oppenheimer wrote, "We are in what can only be described as a desperate need of your help. It may have come to your attention that we have a good many theoretical people working here, but I think if your usual shrewdness is a guide for you about the probable nature of the problem you will see why even this staff is in some respects critically inadequate."[40]

With the candor of a close friend, Oppenheimer told von Neumann that Captain Parsons, former head of Section T and now head of "one of our divisions," would be coming to Washington "within a fortnight or so and will attempt to disengage you from your present niche." He then cautioned von Neumann not to discuss the matter with his boss or others in the Bureau of Ordnance "lest they accuse us of using underhanded methods of recruiting." He closed with the suggestion that von Neumann follow up his discussion with Parsons by visiting the Y site because that would give him "a better idea of this somewhat Buck Rogers project than any amount of correspondence."[41]

According to Parsons' log, his conversation with von Neumann began at 4 P.M. that Saturday afternoon. Within the first few minutes Parsons realized that there was no hope, fight talk or not, of "disengaging" von Neumann from his BuOrd position and his obligations to the Aberdeen Proving Ground, to the National Defense Research Committee, and to Princeton University, where he was involved in special studies with Einstein. Rather than take a total loss, Parsons and Oppenheimer settled for a part-time arrangement by which von Neumann would do theoretical work for Y in Tolman's office and make occasional visits to the New Mexico site.[42] It was a decision that would have a profound effect on the nation's future ability to produce plutonium bombs.

By mid-August 1943 Parsons had selected most of the section heads for his Ordnance Division (see table).[43] Within his first two months at Los Alamos, Parsons pulled together a top-notch ordnance development team, began the design of the nuclear gun, brought new support to the implosion method of nuclear assembly, readied the test range at Anchor Ranch, began the planning for the tactical delivery of the bomb, and started testing scale models.

In the midst of this flurry, Hazel Greenbacker, a prim young woman, stepped off the train at the desolate railway stop at Lamy. There she met her new employer, who she had been told was a navy captain on a medical assignment. She had been better informed than many who disembarked at Lamy, the closest railway stop, fifty-five miles from Los Alamos (fifteen from Santa Fe). Although her new boss had nothing to do with medicine, he was a navy captain, and she soon found that he fit the description given her of "a very fine gentleman." By Hazel Greenbacker Carmondy's later account, "I liked him immediately; quiet speaking, but very firm . . . the type of man you would follow and you wouldn't ask questions."[44]

With a good secretary aboard, Deak Parsons was now fully ready to go to work.

Proposed Organization of Ordnance Division, Mid-August 1943

Group	Personnel[a]	Head
Proving Ground Group (later, Gun Group)	13	Edwin McMillan (original group head)
Instrumentation Group	18	Kenneth Bainbridge (joined in September)
Fuze Development Group	16	Robert Brode (still employed at APL but working for Y)
Projectile, Target, and Source Group	14	Charles Critchfield (original group head)
Implosion Group	8	Seth Neddermeyer (original group head)
Engineering Group	39	George Chadwick (at Detroit, reluctant to come to Y)
Delivery Group	5	Norman Ramsey (with War Department but working for Y)
Interior Ballistics	[b]	Joseph Hirschfelder (to report to Y in September)

[a] 29 June 1943 estimates of number of personnel in 1944.

[b] No estimate made.

·11·

Thin Man versus Fat Man

He had a knack of asking, "How's it going" in a stimulating way.
Dr. Norris Bradbury

Los Alamos had only two hundred employees when the Parsons family arrived in June 1943. By August 1944, when the laboratory underwent a major reorganization, the number had risen to eleven hundred, and the community itself was well on its way to its peak wartime population of over five thousand scientists, technicians, military personnel, and their families.[1]

Brain power, remoteness, secrecy, and intensity of life set wartime Los Alamos apart from any other town. Army-built and army-controlled, the town had no unemployed, no poor, no jails, and, as one resident proclaimed, no in-laws. Neither did it have sidewalks or paved streets.

A strange mix of young people (average age twenty-five) made up most of the population. Initially most were civilians, but in time the blend became half civilian and half military, each half regarding the other with a certain apprehension. The civilians included Nobel laureates and deans of science as well as engineers, explosives specialists, and technicians. It was an all-American team except for twenty scientists of the British mission. The chief army contingents included Women's Army Corps soldiers for administrative services and Special

Engineering Detachment soldiers for technical assignments at the laboratories and test sites. The SEDs were enlisted men with technical training, in some cases advanced degrees. Many had been caught in the military draft and were headed for combat assignments when they were abruptly reassigned to this secret site. Although the SEDs lived in barracks like soldiers, dressed (more or less) like soldiers, and were soldiers, they floundered when it came to discipline, saluting, and close-order drill.

Because of Parsons and his navy support, a sizable number of naval reserve officers, many with advanced degrees, filled technical positions and worked directly with the civilian scientists. By the end of the war there would be thirty-eight of these naval reserve officers and three officers of the regular navy.[2]

Guard gates, fences capped with barbed wire, armed guards, passes and badges, car inspections, fingerprinting, and censorship of mail aggravated daily life for civilians, particularly those from academia. So too did army regulations, forms, arbitrary housing assignments, telephone limitations, and controls over travel. The problems were not helped by the difficulties General Groves had in acquiring base commanders sensitive to the needs of an intellectual community. It took a succession of army colonels before he finally found one who understood that civilians were not to be ordered about like army recruits.

Despite its isolation and military flavor, Los Alamos had its charms: magnificent scenery, crisp mountain air, enticing hiking trails, horseback riding, skiing, square dances, and theater. The town sparkled with stimulating people. Edwin McMillan's wife, Elsie, said, "I don't think I shall ever live in a community that had such deep roots of cooperation and friendship." The intensity of the work spilled over into community living and recreation. Parsons, leading a school board meeting, made fun of the community's inability to discuss its underlying mission: "Isn't it wonderful to see five thousand people intent on a single purpose—skiing!"[3]

The scientific work force labored six days a week, often into the night. With some exceptions, however, they held to the rule "Never on a Sunday." On Sunday mornings Oppenheimer could be seen on his chestnut horse headed for the mountain trails. While Enrico Fermi might be heard discussing physics on this day of rest, that would be just his way of relaxing with a fellow physicist on some mountaintop. While Sundays were reserved for outdoor recreation, Saturday nights were for cocktail parties, usually in homes, including Parsons' home, a favorite because of its size. On these occasions physicists proved that neither science nor a weighty military mission limited wit and laughter.

Shopping was confined to the military commissary and infrequent trips to Santa Fe. A small military hospital served the community with free medical services. Half of the hospital's capacity went into maternity care and a nursery. Just as everyone's mail went to one address, so too were the birthplaces of all the Los Alamos babies listed as P.O. Box 1663, Sandoval County. As Elsie McMillan exclaimed, "My God, was that box ever full of babies!"[4]

Some people felt that the isolation and restrictions placed them in a peculiar variation of purgatory; others found it an idyllic intellectual retreat. Deak and Martha were among the latter even though they, like Robert and Kitty Oppenheimer, led the most restricted lives of all. Guards patrolled their houses night and day. Any time Deak left the base he had to be accompanied by a security agent. And because of his own distrust of airplanes, General Groves forbade Parsons and Oppenheimer to travel by air up until the project's final months. But these were inconveniences Deak understood and accepted. He thrived on the community's intellectual atmosphere and the opportunities for exchanging ideas with some of the greatest minds in the world.[5]

As for Martha, things that bothered the scientists' wives did not upset her at all. Having security officers monitor her conversations in the commissary was a small price to pay for the outdoor life she enjoyed there on the mesa. With Deak's help on the Fourth of July, 1943 (after he left Neddermeyer's implosion test), Martha bought "Diamond," half western pony and half Morgan. From then on she and Diamond were a common sight on the Los Alamos trails. Delighted with one horse, Martha searched for another. When a horse trader showed them Dolly, there was some concern over her being swaybacked, but Dolly appeared to be gentle enough for the girls to ride. After bringing Dolly to the army stables, Martha became concerned over the mare's voracious appetite. Deak, despite his country upbringing, professed ignorance of the eating habits of equines. The army vet did better: a quick check revealed a second heartbeat beneath the sway. To the delight and wonderment of Peggy and Clare, Dolly in time gave birth to Charley.[6]

Deak occasionally joined Martha on a Sunday morning ride. More often she rode alone or with Kitty Oppenheimer. Peggy also joined Martha on the trail, but Clare, the daredevil of the two sisters, had suffered a fall on her first try and gave up any pretensions to being a cowgirl.[7]

Martha's challenge came in the kitchen. After fourteen years of marriage her secret was out: she knew little about cooking except that she hated it. She had always had a maid to do the cooking, but that was impossible at Los Alamos. Her own culinary offerings were limited to one menu: steak, potato chips, and salad. Rising to the new challenge, Martha taught herself how to cook, not well but sufficiently to expand her menu from one to seven standard dinners a week. Preoccupied with work, Deak never complained. However, he did join his daughters' merriment in calling Martha's home-baked biscuits "mother's bullets." They were, it seems, more appropriate as munitions than food.[8]

If the pressures of Deak's work had any effect on their home life, it took the form of his increasing firmness in family decisions. "There were times," Martha later reported, "when it was very hard to cross him. . . . He used to make me quite angry because we'd run up against a stone wall over something that to me wasn't very important." In those instances Martha would say, "We're going to do this." Deak would reply, "No we aren't going to do this." And as Martha observed, "By George that's what we did! And quite often it was the right thing to do, but I sometimes wonder if other people ran into this same thing. I mean that's a human failing."[9]

At work Deak Parsons had strong views on key issues related to engineering and delivery of the atomic bomb. As Norman Ramsey observed, "Deak was marvelous if he took a firm position on your side, but if he took a firm position against you it was sort of, well, he was equally firm!"[10] Parsons' calm logic made him a hard man to argue with. Difficult, yes, but not impossible. And for this we have the appraisal of officer-scientist Norris Bradbury:

Parsons was firm, but never, to my knowledge, arbitrary. One of his virtues was that he could argue on those things he knew about. He would press his points on weapon feasibility, military practices, and needs for practical ordnance tests, but did not press his opinions in areas in which he was not knowledgeable. . . . He was a good man at exploring various possible approaches to a problem with others. But once a problem had been explored and an approach agreed upon he could be quite firm in its execution.[11]

Parsons' firmness has sometimes been misinterpreted, particularly in respect to his views on implosion. At the start, like most of the Los Alamos scientists, Parsons saw the gun method as the simplest and most reliable way to achieve a nuclear reaction. Neither he nor the scientists knew as much about the character of plutonium as they would by the summer of 1944. In the early period, Parsons opposed any shift of resources that would delay the gun program. However, he actively supported Neddermeyer's implosion research, as is borne out by correspondence of the time and by Parsons' daily log.[12] But he did have reservations about Neddermeyer's approach to implosion, and probably about his leadership as well. Instead of relying solely on Neddermeyer, Parsons sought von Neumann's help in putting implosion on a better and faster track.

Von Neumann paid his first visit to Los Alamos on Monday, 20 September. He stayed for two weeks. During that time he spent several days closeted with Parsons in an office with a blackboard. By one account, they agreed not to come out until they had found a solution to implosion.[13] In any event, Parsons joined von Neumann in advocating a new method known as "fast" implosion. This made use of "lenses": precisely shaped sections of high explosives designed to focus the detonation waves on a ball of plutonium at the center of a sphere. With proper placement of the lens it would be possible to focus the pressure from the different sections of explosives and make the implosion proceed symmetrically, compressing the plutonium into the critical state needed for a chain reaction.

While still holding fast to the gun as the preferred method, Parsons now sought expansion of research on fast implosion. Oppenheimer and Groves received von Neumann's concept with great enthusiasm because the compression of the nuclear core of the bomb by fast implosion would require less fissionable material. Because of the high speed of assembling a critical mass, the purity of the material would be less critical in respect to the predetonation problem.

Like the sudden blast of a rocket, the von Neumann approach accelerated the implosion program. Neddermeyer's group expanded, albeit slowly at first, from eight to fifty persons. But solving implosion problems required not only more people but more effective leadership as well.

When Oppenheimer proposed bringing George Kistiakowsky to Y to strengthen the implosion work, Parsons quickly joined the cause. Both knew the difficulties they faced in trying to bring this eminent Harvard chemist into the fold. Director of NDRC's Explosives Research Laboratory at Bruceton, Pennsylvania, Kistiakowsky was thought by many to be the nation's leading explosives expert.

James Conant, head of NDRC, became the key. Conant first arranged for Kistiakowsky to visit Y as a consultant. The October 1943 visit reveals that Kistiakowsky's interests at Y went beyond the chemistry of high explosives to the personal chemistry among project leaders. Upon returning east, Kistiakowsky wrote Conant, "Capt. Parsons is now committed to a vigorous prosecution of the project (implosion), although it is doubtful that he believes in its success." At the same time, Kistiakowsky reported Neddermeyer reluctantly abandoning personal experiments in favor of building an organization. "The real difficulty," Kistiakowsky wrote, "is that there is a serious lack of mutual confidence between Parsons and Neddermeyer."[14]

The solution, Kistiakowsky thought, would be the appointment of a deputy for implosion under Parsons. He thought this would work well "because Capt. Parsons is an unusually capable and pleasant man and I could think of no other officer better qualified to direct the project." Kistiakowsky then added a contradictory appraisal that some later writers have incorrectly used to stereotype Parsons as an old-style navy autocrat: "But as things stand at present, [Parsons'] concern with the details irritates and offends former college men who are accustomed to work pretty independently and who think him domineering. Capt. Parsons, on the other hand, considers them uncooperative and impractical, in short 'long haired,' so the situation is a mess, although nobody is directly at fault."[15]

This judgment is not consistent with recorded recollections of Parsons' contemporaries, including Kistiakowsky. When later asked if his early criticism of Parsons was based on his military attitudes, Kistiakowsky responded, "Oh no. He was accepted as a technical member of the senior staff of the laboratory without any challenge, and I think had on the whole very good relations with almost everybody, but not everybody had good relations with everybody anyway."[16]

When he recommended that Parsons should have a deputy in charge of implosion, Kistiakowsky said he did not think he himself needed to be that deputy. Groves, Oppenheimer, and Parsons believed otherwise. To this end, Parsons met Conant for lunch on 3 November and described for him "the bright possibilities and the serious difficulties" of fast implosion. If implosion was to succeed it needed the best brains the nation had to offer. By the end of lunch Conant had concluded that Kistiakowsky had to be made available full-time.[17] Although Kistiakowsky did not report to Y as Parsons' deputy until January 1944, he began the reorganization of the implosion program through frequent visits. During these visits, Kistiakowsky found himself administratively and technically between Parsons and Neddermeyer. He did not agree with Neddermeyer, who wanted a small, tightly knit group that would somehow come up with a great invention or scientific insight that would miraculously save the day. He also found fault with Parsons' "more classical ordnance way of handling explosives." However, he added, "My disagreements with Deak Parsons were very minor compared to my disagreements with Neddermeyer."[18]

Parsons eliminated many of Kistiakowsky's early complaints by absolving him from the safety requirements imposed by David Busbee, an old-time ordnance chief Parsons had brought in from Picatinny Arsenal to head the manufacture of explosives. The Kistiakowsky-Busbee issue was over who knew the most about explosives: a Harvard professor or an old ordnance hand. What infuriated the fiery Kistiakowsky most was that when he and Busbee disagreed over what was safe or unsafe, Busbee's retort was invariably, "Have you ever picked up the remains of a man on a shovel after an explosion?" To this the scientist would respond, "No, I haven't, but if we do it my way, we won't have to."[19]

The direct disagreements between Kistiakowsky and Parsons were on a higher plane. The two men had a high professional regard for one another. Their skirmishes took place between equal but stylistically different gladiators: Parsons calm, logical, and firm; Kistiakowsky excitable, acerbic, and firm. Parsons put his confidence in traditional tried-and-true ordnance procedures; Kistiakowsky believed that success depended on breaking new ground in explosives technology, particularly in the precision machining of high explosives—a horror to old-time ordnance men. Kistiakowsky also argued against making large-scale trials of the implosion device "early in the game," as advocated by Parsons.[20]

Ultimately their ideas clashed over the design of the explosive lenses. Having achieved a workable design for the lenses of the implosion bomb, Kistiakowsky wanted to freeze it so that they could push forward with lens production. Parsons, who had originally promoted fast implosion, now believed that the design was too complicated to be produced on schedule. He believed that more experimental work could lead to a simpler design. As was typical at Y, both men presented their arguments before an appropriate committee. In this case the vote favored Kistiakowsky, but, as the Harvard professor recalled, "Parsons took it with very good grace—though also saying that we probably wouldn't be ready in time."[21]

Skeptical or not, Parsons strove to solve the lens design problem. Among other actions he raided Hedrick's proving-ground staff to bring Lt. Comdr. Norris Bradbury to Project Y to perform lens research. When Bradbury resisted Parsons' appeals, Parsons asked only that he see Admiral King before making a final decision. Bradbury responded that if ordered to Y he would willingly come. He saw Admiral King, and he came.[22]

The Bradbury and other abductions from Dahlgren did not sit well with Captain Hedrick, but with Admirals King and Blandy supporting the transfers, he had to muffle his complaints. After some months of not encountering each other, Hedrick and Parsons met by chance in a Main Navy hallway. Instead of saying, "Hello Parsons, how are you?" or "Hello Parsons, we need to talk about these people you are stealing," he said, "Your wife still owes me for some chickens."

With this well-aimed shot, Hedrick penetrated Parsons' thick emotional armor. Back at Los Alamos, Deak confronted Martha: "You didn't buy any chickens from Hedrick, did you?"

Martha had to confess that she had, pleading, "Yes, I did but I paid him that very day with a check." For once family matters took precedence over Project Y. All else had to wait until the canceled check could be found and photostatted, and the copy mailed to Captain Hedrick.[23]

•

In June 1943, when Parsons brought Norman Ramsey into the project, the best assumptions pointed to a skinny seventeen-foot bomb. That fall, equal billing was given for a fast-implosion bomb—that is, a fat, squat bomb built around a fifty-nine-inch-diameter sphere. Parsons' insistence on full-scale tests of both bomb shapes placed a priority on Ramsey's search for aircraft capable of delivering these unorthodox bombs. Ramsey believed that the critical shortage of the new American B-29 bombers and the mechanical problems they were then experiencing might delay the drop tests. He therefore proposed that the early testing be done with British Lancasters. By this time, however, Parsons had opened the way for a few select officers of the Army Air Forces (AAF) to be briefed on the secret project. These AAF officers, as Ramsey conceded, "wisely recommended" that B-29s be used from the start, as that would add cumulative experience in B-29 operation with the revolutionary bomb.[24]

Hence, the Army Air Forces entered the project with the immediate task of modifying a B-29 to accommodate two radically different bomb configurations. As security cover, the AAF officers designated the Manhattan Project as "Silver Plated," and these words soon became an open sesame to high-priority handling. At the same time, they named the long bomb Thin Man and the squat one Fat Man in order to give any surreptitious telephone interceptors the notion that a plane was being modified to carry Roosevelt (Thin Man) and Churchill (Fat Man).[25]

The Army Air Forces connection opened the way for Parsons to transfer future air drops from Dahlgren to the more convenient Muroc Army Air Base (now Edwards Air Force Base) in California's Mojave Desert. With that site in mind, Parsons scheduled the first drop tests of full-scale Fat Man and Thin Man models for mid-January 1944.[26] One action triggered another. To meet the test schedule, Parsons needed Triple X priority—that is, next to that of the president—for the manufacture through Chadwick of forty Fat Man and twenty Thin Man inert models. Likewise, early scheduling of the Muroc tests pressed Robert Brode to hasten the development of prototype proximity fuzes for triggering the bomb at the desired altitude above the earth. Parsons saw a controlled airburst as essential to achieve maximum blast damage and to avoid long-term radiation contamination of the target area.

As Parsons expected, the early scheduling of full-scale drop tests pushed his teams—and himself—to the limit. Expecting surprises, he got them.

The first trouble came in mid-December from Chadwick. He informed Parsons that the Thin Man and Fat Man models could not be delivered to Muroc on schedule. He cited contract problems, the poor quality of the Los Alamos engineering drawings—"which look like high-school stuff"—and the flu epidemic. The prospects looked better by New Year's Eve, when trucks with military escort left the manufacturer for Wright Air Force Base with the first two Thin Man models of an atomic bomb. But luck changed again when the two Fat Man models that followed were seriously delayed by a sleet storm.[27] When Parsons learned that the suspension lugs for the Thin Man would have to be remade, he left for Dayton to investigate the problem personally.

On arrival at Wright Field, Parsons watched as technicians suspended a "fully loaded" Thin Man—that is, a model filled with lead and concrete to the anticipated 7,480 pounds of the combat bomb—inside a B-29 bomb bay. He then witnessed the suspension of an "unloaded" Fat Man. As if suspicious when things went smoothly, Parsons left instructions for Chadwick and Captain Roarke, the air force officer in charge of aircraft modifications, to suspend a Fat Man in the B-29 and taxi the loaded bomber about the airfield doing turns and rapid braking. Even with this additional testing, Captain Roarke assured Parsons that he would be ready by mid-February to fly the modified B-29 to Muroc for the air-drop tests.[28]

The events that followed might well have caused anyone less optimistic than Parsons to wonder if the gods of war, whom Parsons sometimes invoked, viewed the creation of an atomic bomb with displeasure.

Parsons' and Ramsey's arrival at Muroc on 20 February coincided with a cloudburst of unprecedented ferocity, even for the Mojave Desert with its legendary flash floods. Surely a portent of the gods, the downpour turned Rogers Dry Lake from a natural landing field of compact sand back into a wet lake. Access roads to observation towers and the project's SCR-584 radar were covered with water. For the next nine days trucks and jeeps that challenged the storm became mired in the mud.

As the weather cleared, Captain Roarke still had not arrived in the B-29 from Wright Field. Rather than stand by any longer, Parsons began rehearsals using a B-24 bomber as a substitute for the B-29 and scale models for bombs. Parsons noted in his log, "Many loose ends still apparent."[29]

A month and a half behind the original schedule, the first air drops of full-scale models were made from the B-29 in early March with, it seems, the gods of war still displeased. On the first drop of a Thin Man, the bombardier sang out, "Bombs away" and simultaneously sent a radio signal to the ground crew at the moment the bomb was triggered for release. But twenty seconds elapsed before the reluctant bomb fell through the bomb bay doors, enough of a hang-up to make a combat bomb miss its target, and enough on this first drop test to leave the cameras and radar operators tracking a bomb that was yet to appear. It is little wonder that Colonel Cork, the commanding officer of Muroc—who was told only that the project was important—was not impressed.[30]

Despite on-site modifications, the next two Thin Man models also had delayed releases. While no hang-ups occurred in the first drop tests of the Fat Man models, the bulbous bombs wobbled unacceptably in flight. Brode's fuzes malfunctioned. Still, it was not these failures but the 16 March Thin Man test that shook the hopes of Ramsey's delivery team.

At twenty-two thousand feet, as the B-29 was still climbing to bombing altitude, the shackle holding the Thin Man let go. A full twenty minutes before the scheduled release, the 9,000-pound inert bomb crashed down upon the yet unopened bomb bay doors. With the doors badly damaged, the flight crew had a struggle jettisoning the derelict weapon. As difficult as this was with an inert bomb, it could not match the nightmare of a fully armed nuclear bomb caught in bomb bay doors while flying over enemy territory. In recording the episode Ramsey wrote, "With this accident the first Muroc tests were brought to an abrupt and spectacular end."[31]

Deeply disappointed at the time, Ramsey later recognized the early Muroc tests as vindication of Parsons' determination to press for an early solution to the delivery problems. Ramsey concluded, "The negative results of most of these tests thoroughly justified the holding of preliminary tests at such an early date." Parsons himself, conditioned to expect the unexpected in weapon testing, had anticipated some early strikeouts. During the March failures he wrote in his log, "In comparison with other experimental tests involving a combination of new plane, new bomb, and new observation groups, the progress is considered remarkably good."[32]

By pressing Ramsey's delivery group into early testing, Parsons had also forced his embryonic engineering and production forces headlong into crises. But this was only one of the pressures on engineering. At the same time that Chadwick was pressing production of the full-scale bomb models, he also had to arrange the manufacture of hundreds of small hollow metal spheres (ca. twenty inches in diameter) and scores of full-scale spheres for Neddermeyer and Kistiakowsky's implosion experiments. New data called for constant modifications of designs. Everything produced was unconventional, pushing Parsons' engineering group and Chadwick's Detroit office constantly into unexplored technology.

In engineering as elsewhere, time was the adversary, and General Groves made sure no one forgot it. The general no longer predicted a German atomic bomb in 1944, but he warned of the German military possibly spreading large quantities of radioactive materials. Parsons needed no "fight talk"; he was already doing his best to fix the weak link in his organization. He desperately needed a seasoned engineer at Y to take over what he called the "orthodox" engineering that encompassed design, drafting, and operating the machine shops.[33]

The chief engineer's salary was higher than that of most scientists, but the glamour that Los Alamos held for nuclear physicists did not apply to engineers. The first three men to head the Engineering Group threw up their hands and left after short tries at the job. Oppenheimer blamed the departures on the "incompatible snobbisms between engineers and scientists." Parsons saw the cause as "the frustrations which these people experienced when one week they thought they had a problem in mind and had evolved a solution, only to find, when they proposed it, that the concept of the problem had changed in the meantime and their solution was irrelevant."[34]

In the rush to develop the bomb, Parsons' Implosion Group had its personality clashes, the Delivery Group its test failures, and the Engineering Group its frustrations, but the Gun Group moved steadily forward with remarkable harmony.

Although Parsons remained in full charge of gun design, he delegated the day-to-day conduct of the program to its group leader—first McMillan, who set up the experimental facilities at Anchor Ranch, and soon afterward McMillan's replacement, navy commander A. Francis Birch.

Birch was a windfall. A Ph.D. physicist from the Harvard faculty, he had received a navy reserve commission at the start of the war and was on duty at the Radiation Laboratory under Bainbridge when the latter agreed to serve at Y. Birch's background in physics, electronics, and mechanical design made him particularly attractive to Parsons. And in this case there was no need for the "fight talk." Birch wanted to join Bainbridge at Los Alamos and was in uniform. All Parsons had to do was ask Admiral Purnell to press the proper button in the navy, and Birch received orders to Y.[35]

As with other scientists that Parsons brought into the project as naval officers, Birch was known at Los Alamos as a physicist who just happened to be in uniform. As the new head of the Gun Group, Birch saw "our special gun as a kind of physics experiment set up for a very specific purpose." And he viewed Parsons as a navy superior who "kept very much in touch with what was going on." He found Parsons "a very amiable fellow" who encouraged his people to take initiatives on their own.[36] One result of the innovative environment Parsons created was the alternate breech block Birch designed for the gun. This adaptation would make it possible to add the high explosives for triggering the gun after the bomb was on the plane and en route to its target. At the time Parsons thought the adaptation would not be necessary, but he encouraged its development nonetheless.

Initially, the central problem of the Gun Group was to find a way to fire a plutonium projectile at 3,000 feet per second into a plutonium target a dozen or so feet away in a manner that would not shatter the target before a neutron source had initiated a nuclear reaction. To this end, the Gun Group began systematic testing at Anchor Ranch in the fall of 1943 with a 3-inch naval gun. Among other things, the early tests provided information on projectile strength and workable shapes for the full-scale plutonium projectile and target. In time the most critical testing shifted to full-scale prototypes of the gun that would fire the plutonium bullet.

As with gun design, success in getting the Anchor Ranch testing off to an early start is attributable to Parsons and the solid support given him by the navy's Bureau of Ordnance. When Deak Parsons wanted guns, he got guns. When he wanted gun forgings from BuOrd suppliers, he got them. When he wanted key people, he got them. When he wanted the help of the Naval Gun Factory or the Naval Proving Ground or any of BuOrd's facilities, he got it.[37]

This power extended to BuOrd suppliers as well. When Midvale Steel quoted three months' delivery time to forge the experimental guns, Parsons informed them that that was not soon enough. He then sent a teletype to Blandy requesting the priority needed to bring the job to completion within a month. Four weeks later, Midvale delivered the guns.[38]

Following the arrival of the forged guns at Anchor Ranch, full-scale experiments were begun using iron projectiles as substitutes for the plutonium bullet. Iron, however, proved unsatisfactory for many of the tests because of its dissimilarities to plutonium. To approximate the physical characteristics of plutonium-239, the scientists considered using gold for the 50-pound projectile and the target sleeve. They finally settled on unseparated uranium (code-named tuballoy) because it had physical properties close to plutonium but not its fissionability.[39]

In pushing development of the high-velocity gun, Parsons suffered no illusions as to the gaps in the scientists' knowledge of plutonium. In the Steering Committee meeting of 21 April he pointed out, among other problems, their lack of knowledge about the nuclear and mechanical properties of plutonium. He had a right to be concerned, as was soon borne out by some of the physicists. They found that the first samples of pile-produced plutonium contained not only plutonium-239, the desired isotope for the bomb, but also significant amounts of plutonium-240, whose fast neutrons could cause predetonation—that is, a fizzle—in the Thin Man gun.[40]

Growing awareness of the plutonium gun's potential predetonation problem was matched in the spring of 1944 with reports on the abysmal rate at which uranium-235 was being produced at Oak Ridge. The only hope for a second uranium bomb by the summer of 1945 would be in finding a way to produce enriched material to feed into the isotope separation.

Although production was well outside Parsons' ordnance duties, he visited a small thermal-diffusion plant that Ross Gunn (his old friend at the Naval Research Laboratory) and Gunn's associate Philip Abelson had set up at the Philadelphia Navy Yard to produce uranium-235 concentrates of 5 percent.[41] As Parsons knew, if Oak Ridge had concentrates of this order, it could increase the rate at which it was producing nearly pure uranium-235 for the bomb. Through Parsons' connection with Gunn, the way was opened for NRL to provide information on its processes and plant, thus clearing the way for rapid construction of a larger thermal-diffusion plant at Oak Ridge.[42] Without this NRL involvement that Parsons opened up, there could not have been a uranium-235 bomb by the summer of 1945.

By July 1944 the prospects for a plutonium bomb had also become questionable. Parsons then learned from the scientific testing that the plutonium high-speed gun the Gun Group had spent a year developing would not work because of the predetonation problem. If they were to have more than one atomic bomb by the summer of 1945, they would have to use the implosion method.

William Parsons snake-hunting behind the Parsons home with a .22-caliber rifle, ca. 1915
Courtesy of Harry R. Parsons Jr.

William "Deak" Parsons' Naval Academy portrait, 1922
Courtesy of Harry R. Parsons Jr.

Hyman "Rickie" Rickover's
Naval Academy portrait, 1922
U.S. Naval Institute

Parsons served as gunnery officer on the USS *Idaho* from August 1922 to May 1927.
U.S. Naval Institute

Deak Parsons with his sister Clarissa while on leave from the *Idaho*, December 1922 *Courtesy of Harry R. Parsons Jr.*

Parsons (*right*) with his scientific mentor, L. T. E. "Dr. Tommy" Thompson, ca. 1930 *Courtesy of Charles C. Bramble*

Merle A. Tuve, chief scientist and close associate of Parsons in the development of the proximity fuze *Courtesy of The Johns Hopkins University Applied Physics Laboratory*

The inconspicuous garage in Silver Spring, Maryland, that housed the highly secret proximity fuze project *Courtesy of The Johns Hopkins University Applied Physics Laboratory*

J. Robert Oppenheimer,
wartime director of Los Alamos
Los Alamos Historical Museum

Captain Parsons filled numerous roles at Los Alamos, including head of
Ordnance, associate director, and head of Project Alberta, 1945.
National Archives

The Oppenheimer (*left*) and Parsons (*right*) homes on Bathtub Row were continuously patrolled. *Laura Gilpin, Los Alamos Historical Museum*

Martha Parsons and her horse Diamond were a familiar sight on the Los Alamos trails. *Courtesy of Clara Parsons*

Nine-year-old Peggy (*left*) and six-year-old Clare Parsons at Los Alamos
Courtesy of Clara Parsons

Inert models of the Little Boy (*left*) and Fat Man atomic bombs
Los Alamos National Laboratory

Test preparations at Trinity site for the first nuclear explosion, July 1945
Los Alamos National Laboratory

Aerial view of Tinian, overseas base for the final assembly and combat delivery of the first atomic bombs *Los Alamos Historical Museum*

The "Tinian Joint Chiefs" (*left to right*): Capt. William "Deak" Parsons, officer in charge of Project Alberta; Rear Adm. William Purnell, representative of the Military Policy Committee and of Commander in Chief, U.S. Fleet; and Brig. Gen. Thomas Farrell, deputy director of the Manhattan Project *National Archives*

A moment of relaxation at Tinian for some Project Alberta leaders (*left to right*): Norman Ramsey, deputy director; Captain Parsons, head of Project Alberta; Edward Doll, head of the atomic bomb fuzing team; Col. Ernest Kirkpatrick, coordinator of Alberta overseas construction; and Comdr. F. L. Ashworth, Alberta operations officer and Parsons' military alternate *Courtesy of Clara Parsons*

Capt. Deak Parsons and Col. Paul Tibbets
briefing crews for the Hiroshima mission
National Archives

B-29 bombers of the 509th Composite Group on Tinian with an assembly of military and Project Alberta technical personnel *National Archives*

Interior of the *Enola Gay*'s forward compartment, occupied by Parsons during most of the flight to Hiroshima. An unidentified airman is in the tube connecting the forward and aft compartments. The sealed door below the airman leads to the bomb bay where Parsons made the final assembly of the first atomic bomb. *National Archives*

Destruction at Hiroshima near the aiming point for the first atomic bomb
Smithsonian Institution

Deak Parsons (*right*) was awarded the Silver Star by the Army Strategic Air Forces while still wearing the shirt stained by sweat and blackened by graphite from his making the final assembly of the bomb during the *Enola Gay*'s flight to Hiroshima. Brig. Gen. John H. Davies presented the award. The navy later awarded Parsons the Distinguished Service Medal for his leadership in the development of the atomic bomb. *National Archives*

Mushroom cloud from the atomic explosion at Nagasaki *Smithsonian Institution*

Featured speakers at the postwar award of the Army-Navy E to the Los Alamos Laboratory (*left to right*): J. Robert Oppenheimer, laboratory director; Maj. Gen. Leslie Groves, director of the Manhattan Project; Robert Sproul, president of the University of California; and Commodore William S. Parsons, chief of Ordnance and associate director of the Los Alamos Laboratory, late 1945 *Los Alamos National Laboratory*

Promoted to rear admiral at the end of World War II, Deak Parsons led the technical effort at Operation Crossroads and set the direction of much of the navy's nuclear policy. *U.S. Navy*

The explosion of an atomic bomb underwater in the Baker test at Crossroads created a mile-and-a-half tower of water. *U.S. Naval Institute*

High-line transfer of Rear Admiral Parsons to the USS *Macon,* his flagship as commander of Cruiser Division Six *U.S. Navy*

Commissioned in 1958 as a conventional destroyer, DD-949, the USS *Parsons* was later converted into a guided-missile destroyer, DDG-33. *U.S. Naval Institute*

·12·

Common Sense and Hypotheticals

**It is impossible to overestimate the value which
Captain Parsons has been to the project.**
Dr. J. Robert Oppenheimer

The American impetus to build an atomic bomb grew out of the realistic fear in 1939 that Nazi Germany, with its nuclear head start, was preparing to build this weapon of unprecedented power. Had American scientists known then what they had come to know by the summer of 1944, they might well have concluded that a Nazi nuclear threat was unlikely. But they had no way of anticipating the complexity of turning nuclear theory into industrial and military reality. They expected breakthroughs in the separation of the fissionable uranium, but these did not occur. The severity of the predetonation problem with plutonium was not foreseen. And even the early advocates of implosion did not recognize how difficult that would prove to be.

By the time the scientists and the military fully grasped the magnitude of the undertaking, the Manhattan Project had become an organizational giant that encompassed laboratories, industrial plants, and test ranges. It had become the greatest assemblage of military-scientific talent ever pulled together for a single objective. The atomic bomb now had a life of its own. There was no pause at Los Alamos to reexamine the original decision; the objective merely changed from beating the Germans to the draw to completing the bomb and ending the war.

In the summer of 1944, following the Allied landings at Normandy, Robert Oppenheimer was planning a different kind of attack. With all hope gone for a plutonium gun-type bomb, he planned an all-out assault to create the implosion bomb. To do this he had to reorganize his forces.

In the "August reorganization," Oppenheimer created two associate directors: Parsons for ordnance, engineering, assembly, and delivery, and Enrico Fermi for research and theoretical work.[1] In addition to being named associate director, Parsons remained in charge of the Ordnance Division. He retained direct responsibility for the uranium gun, off-site production for the total laboratory, final weapon design, and combat delivery preparations for both bombs. However, parts of the old Ordnance Division, which had outgrown itself, split into two newly created divisions. The Gadget Division for the applied physics of the implosion weapon went to Robert F. Bacher, former head of the Experimental Physics Division and a forceful manager. The Explosives Division for the explosive components of the bomb, including the explosive lenses, went to Kistiakowsky.

In the shuffle, Oppenheimer ended the Neddermeyer skirmishes with Parsons and Kistiakowsky by moving Neddermeyer out of implosion research into betatron diagnostics in the Gadget Division. Parsons recognized the need for the move but would later applaud the "stubborn refusal of Neddermeyer to give up work on implosion in the early period."[2]

In separate memoranda to Kistiakowsky and Bacher, Oppenheimer stressed the importance of their keeping Parsons promptly and fully informed of the developments in their divisions and of their plans for the future.[3]

In addition to being a division head and the associate director, Parsons kept his hand on the Los Alamos pulse through key committees, including the Intermediate Scheduling Committee, which he chaired, and the Weapons Committee, which reported to him. With his interlocking positions and committee connections, just how important was this naval officer in the Los Alamos structure? Kistiakowsky tells us: "When Oppenheimer was away, which was fairly frequent, Parsons was the boss." From Ramsey: Parsons was "sort of second in command." From Norris Bradbury: "If there was a number two man it was Parsons."[4]

•

Deak Parsons' effectiveness stemmed from something beyond his ord-nance knowledge, the strength of his organizational position, and his Washington power base. According to Bradbury, Parsons' main con-tribution to the Manhattan Project was "common sense." Or as Charles Lauritsen put it, "He sliced through funny ideas." Some of the scientists might not have agreed. "There certainly were a fair num-ber of people," Ramsey tells us, "who were in one way or another irri-tated by him." These scientists objected to his insistence on more tests than they believed necessary. They saw him as overly concerned with future problems and prone to creating seemingly unrealistic deadlines. The validity of these objections should be measured by the results, which no one was in better position to judge than Robert Oppen-heimer. He wrote, "[Captain Parsons] has been almost alone in this project to appreciate the actual military and engineering problems which we should encounter. He has been almost alone in insisting on facing these problems at a date early enough so that we might arrive at their solution."[5]

Parsons' attention to detail should not be interpreted as inability to delegate. Once he had his gun team organized and the basic design parameters established, he stepped back and let McMillan, Birch, and Hirschfelder run their own shows. Through them he still kept track of every detail that could affect on-time completion of the bomb and the success of the ultimate mission.

The scrubbing of Thin Man as the means of assembling plutonium caused Parsons to refocus the gun work on the new member of the nuclear family, Little Boy. This new gun-type bomb with a uranium-235 bullet became a quickly resolvable challenge because of the exper-imental data already accumulated for the plutonium gun. As there was no predetonation problem with uranium-235, the new gun could be fired at 1,000 feet per second, or one-third the velocity specified for Thin Man. The length of the gun could be reduced from seventeen to six feet, allowing the bomb an overall length of ten feet and a con-ventional shape for which well-established ballistics data existed. The limitation on Little Boy was not its design but the slow, difficult process of separating uranium-235 from ore-grade uranium. After millions of dollars and months of work, the ability of the Oak Ridge plant to produce enough uranium-235 for more than one bomb by

August 1945 was problematical. This meant no advance testing of a complete uranium bomb; its first use would be against the enemy. Parsons and his gun group were confident that no advance test was needed. Much of this confidence stemmed from the rigorous tests Parsons had demanded of all the non-nuclear components.

By the time of the August reorganization, Ramsey had completed a second series of drop tests at Muroc with various models of Thin Man and Fat Man. The latter still dropped like a 9,000-pound brick, but Ramsey's new box-tail design with baffles brought Fat Man closer to a predictable trajectory.[6] Parsons witnessed some of these tests in June 1944 both from the ground and from within the B-29 in flight. He concluded that the aerodynamic problems of Fat Man were coming under control.[7]

By the summer of 1944, when Little Boy models made their appearance, aerial testing had expanded from Muroc to two other sites in the California desert: Salton Sea and the Naval Ordnance Test Station, Inyokern. NOTS was then being built in the Mojave Desert to test rockets created under the Office of Scientific Research and Development by the California Institute of Technology. The CalTech-NOTS rocket work had become the belated fulfillment of Goddard's proposal for a major wartime rocket program, but without Goddard. In one of the first tragedies of Big Science, the American rocket pioneer became isolated from the nation's main World War II military rocket program. Instead he directed a small rocket research group working on a jet-assisted takeoff device for aircraft.[8]

The first Little Boy dropped at NOTS Inyokern proved itself not only aerodynamically sound but also, unfortunately, quite proficient at ground penetration. Digging for the errant Little Boy created a hole the size of a four-story building. As one officer said, "It went down a hell of a way."[9] To hell or not, Parsons was intent on knowing what happened to the innards of the bomb upon impact, in particular whether it would assemble itself and explode. The worst thing about dropping a nuclear dud in combat would be having the enemy retrieve it and learn its secrets.

The effects of ground impact was but one of many questions raised by Parsons, the master of hypotheticals. What would happen if the bomb fell into a body of water? What if the plane crashed and burned on takeoff? What if enemy machine-gun bullets struck the bomb?

"What if" constantly played in Parsons' mind. For answers he sought the results of the tests at Muroc, Salton Sea, and Inyokern.

Prior to August 1944 only two top officers of the Army Air Forces had been fully informed about the atomic bomb development. Parsons saw this as a danger and pressed Groves to increase Air Forces involvement. In particular he wanted access to an Air Corps officer of high technical qualifications, emphasizing that "the success or failure of this project will depend upon adaptation of airplanes and tactics to deliver a bomb which is radically different in characteristics and effect from any hitherto carried."[10]

Groves agreed, and the Air Forces responded by naming Col. R. C. Wilson as the link. On 12 and 14 April, Wilson met with Oppenheimer, Parsons, Ramsey, and others at Los Alamos. Ramsey, who kept the minutes, identified the subject as "Air Forces Organization for Our Project." The "Our Project" may well have been a subtle reminder by the scientist of who was inviting whom into the tent.[11] If so, it was a message ultimately lost.

A fundamental question posed at the meetings was how far ahead of bomb availability an air force combat unit should be formed. Starting early might avoid a crash program later. But it could also create morale problems should the crew be put on standby too long. Colonel Wilson, wanting no delay, took immediate steps to assign fifteen B-29s to the project.[12] Within the week he had three strong candidates as the commander of the air force unit. Among them was Paul Tibbets, a twenty-nine-year-old lieutenant colonel who had not only proved his piloting skill in bombing missions over Germany but also had a year's experience testing the B-29.

When Tibbets reported to Gen. Uzal G. Ent's Second Air Force Headquarters at Colorado Springs, he found himself facing not only General Ent but also a naval officer and a civilian: Captain Parsons and Dr. Ramsey. Before the morning was over, Tibbets found himself in an environment unlike anything in his previous military experience.[13]

Ramsey described the basic features of the 9,000-pound nuclear bomb the Air Corps officer would be responsible for dropping upon the enemy. It should explode, he said, with the force of several thousand tons of TNT—but having never tested it, they did not know just how powerful it would be. When Tibbets asked how far away the plane had to be from the explosion to be safe, Parsons responded, "We're not sure, but our best calculations indicate an airplane should be able to withstand the shock waves at a distance of eight miles."[14] Conventional delivery tactics with a B-29 would leave the airplane closer than that. Part of Tibbets' job would be figuring out how to increase that distance.

The dangers of the mission would come up again when Tibbets paid his first visit to Los Alamos. On that occasion Oppenheimer let him know that Captain Parsons would be accompanying him on the first bomb drop. "Good," Tibbets said, "then if anything goes wrong, Captain, I can blame you." "If anything goes wrong, Colonel," Parsons replied, "neither of us will be around to be blamed."[15]

Paul Tibbets was not the only aviator thrust without warning into the secret world of Project Y. At 1500 on a Friday in November, Comdr. F. L. "Dick" Ashworth, an ordnance postgraduate and the senior aviator at Dahlgren, was told by Captain Hedrick, "Don't worry about your uniform, get an airplane and fly to Washington and you'll be met at Anacostia [Naval Air Station]." At Anacostia a station wagon whisked Ashworth to the National Academy of Science. There he was met by Captain Parsons and Dr. Ramsey, who wanted to know if he would be interested in working with the Army Air Corps on B-29s. Ashworth, who knew Parsons' technical reputation, responded, "Well, I don't know what you are talking about, but if you want me, I'll go."[16]

Ashworth left on Sunday morning for a mysterious site called "Kingman." This was the code name for the Second Air Force's Wendover Airfield, the center for training Tibbets' 509th Composite Group and the new site for most of the flight testing previously done at Muroc for the atomic bomb. The 509th was as radical in structure as in mission. Besides an aerial squadron with fifteen B-29s, it had a transport squadron and an ordnance squadron for the assembly of the world's most awesome weapon. Completely self-contained, Tibbets' group had its own engineering, maintenance, and military police.

Upon arriving at Wendover, Ashworth received a briefing from Ramsey on the bomb and the existence of Los Alamos. All the while, Ashworth contemplated the utter desolation of Wendover, finally pleading, even though he had not seen the New Mexico site, "Please don't leave me here; let me go to Los Alamos." In all likelihood, Ashworth was more concerned for his wife than himself. Parsons approved the arrangement and the Ashworths, with bulldog, were assigned quarters at Los Alamos. Ashworth typically spent three weeks a month at Wendover, where he relieved Ramsey of direct technical supervision of testing.[17] On the fourth week he would return to Los Alamos, via the 509th's "Green Hornet" flights between Albuquerque and "Kingman" to get ready for the next series of tests.

As a Green Hornet regular, Ashworth witnessed a continuing airborne masquerade. Since Groves did not want any of the military at Wendover other than Tibbets and the head of the ordnance squadron to know about Los Alamos, scientists going to Wendover to participate in tests were identified as safety engineers or anything other than scientists. Sergeants and corporals from SED put on officer's uniforms and insignia so that they would have the proper clout with the Air Corps technicians at Wendover. On flights from Wendover, Ashworth would see officers exchange their Air Corps insignia for the castles of the Corps of Engineers in order to cut speculation at Los Alamos on the level of Air Forces involvement. The Los Alamos security office orchestrated these deceptions, but some of them may have originated with Parsons, whose creativity in making identity switches went back to the time of the proximity fuze program, when he turned civilian scientists into officers overnight.

What is clear is that Parsons set the technical agenda for Wendover. In Ashworth's words, "Parsons was darn well on top of Tibbets and his whole operation with the airplanes."[18] This was not a direct command relationship but a practical resolution of how to provide air support to the Manhattan Project. The project's master planner for delivery was Deak Parsons, and the final means for that delivery was the 509th. General Groves, with the backing of air force generals Henry "Hap" Arnold and Lauris Norstad, looked to Parsons to bring together the weapon and the aircraft and the expertise necessary to assure successful delivery.[19]

In addition to his other responsibilities, Parsons was, as one Los Alamos officer said, "kind of a granddaddy for all the military."[20] This role fell to him not just because he was the senior military officer on the technical side of the house but also because he had brought the project's naval officers to Los Alamos. Groves twitted Parsons about having a navy bias in filling key positions. Although there was some truth to that, the main reason Parsons chose naval officers was that he had access to them through Admirals King, Purnell, Blandy, and George Hussey. He had no clout when it came to prying loose army ordnance or engineering officers.[21] Parsons accepted the "granddaddy" burden, and, according to his secretary, "never forgot his men even though he had all this serious technical business of the bomb on his mind."[22]

To help with the extra work, Parsons requested a yeoman to work with Hazel Greenbacker; instead, the navy sent an officer, Ens. Louise Newkirk. There were three hundred army WACs at Los Alamos, and now with Ensign Newkirk's arrival there was one navy WAVE. And so it would be to the end of the war. Ensign Newkirk, whom Parsons commended for "outstanding initiative and industry," took over the record keeping for the project officers.[23]

Parsons could not avoid the extra responsibilities that went with being the senior naval officer at Y, but many of the tasks that he took on were self-imposed. In July 1944 he did not have to personally investigate the explosion of two ammunition ships at Port Chicago northeast of San Francisco. It was, however, something he felt he had to see for himself. As the chief planner for the military delivery of an explosion of unprecedented size, he recognized the Port Chicago disaster as a chance to examine the effects of the largest explosion ever to occur in the United States.

On 20 July, accompanied by a Los Alamos officer and a scientist, Parsons joined his brother-in-law Capt. Jack Crenshaw (a member of the official inquiry into cause) at Mare Island, and they went together to the Port Chicago site. There they observed what had happened when over 1,500 tons of high explosives and additional tons of shells, smokeless powder, and incendiary clusters exploded in a harbor: the USS *E. S. Bryan* "fragmented and widely distributed"; the USS *Quinalt* (waiting to be loaded) torn into large pieces; three hundred and twenty men killed (of which two-thirds were African-American seamen loading ammunition); nothing left of the pier within four hundred feet of the detonation; a wood-frame shop demolished; freight cars buckled. Of the persons killed, all but five were at the center of the explosion. All of the serious damage took place within a one-mile radius.[24]

Parsons' Port Chicago trip was not a major incident in Project Y history despite subsequent sensational attempts by a historical revisionist to make it so. Parsons' appearance at the site, plus the report of a mushroom cloud, contributed to erroneous charges starting in the 1980s that this had been a nuclear explosion and hence the subject of a government coverup. The story resurfaces from time to time despite a clear case to the contrary by historians Lawrence Badash and Richard G. Hewlett assisted by fifteen other established scholars.[25]

The adaptability that allowed Parsons to rush off to Port Chicago also made it possible for him to move from the pressing work of war to postwar planning. These were not things he was asked to do, but things he felt compelled to do. In July 1944, with battles raging in Europe and the Pacific, Parsons paced the floor of his office dictating to Hazel Greenbacker his ideas on what form army and navy postwar research should take.[26] Many of these ideas, forged in the heat of war, will be presented in the postwar chapters of this account. We need only note here the degree to which Parsons drove himself not only for the immediate but also for the long-range objectives of the navy and the nation.

Parsons could not foresee that he would become the Atomic Admiral of the postwar world. He believed that his next peacetime assignment would be his long overdue command at sea. However, in his correspondence with Dr. Tommy he acknowledged the possibility of cutting his future sea duty short in order to fulfill their dream of a "super" laboratory. By the fall of 1944 Parsons and Thompson foresaw the possibility of the secret rocket station at Inyokern becoming their dream laboratory.[27]

As Parsons knew, the Naval Ordnance Test Station, Inyokern, had grown out of the California Institute of Technology's need for a large instrumented range for testing the rockets it was developing for the navy. Blandy had turned the proposal for a rocket test facility into an opportunity to create a large permanent proving ground where the navy could do research, development, and testing of weapons with the kind of military-scientific cooperation characterized by the navy's wartime work with OSRD scientists. Blandy struck while the iron was hot and wartime funds were still flowing.[28] The station became a reality on 8 November 1943 under the command of Capt. S. E. "Ev" Burroughs. The young CO called on Dr. Tommy as his principal adviser. Thompson immediately involved Parsons, informing him, "There are now 7,000 men working on the building program. It is going to be a magnificent plant, the sort of place we always dreamed about but never expected to see."[29]

When Thompson learned that Burroughs was going to sea, he wrote Parsons, "I think the most important point now is to see that the right successor to Captain Burroughs is selected. I think you should be his successor."[30]

Parsons tossed the ball back to Thompson. He believed that Thompson's task of planning the NOTS postwar organization should be expanded. He used his Washington connections to obtain a contract putting Thompson in charge of the facilities planning and the organizing and recruiting of the technical staff for the station. As for becoming the future commander of NOTS, Deak assured his old friend that if Inyokern should get into the kind of problems they had experienced at Dahlgren, he would be prepared to cut his expected sea duty short and come to the rescue. If Dr. Tommy would organize their dream laboratory, Deak was prepared, if necessary, to command it.[31]

Although Deak found time to plan and promote future military research, he had little time to revisit the past with his sister in Albuquerque. "Once in a awhile," Clarissa Fuller reports, "Deak would call, 'Sister, I'm going to be here for 15 minutes.' And I'd go down and he'd be with some of these men [most often Brode, Ramsey, and Bradbury], and they'd be here for just a short time." Clarissa sensed a deep "feeling of kinship among these men." The kinship included a common reverence for the name Oppy: "Oppy would like that," "Oppy would be pleased with this."[32] Even before she met Robert Oppenheimer, Clarissa recognized that Deak's esteem for the man bordered on veneration. What she did not know about were the tensions that tested the alliance between physicist and officer.

The strength of the Parsons-Oppenheimer relationship lay not only in mutual respect but also in the ease with which they could agree to disagree. Oppenheimer, for example, ended one bout with the comment, "I wanted to make my own views clear since I respect yours but do not share them."[33]

One contest of wills was not so much a matter of viewpoints as one of power. In a September memo Parsons told Oppenheimer that he believed that as the associate director he should be on all councils in which long-term basic policies and schedules were determined. To this Oppenheimer agreed. Parsons then sought "full authority with backing above and below" to carry out the established policies and schedules for the design and production of all mechanical, electrical, and explosive parts of the gadget. Next we have Deak Parsons, the long-standing opponent of autocratic management, claiming exceptional powers for himself. He wrote Oppenheimer, "It is clearly proper for me to assemble the interested parties and to reach a decision (if necessary on my own), and to express this decision in a binding directive, schedule, design or production order as the case may be." This bid for extraordinary powers came, it seems, out of desperation. Boards and committees were fine, but Parsons at this point believed that once policy and schedules were defined, a qualified individual should be empowered to make final decisions and take vigorous action. Otherwise, he prophesied, the project would fail. Oppenheimer responded, "The kind of authority which you appear to request from me is something I cannot delegate to you because I do not possess it."[34]

Oppenheimer explained that he could not ask scientists to execute decisions they did not understand or approve of. "I do not mean by this," the director said, "that in the case of a divided opinion it is not appropriate for you and for me to let our own views render the decision." Because of the advanced state of the gun program, Oppenheimer rationalized, "centralization of responsibility and authority in one man is essential."[35] He also left Parsons broad authority for the weaponeering on the Fat Man and Thin Man bombs. But when it came to research and development policy for implosion, Parsons would have to argue his views right along with the others. As yet, Oppenheimer was not ready to hand a whip on this to anyone, much less a military officer.

Deak Parsons' uncharacteristic bid for power came, it seems, from his concern over the deep consequences of failure: a $2 billion dud, a lost opportunity to shorten the war, and, not least, the likelihood of personal blame for the failure. In a letter to Groves, Parsons gave one of his characteristic hypotheticals to illustrate his concern: "If the first gadget is, through mechanical failure, dropped in the sea shortly after take-off, it will be the fault not of the Material Command of the Army Air Corps nor of Army or Navy Ordnance, but will be chargeable to the group including yourself, Drs. Bush, Conant, Oppenheimer, and myself."[36]

Parsons identified a series of problems that could lead to failure. Among them was the discord he witnessed between scientists and engineers. This accounted for the difficulties he was having in bringing in and keeping a top-flight chief engineer. Parsons believed that the solution called for "heroic action" on the part of the laboratory director and other senior scientists in backing engineering with the same kind of fire they had for the "elegant research solutions." In his words, "Scientists engaged in the most exciting physics work of the century, should be simultaneously excited about and welcome the problems of detailed design, fabrication, and bomb delivery."[37]

Parsons also saw a vulnerability in the reluctance to recognize the magnitude of the delivery problems. As he pointed out, these problems went beyond combat delivery of an entirely different bomb in a new type of airplane. In this case, the airplane had a "notoriously unreliable engine." And the Army Air Forces' mass-bombing psychology aimed at statistical success—large numbers of planes on repeated missions—could endanger a mission needing sure-fire excellence on just a few flights.[38]

Parsons concluded that the mission could also be jeopardized by a weakening resolve to use the final weapon. He wrote Groves, "Some tender souls are appalled at the idea of the horrible destruction which the bomb might wreak in battle delivery. I believe these imaginations magnify the horror beyond what they read about in thousand-bomber raids." Parsons felt it would be but a short leap from "this loose reasoning to the expressed or unexpressed hope that 'We may never have to use this weapon in battle.'"[39] Once that happened, in his view, the drive necessary to complete the project would be lost.

Parsons noted that he had not encountered this wishful thinking at Y. He alluded instead to people elsewhere in "high and responsible quarters" who held that "if we are winning the war anyway, perhaps the best use of the gadget is in a staged field test in an American desert." For this demonstration the United States would invite those foreign observers it wished "to impress with our victory over the atom and our potential power to win victories over our future enemies."[40]

Based on his observation of the Port Chicago explosion, Parsons assured Groves that the reaction of foreign observers to the desert shot would be one of "intense disappointment." He noted, "Even the crater would be disappointing." In his conclusion Parsons wrote, "The principal difficulty with such a demonstration is that it would not be held one thousand feet over Times Square, where the human and material destruction would be obvious, but in an uninhabited desert, where there would be no humans and only sample structures." To Parsons the demonstration idea was an invitation to "a political and military fizzle, regardless of the scientific achievement." If the demonstration failed in psychological impact, as he believed it would, the Japanese mainland would have to be taken by troops, not technology—with American blood, not Yankee ingenuity.[41]

·13·

Homestretch

There is no one more responsible for getting this bomb out of the laboratory and into some form useful for combat operations than Captain Parsons, by his plain genius in the ordnance business.
Vice Adm. F. L. Ashworth, USN (Ret.)

In February 1945 Parsons sounded the alarm. Unless Oppenheimer made drastic changes, an implosion bomb could not be produced in time to meet the operational plan. The plan's objective was to render unnecessary a U.S. invasion of mainland Japan. It called for the military use in the summer ahead of Little Boy and one or two Fat Man bombs, followed by more if necessary.

Parsons addressed the problem in a brisk memo to Oppenheimer titled "Home Stretch Measures." He began, "We embraced lenses as our first love in July 1944." But because of unmet schedules, that love had failed. He tartly declared that it would be "difficult in cold blood to look for an adequately tested lens implosion gadget in 1945." Parsons believed that explosive lens research should be continued but advocated putting the main effort into a more straightforward nonlens implosion model.[1]

There was plenty to back this argument. Over twenty thousand cast lenses had been exploded in tests, yet the right design still eluded Kistiakowsky. The rejection of another forty thousand castings as unfit testified to the difficulty of casting explosives into the precise geometric forms required. At the same time, scientists designing detonators had difficulty achieving the extreme precision required to fire several dozen detonators simultaneously from different points of the explosive sphere. To this end, hundreds of variously designed detonators, as well as detonators in combination with explosive Primacord, were being test-fired every day. Despite all the explosions echoing through the Jemez Mountains, a nuclear explosion by implosion remained undemonstrated theory. Parsons heard the ticking of the clock.

Parsons proposed that Oppenheimer empower a select committee to make and enforce technical decisions. "Ruthless, brutal people must band together," he wrote, "to force the Fat Man components to dovetail in time and space"—that is, fit the tight time schedule and fit within the fifty-nine-inch-diameter sphere. Parsons named ten of the laboratory's elite as candidates for this ruthless band, including Oppenheimer, Kistiakowsky, and himself. The members of this band, he said, "must feel that they have a mandate to circumvent or crush opposition above and below, animate and inanimate—even nuclear!"[2]

Oppenheimer took Parsons' warning seriously. Within four months they would have enough plutonium for a bomb, but unless drastic action was taken they would not be ready to make this fissionable material into a bomb. Reacting to Parsons' admonitions and the situation itself, Oppenheimer made a series of homestretch decisions. No more arguing over whether the Fat Man plutonium core would be a hollow or a solid ball; it would be solid. No more quibbling about detonation; electric detonators would be used. As for kick-starting the nuclear reaction, a modulated initiator was the answer. And, despite Parsons' arguments to the contrary, research would concentrate on a bomb imploded by explosive lenses. Any additional research on the nonlens model would fall to CalTech.[3]

As Parsons had advocated, Oppenheimer crushed the opposition—and that included Parsons himself. But what was more important to Parsons was that Oppenheimer had shifted into high gear for the homestretch. As part of his new stance, Oppenheimer formed the powerful Cowpunchers Committee to "ride herd" on implosion. He had his own ideas on membership but included most of the individuals suggested by Parsons. Samuel Allison, a scientist of stature on both lists, was made chairman of the Cowpunchers as well as the Technical and Scheduling Conference.[4] In effect Allison became the whip Parsons had sought. This former director of the University of Chicago's Metallurgical Laboratory (under Arthur Compton, director of the Metallurgical Project) had pioneered with Fermi in early nuclear research. He had the stature to wield the Cowpunchers' whip.

After freezing implosion design and forming the Cowpunchers, Oppenheimer initiated the most important homestretch measures of all: in March 1945 he created Projects Trinity and Alberta. Superimposed upon the existing organization, these projects split the main thrust of the laboratory's work in two. Bainbridge as head of Trinity had the task of setting up an experimental test site in the desert and firing the first nuclear device, perhaps the most momentous scientific event of the century. Parsons as head of Alberta had responsibility for laboratory activities leading to the delivery of the first atomic bomb in combat.

Many of Parsons' Alberta responsibilities were part of the ongoing operations of his Ordnance Division: converting nuclear devices into weapons with predictable ballistics; modifying aircraft to accommodate the bombs; coordinating a delivery plan with the Air Forces; supervising field tests of non-nuclear components and full-scale bomb models; developing fuzes to fire the bomb at the chosen altitude; selecting an advance base within bombing range of the enemy; and planning the facilities and procedures for assembling the bombs overseas. Many hurdles lay ahead, but scientists who had once scoffed at Parsons' early emphasis on delivery problems could now recognize the magnitude of these problems and the validity of his early concerns.

Parsons began Project Alberta with a first-class, proven team in place. Ramsey's manuscript history of the project identifies the key players in March 1945 when the project was established:

> Captain W. S. Parsons was Officer in Charge of Project A, N. F. Ramsey was his deputy for scientific and technical matters, Commander F. L. Ashworth was operations officer and military alternate for Captain Parsons, Commander Norris Bradbury and Roger Warner were in charge of Fat Man Assembly, Commander Francis Birch was in charge of Little Boy Assembly, R. B. Brode was in charge of fusing, Lewis Fussell was in charge of the electrical detonator system, Philip Morrison and Marshall Holloway were in charge of the pit (active material and tamper), Luis Alvarez and Bernard Waldman were in

charge of airborne observations of the combat explosions, George Galloway was in charge of engineering, Lt. Col. R. W. Lockridge was in charge of supply, Maurice Shapiro was in charge of ballistics and Sheldon Dike was in charge of aircraft problems.[5]

Parsons already had the delivery program at full throttle when Alberta went into effect. In the Pacific theater of war, Commander Ashworth selected the island of Tinian, fifteen hundred miles from Japan, as the project's advance base. There bombs would be assembled and from there the nuclear attacks launched. In the communications that followed, Tinian was known simply as "Destination."

By the end of March, Parsons and Ramsey had completed the plans for what Parsons described as the most complex technical operation ever conducted overseas by American armed forces.[6] From their Los Alamos offices, eight thousand miles from "Destination," they defined requirements for everything from screwdrivers to loading pits to air-conditioned assembly buildings. They simplified the problems of purchasing and shipping these assorted materials overseas by the innovative use of the word *kits*. One "Kit, Bomb Assembly, Heavy," for example, covered a multitude of items from hand tools to Quonset huts. Each kit passed through the Port of Embarkation as a single item.[7] Characteristic of the Parsons thoroughness, all critical kits were ordered in triplicate so that a complete facility for assembling the bombs could be constructed at each of three sites: Tinian, Iwo Jima, and NOTS Inyokern. The latter was to be constructed first to provide stateside proof that the facilities went together as planned and that nothing, down to the smallest tool, had been forgotten. The full array of assembly buildings, equipment, and loading pit at Iwo Jima was for backup in the event of eleventh-hour operational problems at Tinian.

The stream of shipments by sea and by the three C-54 and four C-47 cargo planes of Tibbets' Green Hornets began in April. Also in April navy Seabees began construction at "Destination" under the direction of Lt. Col. E. E. Kirkpatrick of the Army Corps of Engineers. Kirkpatrick had worked with Groves on previous projects and was the general's personal representative in getting the work under way on Tinian. Working with the plans provided by Parsons and Ramsey, Kirkpatrick oversaw the construction of fourteen buildings for bomb assembly, shops, and storage as well as explosive magazines and the loading pit.

Parsons' homestretch measures went beyond completing the bombs on time and preparing assembly facilities on Tinian. Mission success also depended, as he told Groves, "on really smart delivery of our gadget."[8] In connection with the general's Military Use Committee, Parsons involved himself in the analysis of the kinds of targets and delivery that would produce the most devastating results. The premise being that if two atomic bombs were to shock the enemy into surrender, the military damage had to be conclusive.

From the various studies it was concluded by all concerned that the most effective use would be an airburst over a military industrial center. To this end, Parsons had a great deal of analytical work done to determine the height at which the bomb should be exploded. The studies indicated that the optimum height for the burst would be about two thousand feet above ground. Radiation effects from an airburst seem not to have been taken into account, under the mistaken belief that the explosion would kill anyone in the target area before the radiation could affect them.

Throughout the studies of the bomb's killing power, Parsons remained an objective, unemotional military officer doing his job. In this he was not alone: he was part of a powerful military-scientific-industrial team intent upon its wartime mission, winning the war. The atomic bomb, the ultimate product of the weapons revolution, had a momentum of its own. If anyone were to halt or delay its use in the war, it would not be Deak Parsons or those at Y immersed in its creation.

During the homestretch Parsons wrote Groves, "As I understand your wishes, it will be my duty to represent you in the initial battle delivery. This has been my aim since joining the project."[9] Whether the general held to his word or not would not diminish Parsons' commitment to a mission that could shorten the war. But his belief that he would accompany the first bomb helps explain his uncommon drive and his close attention to every detail affecting combat delivery. He wanted no surprises at the end.

In particular, Parsons wanted no last-minute interference from outsiders. In the closing weeks he wanted to be free to concentrate on the gadget and the delivery plan. He wanted to avoid the last hours being taken up, as he wrote Groves, "arguing over tactical plans with operational research people who previously receive only sketchy and over-simplified versions of what our gadget can do."[10] To avoid this, Parsons proposed the formation of a two-man operational group under Brig. Gen. Lauris Norstad, chief of staff, Army Strategic Air Force, and spokesman for Gen. H. H. Arnold on all air force matters related to the atomic bomb. On Parsons' recommendation, Dr. David Dennison, professor of physics at the University of Michigan, and Dr. E. J. Workman, head of physics at the University of New Mexico, took on the operational analysis, working both with the Strategic Air Force and Los Alamos. By bringing in Dennison and Workman as analysts of his own choice, Parsons turned a potential problem into assets.

Parsons' previous connections with Dennison are not known, but he had a close ongoing relationship with Workman. In fact, Workman was already involved in Project Y as security cover by which technical materials were shipped to Los Alamos via the proximity fuze test range that he operated in New Mexico for the Applied Physics Laboratory.

Among Workman's recommendations as operational analyst was the stripping of delivery planes of virtually all armaments. He concluded that the speed and maneuverability gained through diminished weight would more than offset the defensive value of the guns. At the same time, Dennison recommended that Tibbets' group have combat experience dropping high-explosive bombs over Japanese territory as dress rehearsals for the big event. He advocated the dropping of the second bomb within six days of the first in order to convey to the enemy that the nuclear bombing would be continuous until surrender.[11]

From his proving-ground days Parsons knew that weapon hardware as well as people could provide surprises. Imperfect soldering in the circuitry or the failure of a small switch could spell disaster; hence he called for a reliability rate such that there would be less than one chance in ten thousand of failure from the non-nuclear parts of the bombs. He designed redundancy into the system. If the electronic circuitry on one side of the plane was knocked out by enemy gunfire, the electronic signals would be transmitted by circuitry on the opposite side. He required a combination of fuzes, electronic circuits, and clock switches with built-in redundancy to control the triggering of the bombs. These included barometric switches to prevent the bomb from exploding until it was at least 15,000 feet below the drop plane; a proximity fuze (later replaced by an Archie radar device) to trigger the bomb when it reached the desired distance (ultimately determined to be 1,750 to 1,850 feet) above ground; and finally contact fuzes to explode the bomb in case the other fuzing failed and the bomb struck the ground.[12]

As head of Project Alberta, Parsons was in charge of the Manhattan Project's overseas operations for bomb assembly and delivery. What Parsons did not have was authority in the conventional military sense over the aircraft and aircrews it would take to deliver the bomb. To explicitly put a naval officer in charge of a flight mission would have been heresy of the same magnitude as placing an Air Corps officer in command of a battleship going into action. Hence, Parsons' control over the air arm of delivery was not direct but was exercised through the command arrangements previously described. Transcribed telephone conversations between Ashworth at Wendover and Parsons at Los Alamos confirm that Parsons was ready to start action at the top in the case of noncooperation from the 509th Composite Group. In practical terms this meant a telephone call from Parsons to Groves and a second call from Groves to Norstad.[13]

As a case in point, when Parsons asked Ashworth over the telephone if he thought corrective action was needed on some rather large bombing errors, Ashworth replied, "I had some discussion on that with Tibbets, and he doesn't feel so. He feels his setup is all right there." "That might be the worst situation," Parsons replied. "I mean [if] he feels it's all right when it isn't. . . . The question is whether he is unduly complacent. . . . If he's not taking the responsibility that should be his as a senior man, then corrective steps must be taken. And if Paul doesn't take them, then they will be taken somewhere else. . . . If action starts, you know, via Mr. N. [General Norstad], you can imagine that there might be some rather serious repercussions." After quizzing Ashworth, Parsons concluded that Tibbets had a "very progressive attitude."[14] It was a view Parsons would have no reason to question for the remainder of the war.

However, Parsons did have continuing concerns about the effect on the mission of the mass-bombing psychology that prevailed in the Strategic Air Force. In the raids against industrial targets in Europe, scores of bombers would follow a lead plane and release their bombs in unison. In a nuclear attack, only one plane would carry a bomb, and that plane needed to operate largely on its own. Parsons' concerns, relayed through channels, resulted in Tibbets' flight crews being sent off to the Caribbean where they underwent intensive navigation training and flew thousand-mile triangular courses over water. As a result, according to Groves, "our navigators were all top-notch."[15]

The next concern Parsons brought to Groves had Tibbets' endorsement. Both he and Parsons wanted a real bomb with which the 509th could gain combat experience before the nuclear mission. The result, after some original objections by Groves, was the bomb known as the Pumpkin. This bulbous copy of Fat Man was painted orange to distinguish it from its powerful look-alike with a nuclear core. When packed with high explosives, the 5,500-pound Pumpkin could pack a respectable wallop. To keep its development from interfering with Fat Man production, the Pumpkin was designed and manufactured through CalTech. By May 1945, Pumpkins were being shipped overseas at the rate of twelve to sixty a month, adding significant logistical problems at Mare Island and Port Chicago. Parsons displayed his proving-ground heritage in his response to these mounting problems: "There are enough new features to our problems of storage, handling and shipment to justify that until we have done something at least once, we cannot count on it being done."[16]

The Pumpkin was but one item that Parsons and Tibbets worked on together. Tibbets turned to Parsons when he wanted to replace the first batch of B-29s with the latest model. Parsons simply told Groves that the existing B-29s were worn out and could become the fatal weak link in the chain of final events. Groves observed, "It was the kind of thing that Tibbets would tell him [Parsons] but wouldn't tell me because he thought there was just no hope of getting them and I would look on him as a complainer."[17] In March and April the 509th received fifteen new B-29s, the prime pick of the line with all the latest advances: fuel-injection engines, electric reversible-pitch propellers, and pneumatic bomb bay doors. The American bomber for the mission was now one of the strongest links in the chain rather than the weakest.

The first of the fifteen flight crews took off with the new B-29s for Tinian on 5 June. They had been preceded by other elements of the 509th, whose total strength now came to 225 officers and 1,542 enlisted men.[18] The secrecy of the mission brought more ridicule than obscurity to the 509th upon its arrival in Tinian. Among the taunts thrown by the seasoned air force units on the island was the poem "Nobody Knows":

> *Into the air the secret rose,*
> *Where they're going, nobody knows.*
> *Tomorrow they'll return again.*
> *But we'll never know where they've been.*
> *Don't ask us about results or such,*
> *Unless you want to get in Dutch.*
> *But take it from one who is sure of the score.*
> *The 509th is winning the war.*
>
> *When other Groups are ready to go,*
> *We have a program for the whole damn show.*
> *And when Halsey's 5th shells Nippon's shore,*
> *Why, shucks, we hear about it the day before.*
> *And MacArthur and Doolittle give out in advance,*
> *But with this new bunch we haven't a chance.*
> *We should have been home a month or more,*
> *For the 509th is winning the war.*[19]

Although a separate project, Alberta depended on the outcome of the Trinity test scheduled for mid-July at the Alamogordo test site two hundred miles south of Los Alamos. If the scientists failed to achieve a nuclear explosion at Trinity, there would be no second bomb in the summer of 1945. If they succeeded, Parsons' Alberta team and the 509th would have about three weeks in which to complete their overseas preparations and drop the first atomic bomb to be used as an instrument of war. Scores of scientists and technicians worked around the clock for weeks to prepare the Trinity gadget for detonation from a tower in a controlled setting. By contrast, the first combat bomb would have to be assembled in a matter of days on an island thousands of miles away from the base laboratory and delivered by a small crew flying over hostile territory. The only way this could work was if Parsons' two years of planning resulted in a perfect mesh overseas.

Besides his overseas responsibilities, Parsons as a member of the Cowpunchers had a role to play in Trinity. The Cowpunchers selected 4 July as the target date for what Parsons called "the Big Bang at Trinity." Working backward from that date, they derived a schedule that was ruthlessly rechecked every week to determine who was failing to meet his commitments and what to do about it. As Parsons noted with satisfaction, "Allison lashed the guilty one with the title 'pathological optimist.'" Without this internal pressure Parsons was certain that "Los Alamos would still have been fumbling over minor engineering and procurement problems in the Fall of 1945."[20]

Spurred by the Cowpunchers, Project Trinity moved apace. The scientists had to change the target date from 4 to 16 July, but this was still consistent with the objective of having the first combat bombs ready as soon as the fissionable materials became available.

Freed from Groves' restriction on air travel, Parsons entered a burst of whirlwind travels in June and early July, all as a windup of his homestretch measures. These included Air Corps matters at Wendover, project links at Inyokern, overseas support at San Diego, and explosive lens matters at CalTech, Pasadena. Between 2 and 13 July he made a round trip to Tinian, as he said, "to verify that the arrangements and training for combat delivery were adequate."[21] He then returned to New Mexico two days before his scheduled role in the Trinity detonation scheduled for predawn 16 July.

Parsons returned just as the strain of two intense years approached a peak at both Los Alamos and Trinity site. Long hours produced drawn faces among the scientists and their crews. Wives preparing breakfast at three o'clock in the morning worried about their husbands. Despite the tensions, esprit de corps remained high. By this time there was little reason for the Los Alamos scientists to believe that the bomb would not explode. "Human calculation," said Hans Bethe, head of the Theoretical Division, "indicates that the experiment must succeed." Then he solemnly added, "But will nature act in conformity with our calculations?"[22]

The scientists questioned themselves. Had they overlooked something? Just how powerful would the explosion be? The answers lay in the test itself, and they pressed forward.

Martha and the girls welcomed Deak home on Friday evening, 13 July. More like a phantom than husband and father, he appeared for short intervals but then rushed off again.

Sunday afternoon he left for Kirtland Army Air Field to take part in Trinity. Had events gone as planned, he would have been stationed at one of the most dangerous locations when the Trinity bomb exploded. To make the experiment resemble a tactical delivery, he meant to assume the roles of bomb commander and weaponeer that he would fill on the combat run. For Trinity he was supposed to be in a B-29 flying above the tower that held the nuclear bomb. Seconds before passing the tower, Luis Alvarez and his crew on the B-29 with Parsons were to parachute three canisters with pressure gauges. When the plane was out of range and the parachutes still in the air, the nuclear device was to be exploded. Parsons and Alvarez were depending on these pressure gauges to give definitive information on the magnitude of the blast.[23]

But tests do not always go as planned. By 1600 that Sunday a storm began to gather at Kirtland and Trinity site. Lightning crackled at the site, posing a threat to the electrical circuitry for the monitoring and triggering of the nuclear device on the tower, not to mention the multimillion-dollar gadget itself and the men still checking connections.

Oppenheimer, haggard from ceaseless action and sleepless nights, conferred with Groves—now at the test site with Bush and Conant—about possible postponement. Oppenheimer wanted to proceed if at all possible, believing that if the work stopped it would be days before the men could be rested, equipment rechecked, and momentum restored. Groves had a stronger reason to proceed. He alone knew that President Truman, who had just arrived in Potsdam, urgently wanted to know before his discussions with Stalin whether the United States had a new superweapon.

The same rain that threatened the firing circuits at Alamogordo also pelted Parsons that evening as he arrived at Kirtland Air Field. There he joined Alvarez and his team, who were loading the B-29 with radio receivers, cameras to record fireball intensity, and the three canisters with pressure gauges and radio transmitters.

Late that evening Alvarez learned that Oppenheimer had been trying to reach him by telephone from Trinity site. Alvarez called back from a public telephone at the airport, only to receive a disturbing order from Oppenheimer: The B-29 was not to fly over the tower or drop the instruments as planned. Because of the storm Oppenheimer did not want the airplane getting any closer to the tower than twenty-five miles. The canisters would not be dropped. Alvarez argued the case: The plane had radar beacons; an SCR-584 radar would be tracking them from the ground; he and Parsons were both radar experts. They did not need to see the tower to find it. "Robert was insistent," Alvarez later recalled, "and ordered me to abandon the test. I was absolutely furious, angry with him as I have never been angry with anyone before or since, but I had to back down because he was my boss."[24]

Alvarez, a future Nobel laureate in physics, resigned himself to being a mere observer of what would be perhaps the most important scientific experiment of the century. Parsons remained dispassionate. Unlike Alvarez, his primary concern was not so much new science as the final military objective. For this he knew his own eyes were as important as the keenest scientific instrument. They could tell the difference between a fizzle and a bomb powerful enough to shock the enemy into surrender.

Before dawn, Parsons stood behind the pilot, as he would on the combat mission, while their B-29 circled the Alamogordo test site, invisible behind the storm clouds. Alvarez knelt between the pilot and copilot. A few seconds before 0530 they heard the countdown begin over the radio. The pilot banked and headed in the direction of the tower. From twenty to twenty-five miles away and twenty-four thousand feet up they would have grandstand seats at the first display of the atom's awesome power.[25] The countdown droned toward zero. The officers and scientist pulled special Polaroid goggles over their eyes.

Neither the clouds nor the darkened lenses could contain the burst of illumination that filled the sky from the initial fireball. "My first sensation," Alvarez recalled, "was one of intense light covering my whole field of vision." A deep orange-red glow pierced the clouds. Shortly after, a new ball of fire seemed to be developing. According to Alvarez, "This fire ball seemed to have a rough texture with irregular black lines dividing the surface of the sphere into a large number of small patches of reddish orange."[26]

Looking out through the pilot's side window, Alvarez and Parsons could see a glowing cloud push up through the undercast, looking like "a parachute which was being blown up by a large electric fan." After the hemispherical cap emerged through the storm clouds, Parsons and Alvarez observed a stem about one-third the diameter of the "parachute," leading Alvarez to observe, "This very much had the appearance of a large mushroom."[27] After eight minutes the cloud towered an estimated sixteen thousand feet above the bomber—forty thousand feet above the now disintegrated tower.

Down below, Los Alamos scientists along with Bush, Conant, and Groves watched, awestricken, from their trench ten thousand yards from ground zero. They needed no instrument to tell them the bomb was mightier than anticipated. When a scientist decried the wreckage of his measuring instruments from forces beyond expectations, General Groves grinned, saying, "It must have been a pretty big blast and that's what we wanted most." Later he said, "The war is over as soon as we drop two of these on Japan."[28]

Oppenheimer, caught between elation over the scientific success and concern for the human consequences, congratulated Bainbridge for his Trinity leadership. Then, looking the physicist in the eye, he said, "Now we're all sons of bitches."[29]

Oppenheimer sent a message back to Kitty: "You can change the sheets," meaning that the planned victory party would take place.[30] The party at the Oppenheimers' lasted late into the night. Congratulations and liquor flowed. Any second thoughts were submerged in the excitement of seeing scientific theories proven and in the conviction that their gadget was now ready to end the war.

Deak and Martha probably left the party early. Deak—if any man ever did—had work to do. The Trinity scientists had done their job. His was still ahead.

·14·

Tinian

Don't let Parsons get killed. We need him!
Maj. Gen. Leslie Groves

By the time the scientists exploded the first atomic device at Trinity, the Manhattan Project encompassed the work of over forty thousand people in laboratories, universities, industrial plants, test ranges, and military facilities throughout the nation. Costs were approaching the final $2.2 billion.[1]

The project had been formed in order to beat Hitler to the nuclear draw. With Germany's surrender in May 1945, the goal became defeating Japan without having to launch an invasion that could cost tens, if not hundreds, of thousands of casualties, both American and Japanese.

Deak Parsons' two years at Los Alamos had been driven by his desire to win the war at the earliest possible date. This underlying motive was reinforced by the war news and mail awaiting him upon his return from Tinian for the Trinity shot. Headlines from accumulated issues of the *New York Times* proclaimed American successes in the Pacific, but casualty figures testified that these victories had been dearly bought. As American forces battled their way into the Marianas, Japanese resistance became more intense and fanatical. Parsons read the accounts of the Japanese surrender of Okinawa, which had occurred while he was on his travels. This victory had cost the lives of twelve thousand marines. In all there had been thirty-six thousand American casualties, a number with meaning beyond statistics. Each casualty meant somebody's son, brother, friend, classmate, or fellow in arms had been killed, wounded, or captured. Parsons felt the personal pain of war through the loss of officers and men with whom he had served.

The battle for Iwo Jima, a speck compared with mainland Japan, cost twenty-one thousand American casualties. One of the injured was Deak's youngest brother, Bob. Clarissa wrote Deak, telling him that she was with Bob at the San Diego Naval Hospital, where she was helping him recuperate. She later described her brother's condition: "He came back from Iwo Jima with the whole side of his face smashed in, an eighteen-year-old boy. . . . I can't describe to you how awful that was to see this young, this lovely young brother . . . [with] a terrible wound—a rock driven up through his right eye, smashing his jaw, taking his eye."[2] Clarissa's implicit request was, Can you come? She knew that Deak was busy, but Deak was always busy. She had no way of knowing that her brother—the shy playmate of her childhood—was now the pivotal naval officer in the countdown of the millennium.

As a consequence of the twenty-four years that separated Deak from Bob, the two half-brothers had not shared youthful experiences as Deak had with Clarissa and Critchell. But they shared a family bond, and Bob held the special niche reserved for a kid brother. Deak reexamined his priorities and found a way to stop in San Diego on his return to Tinian and the final act in the nuclear saga.

Upon arriving in San Diego, Deak arranged for a government car to convey the recuperating Bob to a navy office where Deak was meeting with Pacific Fleet officials. The younger Parsons later recalled, "There was brass all over the place! It kind of embarrassed me, a poor little Marine Private and here was all this brass." The wounded enlisted man had some compensation for his uneasiness. As he later recalled, "I think I made them a little uncomfortable too! You see I had received an enucleation of the right eye. . . . I had a prosthesis which was not an imitation eye but a pink plastic device."[3] Bob's condition must have left the elder Parsons fighting back tears.

The two men shared a bittersweet interlude in which family ties briefly reigned over affairs of war. Although Deak could not stay to help Bob in his recovery, the shared moments must have reinforced his resolve to end the fighting before a land invasion of Japan multiplied the flow of maimed and bewildered young casualties of war.

In less than a week after Trinity, Parsons flew back to the Marianas, this time, as he reported, with "my briefcase heavy with photographs and films of the big bang."[4] In resuming command of Project Y's overseas operations, he found the project on schedule. His worries and proddings of the past two years were paying off as one accomplishment after another fell into place according to plan.

Even the worries as to triggering the airburst appeared to be resolved. By this time proximity fuzes had been abandoned as unreliable for the purpose. During the final months Parsons encouraged Brode to adapt the APS-13 radar used to warn bomber pilots of enemy fighters attacking from the rear. But these devices, called Archies, also failed reliability tests even as overseas preparations began for the combat missions. Methodical testing finally paid off by revealing the problem to be the premature closing of a relay caused by vibrations in the falling bomb. Once the problem had been identified, a new relay was developed and successfully tested—one more problem put to rest.[5]

While the scientists resolved the last of the technical problems, Tibbets and the 509th Composite Group achieved their own successes. During the time Parsons went back to the States for the Trinity test, the 509th made its first combat missions over Japan with explosives-loaded Pumpkin bombs. Starting 20 July, twelve high-explosive Pumpkin missions were flown. In all, sixteen B-29s dropped eighty tons of Pumpkins on primary targets, including oil refineries and industrial complexes. Another twenty-one B-29s dropped 105 tons of Pumpkins on secondary objectives and targets of opportunity.[6]

Parsons reviewed the progress at Tinian in his usual matter-of-fact way, but Ramsey noted that he was distinctly more relaxed and amiable than usual. No longer was he an officer in a nest of scientists. "He was," as Ramsey says, "in charge rather than being sort of second in command, as he was at Los Alamos; I couldn't have asked for a better man to have worked for in every respect." Ramsey admired the firmness with which Parsons handled and averted last-minute problems: "I mean he got everything he wanted, when he wanted it, [even] if it meant he had to go down [to Guam] to Nimitz. He'd pound the table to Nimitz even if it was an extra chair we wanted. I mean it was the most fantastic amount of excellent support in the right direction."[7]

Parsons set the tone for the fifty-one Los Alamos scientists, SED enlisted technicians, and officers of Project Alberta.[8] Although in army uniform, the civilians in this group wore neither insignia nor markings of rank. Parsons could have enjoyed more comfort in the navy bachelor officers' quarters but chose instead to stay with his team in a camp with orderly rows of four-man tents on wooden platforms. Like everyone else, he had his wood-framed folding cot with olive-drab canvas cover, a wool army blanket, and a bedroll. The one modern convenience was a lone electric light. A plain table and chairs for informal conferences distinguished the Parsons tent from the others, which had packing crates as tables.[9] The only wooden structure in the camp was the open-sided mess hall, which served soft drinks and beer in addition to meals. A water tank on a wooden tower provided open-air showers. Neither Parsons nor anyone else seemed particularly concerned that food left out overnight could disappear into the hands of night-raiding Japanese soldiers still hiding in caves on the island.

In these final days Parsons was joined by two senior officers who were not strictly part of Project Alberta: Brig. Gen. T. F. Farrell, as Groves' personal spokesman, and Rear Admiral Purnell, representing not only Admiral King but the president's Military Policy Committee as well. Upon departing for Tinian, General Farrell had been given a last-minute instruction by Groves: "Don't let Parsons get killed. We need him!"[10] This was not something Admiral Purnell had to be told. He understood Parsons' critical importance from the start. Rather than usurping Parsons' overseas authority, Farrell and Purnell reinforced it. Their prime task was to coordinate the project with army and navy commanders in the theater.[11]

Among themselves Farrell, Purnell, and Parsons avoided questions of authority, rank, and power by forming what they jokingly called the "Tinian Joint Chiefs." They included themselves and Ramsey in this decision-making body and took in Tibbets, Ashworth, and other project leaders when needed.[12] The power of the "Tinian Joint Chiefs" was linked to the unique command lines set up by General Groves to control the combat deployment of the first atomic bombs. This command arrangement had been agreed upon by Groves and General Arnold, the commanding general of the Army Air Forces, and endorsed by General Marshall, army chief of staff. By this agreement, control of the bomb would be exercised by them from Washington, not by the operating forces in the theater of war. Groves originated all orders governing the use of the bomb, and upon Arnold's approval (or that of his deputy, Gen. Lauris Norstad), orders were to be issued down through the Air Forces chain of command.[13]

To accomplish the unusual mission, Groves found it necessary for logistical purposes to attach units to Tibbets' 509th Composite Group that were not in its official manning tables. As described by Groves, "These include scientists and technicians, security personnel, and liaison officers between my office and the overseas unit." To do this without making these specialists subordinate to the 509th, Groves created the "First Technical Service Detachment," which would be, he said, "subject to my direction in the Office of [the] Secretary of War."[14]

The First Technical Service Detachment served its logistical purpose at the time, but later attempts to explain this organizational oddity as a conventional military organization have muddied the Manhattan Project's overseas history, particularly in respect to Deak Parsons. One official military history says that the detachment was commanded by Parsons, which is questionable, and states that "the detachment furnished and tested weapons for the 509th."[15] The implication that Parsons' Los Alamos group worked for the 509th helps explain why some writers, film directors, and exhibit designers in recent years have presented the whole overseas operation of the Manhattan Project as an air force orchestration with Tibbets as the conductor.[16]

Both Ramsey's history, written at Tinian, and the Los Alamos manuscript history of Project Alberta describe the Technical Service Detachment as the administrative, security, and housing organization for Alberta. They name Lt. Col. Peer de Silva as commanding officer. Whether de Silva was formally in command or just filling Alberta's administrative functions in Farrell's or Parsons' name is irrelevant. Neither the detachment nor Parsons' Project Alberta team reported to the 509th.[17]

In contrast to the frenzied late-night vigils that had preceded Trinity, there was little last-minute scurrying on Tinian. Those once critical of Parsons could now marvel as the pieces of his master planning came together. In the early months at Y, Parsons had been almost alone in foreseeing the practical obstacles of assembling and delivering a radically new weapon from an advanced base in a war zone, far from its central laboratory, production facilities, and test ranges. Parsons had foreseen and prepared for these obstacles. As a result, the Los Alamos overseas group had confidence that it would be ready to complete the first two bombs as soon as the radioactive material arrived.

Some milestones leading to and including the final combat missions were set down in contemporary notes by Parsons, Ramsey, Ashworth, and others.[18] In the pages that follow the substance of these notes will be presented, with some additional detail, in the form of a master log. It begins:

Monday, 23 July [Tinian time and dates]
　Assembly facilities for Little Boy are completed.

　The first Little Boy (without nuclear components) is successfully drop-tested.

Tuesday–Wednesday, 24–25 July
　Radar fuzes successfully trigger two air-dropped Fat Man bombs at the prescribed altitude.

Thursday, 26 July
　The USS *Indianapolis* arrives with the main assembly of Little Boy and its uranium-235 projectile.

　Flight rehearsals begin for the first nuclear strike with Little Boy.

The most reassuring moment among these events was the arrival of the *Indianapolis* with her precious, if sinister, cargo. The mighty cruiser had barely laid anchor in Tinian Bay before an LST and a motor launch pulled alongside. Without a moment lost, crated components of the Little Boy gun were transferred to the LST for transportation ashore. Two officers of the Manhattan Project in the guise of field artillerymen were whisked aboard a launch and taken ashore with a lead-lined pot containing Little Boy's uranium-235 projectile. The rapid transfer from ship to assembly building typified the support Parsons received from the Nimitz headquarters at Guam.

The extent of navy support for Project Alberta was not accidental; the designated contact on the Nimitz staff was none other than Deak Parsons' former roommate at Annapolis, T. B. Hill. Once Parsons learned that Hill was on the Nimitz staff, it is quite likely that he influenced Hill's assignment to this position. By the time the *Indianapolis* arrived, Hill had already proven himself a great ally to the program through assistance to Col. Elmer Kirkpatrick Jr., the engineering officer sent by General Groves to prepare facilities on Tinian and Iwo Jima. For example, when normal channels failed to get work under way on schedule for standby facilities Parsons wanted at Iwo Jima, Hill had the necessary concrete, the Seabees, and the equipment transferred from another project.

By the end of July, overseas achievements were occurring at an ever quickening pace:

Saturday, 28 July

The plutonium pieces for the Fat Man pit arrive by courier on a Green Hornet flight.

Near midnight, the first of three otherwise empty C-54s arrives with the uranium insert for the Little Boy target.

Sunday, 29 July

Before dawn two C-54s arrive with the remaining uranium inserts for the Little Boy target.

Gen. Carl Spaatz, new commander of the Strategic Air Forces in the Pacific, arrives at Guam with War Department orders authorizing the dropping of "the first special bomb."

Monday, 30 July

The uranium-235 projectile, the initiator, and one uranium-235 insert are assembled in Little Boy.

Tuesday, 31 July

Strike and instrument planes rehearse the rendezvous over Iwo Jima and practice the rapid-escape maneuver.

Parsons declares testing and training complete for the combat delivery of the first bomb.

With the arrival of the last of the uranium and plutonium components, Parsons knew that, weather permitting, the tactical mission could go forward on 2 August, the earliest date approved by the War Department. Indeed, had the bombing been authorized for 1 August, the first bomb would have been ready. Parsons later commented on its readiness: "In the case of the Hiroshima bomb Los Alamos could trot the last laps and still win."[19]

The momentum of two years' intense preparation continued:

Wednesday, 1 August

The combat Little Boy is ready for loading and delivery.

The first inert Fat Man with fuzing and detonators is dropped.

Storms are predicted over Japan for 2 August.

Thursday, 2 August

Continued storms are predicted over Japan.

Friday, 3 August

Continued storms are predicted over Japan.

Major General LeMay brings orders for Special Bombing Mission Thirteen to Tinian defining the targets as primary, Hiroshima; secondary, Kokura; tertiary, Nagasaki.

Sparks had flown three months earlier when General LeMay was first informed of the atomic bomb. As head of the Twenty-first Bomber Command, LeMay had attempted to impose his command prerogatives on the 509th Composite Group. The cigar-chomping, cocksure general first questioned the need for a special group to drop this new superbomb. Then he questioned the tactics: Why drop it from thirty thousand feet when you could be more accurate at a lower altitude? And then there was the question of why a navy captain would be accompanying the bomb on the first mission. In short, LeMay believed that the bomb, like everything else in his bomber command, should be under his full control. He did not, it seems, see the need for Washington (Groves, Arnold, Norstad) directing events in the field. But all of this was before Tibbets explained that the bombing plane could not escape the blast from altitudes much lower than thirty thousand feet, and before he demonstrated the proficiency of the 509th.[20] And it was before LeMay met in June with Groves, an equally aggressive general.

The potential power clash between two superegos passed without a shout during Groves' and LeMay's hour-long meeting. They came out of the session, according to Groves, "with everything understood and with complete confidence in each other." Groves conceded that the delivery "would be entirely under his [LeMay's] control, subject of course to any limitations that might be placed upon him by his instructions."[21] Groves, of course, knew that the instructions would follow those to which he and Maj. Gen. Lauris Norstad, chief of staff of the Army Strategic Air Force, had already agreed. Norstad set forth these instructions in a June memo to LeMay:

> In its actual delivery it is desired that the B-29 airplane which carries the bomb also carry two military officer specialists. The senior officer specialist will be qualified by familiarity with the design, development and tactical features of the bomb to render *final judgment* in the event that an emergency requires deviation from the tactical plan. Captain W. S. Parsons, U.S. Navy, will undoubtedly be the senior officer specialist for initial battle deliveries.[22]

Discussions also occurred at Tinian among Farrell, Parsons, and Tibbets as to how the pilot and bomb commander would work together. They agreed, according to Farrell, that the project officer (Parsons for the first bomb) would be consulted if there was "any difficulty on identification of the target." Moreover, "it was also understood that there would be joint agreement between plane commander and project officer on questions of ditching the bomb; delivery on a [target] less favorable than the primary target; delivery at lower elevation than ordered or by other than visual observation." However, consistent with Norstad's instructions, if there was disagreement, the bomb commander would make the final decision. This was because the plane commander did not have sufficiently detailed knowledge of the bomb and its operation to make the final judgment.[23]

Parsons recognized what he called "the somewhat anomalous division of responsibility between the Manhattan District and the 20th Air Force." This did not bother him, he said, because he and Tibbets had performed together on many flights and "got along perfectly."[24] Nor, it seems, did the joint command of pilot over plane and of project officer over bomb any longer concern General LeMay by the time of his 3 August visit to Tinian.

The momentum continued:

Saturday, 4 August

Morning. Break predicted in storm over Japan.

Ca. 1445. Tibbets and Parsons brief crews of the seven B-29s selected for the first strike.

The seven designated planes included the B-29 carrying Little Boy, which was to be accompanied to the target by an observation plane for photographic coverage of target events and by an instrument plane that was to drop three parachutes carrying cylinders with blast-measuring devices and radio transmitters for sending the data back to the plane. Typical of a Parsons plan, a fourth plane was provided to stand by at Iwo Jima in case some last-minute problem occurred and it became necessary to transfer Little Boy to another plane in order to complete the mission. The remaining three planes were tasked to fly in advance to Hiroshima, Kokura, and Nagasaki to report back by radio on weather conditions over each potential target.

By Parsons' own account, the decision to brief key crews "on the facts of life DAYS rather then HOURS ahead of time" grew out of the "hectic night of 15–16 July" that he had spent at Kirtland Army Air Field and over Alamogordo on the Trinity test. The difficulties of that experience included bad weather and plan changes—and also the wariness of crew members to participate in a hush-hush flight about which they had heard more rumors than facts. This time Parsons wanted, as he said, "the boys to have a chance to think things through before takeoff." That being the case, he strove to inform them "with as little verbal drama as possible," believing that there was drama enough in the facts themselves.[25]

At the 4 August briefing Parsons advised the crews not to look at the flash without filtered goggles. He added, "I can say that it is the brightest and hottest thing on this earth since creation."[26] Throughout the briefing, Parsons let the facts speak for themselves and deliberately closed without an emotional climax. He merely stepped aside after asking Luis Alvarez to estimate the effect of the blast on the delivery plane, which at the calculated distance was expected to be a jolt.

In Parsons' view, the crews reacted well to the briefing. Whatever curiosity they had was "not articulated" at the time. "If there were any white faces," he said, "I did not see them—only red faces when the 35-mm film I had brought [of Trinity] could not be projected."[27]

Characteristically, Parsons shared only the information that he thought the crew needed. He said nothing about the special emergency measures he would have to take to disarm the bomb in the event that the plane was disabled by enemy fire, or about their choice of suicide or capture if shot down over Japan. He did not mention one as yet unresolved design problem: how to avoid a nuclear cookoff and the release of deadly radiation in the event that the bomb plane crashed and burned.

Parsons retired to his tent the evening of 4 August, to be awakened before dawn by the deafening roar of B-29s taking off from the four parallel runways of Tinian's North Field. He watched as four bomb-laden B-29s crashed on takeoff.[28] The crashes included a particularly fiery display as one plane's bombs and ammunition exploded, turning the predawn sky a blazing red. Parsons could not help but recognize that even greater consequences could result if the plane carrying the atom bomb were to crash on takeoff.

Sunday morning, 5 August
Favorable weather reported over Japan.

Operations Order 13 calls for takeoff of strike, instrument, and observation planes at 0300, 6 August 1945.

Later on the morning of 5 August, after receiving a favorable weather report for the mission, Parsons met with his fellow "Joint Chiefs" and voiced his new concern. According to William Laurence in his 1946 account *Dawn over Zero,* Parsons said, "You know if we crack up at the end of the runway tomorrow morning and the plane gets on fire, there is the danger of an atomic explosion and we may lose this end of the island, if not the whole of Tinian with every blessed thing on it."[29] Parsons later objected when a screenwriter amplified his comment to "We'd blow this island off the map and take 40,000 men and 300 air-planes with us." Parsons suggested that his actual statement was more like, "We'd make a terrible mess of things around here."[30]

Whatever the exact words, a 1945-vintage atomic bomb cooked in the flames of seven thousand gallons of gasoline would have been a nuclear mess, with immeasurable radiation hazards. To stave off such a consequence Parsons proposed that he himself complete final assembly of the bomb in flight using Birch's double-breech plug. Farrell agreed despite an earlier pact with Groves that the assembly be complete on takeoff.

Sunday afternoon, 5 August

A second inert Fat Man is air-dropped.

1400. Little Boy is loaded onto a trailer and pulled by tractor to the loading pit.[31]

Ca. 1415. The strike plane is backed over the pit; a hydraulic lift raises Little Boy into the bomb bay.

Ca. 1530. Parsons enters the bomb bay to practice assembly.

Ca. 1600. Tibbets has his mother's name, Enola Gay, painted onto the strike plane.

1730. *Enola Gay* taxies to the pad for pre-mission testing.

Sunday night, 5 August

Ca. 2000. Preflight briefing for the seven aircrews covers departure times, routes, altitudes, expected weather, location of rescue ships, and submarines along the flight paths.[32]

2200. Catholic services.

2230. Protestant services.

2300. Flight briefing for crews of the weather planes, followed by a meal.

2400. Flight briefing for crews of the strike mission, followed by a meal.

At 0015, 6 August 1945, twelve men in loose-fitting military coveralls, scarcely distinguishable from one another in the moonlight, waited for an air force truck. Only a mix of ski and baseball caps with regulation headgear suggested differences in personalities. Parsons wore a simple khaki field cap set square upon his head, Tibbets a peaked flight cap. Parsons and Tibbets joined the driver in the front seat while the others—officers and enlisted alike—climbed into the back of the truck.

At 0130 the truck pulled into the circle of light that illuminated the *Enola Gay.* A milling crowd, klieg lights, and popping flash bulbs astonished Parsons. He and the crew were conditioned to treat everything about their work with utmost secrecy. But orders from General Groves to record the event for history had triggered the carnival-like scene. As crew members posed for photos, scientists and technicians scrambled in and out of the plane making last-minute instrument checks. Pilots clustered together for a final flight talk; ground crews inspected the plane. Unknown to those in the limelight, a remnant band of Japanese soldiers looked down upon them from a hiding place in the hills. The Japanese were, as later reported, perplexed by the strange activities.[33]

Shortly before 0200 the crew began boarding the *Enola Gay*. Parsons remained locked in last-minute discussion with General Farrell. As they reviewed final details, Farrell suddenly turned to Parsons, asking, "Where's your gun?"[34]

Of the men on the plane, only Parsons, Tibbets, and Maj. Thomas W. Ferebee, the bombardier, knew that the bomb was nuclear. Parsons alone knew all the technical details. Indeed, he was one of the few men in the whole Manhattan Project with access to the bomb's entire range of secrets—scientific, military, engineering, assembly, and delivery. In the event of capture, the pistol was to safeguard the information he carried in his head. Parsons, the master planner for Tinian, had forgotten this crucial detail, perhaps because "his main worries," as he recalled, "had to do with avoiding any hitches or delays anywhere along the line."[35] His focus was on mission success, not the personal consequences of failure. Recognizing his oversight, he turned to a security officer and borrowed his automatic pistol and holster.

With the handgun secured at his side, Parsons took his position on the floor of the plane alongside his electronics assistant, Lt. Morris Jeppson. They sat on cushions before a console that was hooked by cable to Little Boy in the bomb bay below. The bank of green lights on the console told them that the critical circuitry of the bomb was functioning properly. A red light on any circuit would signal trouble. For two years Parsons' life had been directed to one end: "a perfectly delivered, perfectly functioning bomb."[36] The bank of lights, all green, told him that Little Boy was ready.

Now that the time had come, what were the captain's thoughts? To this question he later responded, "I did the usual amount of wondering how it would all work out and where I would be 24 hours later."[37] He described his feelings and those of the others on the *Enola Gay* as resembling those of "assistants who prepare the stage and then raise the curtain on a tremendous performance." As he saw it, "the bomb itself was the star performer."[38]

·15·

Hiroshima

I think he is largely responsible for the success of the first bomb.
Dr. Norman Ramsey

Monday, 6 August [Tinian time and dates]

0137. Three weather planes take off simultaneously from three separate runways.

0245. The *Enola Gay* takes off with the 9,000-pound Little Boy and 7,000 gallons of fuel, using all but the last hundred feet or so of the 8,500-foot runway. Observation, instrument, and standby planes follow.

0300. Parsons and Jeppson crawl down into the bomb bay to complete the assembly of the bomb.

Before opening the door to the bomb bay, Parsons tapped Tibbets on the shoulder and said, "We're starting." Tibbets radioed Farrell at the Tinian tower, "Judge going to work."[1]

Jeppson held the flashlight while Parsons squeezed in behind the tail of Little Boy, easing his feet down onto the narrow catwalk. Although Parsons knew by heart every action he had to take, he had Jeppson methodically check off each step as he performed it. At the same time, Jeppson reported the progress over the intercom to Tibbets, who then relayed it by radio to Farrell. Commander Birch standing by with Farrell in the tower was prepared to give advice in the event of any unforeseen difficulty with the special breech plug he had designed.

The first and last of the eleven steps were so rudimentary that anyone other than a perfectionist like Parsons would not have bothered to write them down: "Step One, check that the green plugs are installed" (i.e., that the bomb is not armed for firing); "Step Eleven, remove and secure catwalk and tools." The remainder, like "insert [explosive gunpowder] charge, four sections, red ends to breech" and "connect firing line," required the skill of an ordnance man familiar with the bomb's innards.[2] By the time Parsons reached the ninth step, the radio reports to Farrell were fading. But the general had heard enough to know that "Judge" had everything under control.

Although acknowledging the cramped workspace and the need for intense concentration, Parsons later discounted Hollywood's attempt to create a "brink-of-the-abyss" impression of the hazards of the task. "The assembly job was exacting," he said, "but not because it was very ticklish, and only a suicidal maniac could have made it dangerous." He then went on to say that his main worries had to do with "mixing up electrical leads, breaking insulators, burring threads, loosing tools." What was needed, he said, was "a little skill and a steady hand plus a good assistant to check off each step." What he did not say was that he was handling explosive gunpowder in close proximity to nuclear subassemblies, and that even a simple wiring mixup or a part dropped on the bomb bay doors could have aborted the mission, or worse. Rather, he spoke of the distress of ending the task with "a pair of dirty, greasy hands and no good place to wash them."[3]

By Parsons' account, the final assembly of Little Boy was accomplished within thirty minutes of takeoff.[4] Upon leaving the bomb bay, Parsons knew that he would be making a return visit before Tibbets began the climb to bombing altitude, when the temperature in the bay would drop below freezing. The return would be to replace the three green plugs with the three red plugs that fully armed Little Boy and in effect cocked the gun. Until then Parsons had little to do but assist Jeppson in the routine monitoring—that is, if all events went according to plan. But as Parsons and Tibbets were fully aware, the main purpose of Parsons' presence as bomb commander was to take charge in any emergency requiring a deviation from the plan.[5]

Parsons had to keep in mind what his response would be to "possible abnormal events"—in particular, what he would do if gunfire disabled the plane and a crash landing was imminent.[6] In that case he would have had to work against the buffeting of the disabled plane as he climbed down into the bay—freezing temperatures or not—to disarm the bomb, dismantle the breech, and remove the powder charges and detonator.

Parsons also had to be prepared to act in the event that combat damage caused an electrical power failure. With that in mind he had designed the system so that the bomb could be released as long as the pilot and one other man survived. According to Parsons, "Neither of these surviving individuals should have to do any special job on the bomb—only open the bomb bay doors and operate the mechanical release."[7] There is little doubt but that if Parsons had been among the plane's survivors in such a case, he would have been the man in the bomb bay performing the emergency procedure.

The compartment Parsons and Jeppson occupied during the six-and-one-half-hour flight was no room with a view. To see out upon the world at all, Parsons had to go forward and stand behind Tibbets, who, like copilot Capt. Bob Lewis, sat in a thronelike seat with commanding forward and side views of a virtually endless stretch of sea. But the person with too much vista for comfort was Maj. Tom Ferebee, the bombardier, who was almost surrounded by panes of Plexiglas in the nose of the plane.

Those sharing the compartment with Parsons and Jeppson were Capt. Theodore Van Kirk, navigator; S.Sgt. Wyatt Duzenbury, flight engineer; and Pvt. Richard Nelson, radio operator. Except for a porthole next to Van Kirk, this compartment was not unlike the inside of a dull metallic gray water tank laced with aluminum tubes and cable conduits.

When seated at the console, Parsons faced the starboard side of the forward compartment. Immediately to his left was a partition that separated him from Duzenbury. To his right was radio operator Nelson and the pressure-sealed door to the bomb bay. Above the bomb bay door was the entry to a thirty-foot tunnel by which crew could crawl to the plane's aft compartment. Those in the aft compartment included air force lieutenant Jacob Besar, an electronics officer monitoring Japanese radio signals for signs of any intercepting aircraft; S.Sgt. Robert Shumard, assistant flight engineer; and S.Sgt. Joe Stiborik, who faced a radar screen for plotting the course of any threatening aircraft. Well beyond the aft compartment was S.Sgt. George Caron's perch in the tail of the bomber. Caron manned the bomber's only armament, twin .50-caliber machine guns with a thousand rounds of ammunition—a limited defensive gesture in the event that Japanese fighter aircraft attacked.

Jeppson, while periodically checking the console, sensed that Parsons would have automatically snapped into action at the slightest flicker of red.[8] But, as if the mission were charmed, the lights remained green. The electronic pulses from the silent, brooding superstar below reassured the stagehands that Little Boy would be fully ready on cue to command the stage. And the *Enola Gay* as best supporting actress churned steadily onward precisely according to plan.

Parsons, as one crew member observed, remained awake but deeply withdrawn into himself for much of the flight.[9] Asked later about his thoughts en route, he responded, "After the job of completing assembly of the bomb was finished I had no more 'manual' responsibility. I kept in mind the succession of normal and possible abnormal events: Iwo Jima, rendezvous, head for the Empire, weather over the primary and other targets, choice of target, arm the bomb, climb to delivery altitude, make final tests of bomb, verify target in sight as Hiroshima and authorize release."[10] Parsons listed "authorize release" as if this were some routine procedure rather than his taking responsibility as bomb commander for unleashing the world's most awesome weapon.

Monday, 6 August

0605. The *Enola Gay* joins up over Iwo Jima with the observation and instrument planes. The trio head for Japan.

0730. Parsons returns to the bomb bay and replaces the green safety plugs with the red plugs. He informs Tibbets over the intercom that the bomb is "final"—that is, armed and ready.

0741. Tibbets begins the climb to bombing altitude. Parsons readies his oxygen mask in the event that he has to return to the bomb bay.

Ca. 0750. Parsons and crew pull on flak suits as the *Enola Gay* approaches the southern tip of Shikoku Island.

The recollections Parsons later shared about his thoughts en route reveal his preoccupation with his responsibilities on the flight itself. They do not tell us how he felt about the consequences of the mission. As the *Enola Gay* approached Japan, did he ever stop to think of Hiroshima as something other than the primary target, the headquarters of the Japanese army, an aiming point, a name on a military map?

Clues to the answers exist in interviews with Parsons' colleagues and in correspondence, but the evidence is sometimes contradictory. After the war, for example, when Merle Tuve questioned Parsons about his role in the Hiroshima mission, he responded, "I had no choice, I was under orders." Tuve, who by then had distanced himself from military research, inferred that Parsons "suffered emotional pain for having triggered the bomb."[11] Yet the weight of the evidence is otherwise. The fact that Parsons actively sought to be on the final mission is well documented; so too, as previously presented, are his arguments against a demonstration bomb.[12] Nothing in Parsons' determined leadership at Los Alamos and Tinian suggests any reluctance on his part to use the bomb to end the war.

Both professional and personal factors contributed to Parsons' relentless drive to complete a reliable weapon on schedule and to deliver it against the enemy. Not the least of these was recognition that failure would be professionally devastating. A $2 billion dud could well become the centerpiece of postwar congressional inquiries, an indignity worse than just the scuttling of his career.

Moreover, like virtually all American servicemen of the time, Parsons viewed the enemy with less compassion than do persons a half-century later who are neither affected nor threatened. Pearl Harbor was the battle cry for many. Others honed their fighting spirit with recollections of Japanese fanaticism in the bloody battles for Guadalcanal, Saipan, Iwo Jima, and Okinawa. When someone expressed concern to General Groves over Japanese casualties, Groves said he was not thinking so much about those deaths and injuries as "about the men who had made the Bataan death march."[13]

Flying over fifteen hundred miles of ocean, Deak Parsons could scarcely have escaped thoughts of academy classmates and former shipmates whose lives had been claimed in the sea war below. We know that his wartime thoughts often turned to the USS *Helena*, which had been torpedoed three months after he had left her. One hundred sixty-eight of his former shipmates perished with the *Helena,* some gunned down by the enemy as they clung to her slowly sinking bow.[14] And he could hardly have escaped thoughts of the USS *Indianapolis.* Only a week earlier she had delivered her mysterious nuclear cargo to Tinian. Now, according to the latest reports from Guam, she lay at the bottom of the sea along with hundreds of her crew (finally tallied at 880). Scrawled in crayon on the sides of Little Boy in the bomb bay below were messages to the enemy, including "From the boys of the *Indianapolis.*"[15]

Monday, 6 August

0830. Tibbets receives a radio message from the weather plane over the primary target. He announces that the target is Hiroshima.

0838. The *Enola Gay* levels off at bombing altitude, 32,700 feet.

0847. Parsons and Jeppson make final circuit tests.

0904. Parsons informs Tibbets that all is in order with the bomb and takes his bomb-run position behind the pilot. Tibbets changes course for bomb run.

0909. Hiroshima comes into sight. Parsons verifies the target and authorizes release.

0913.30. Tibbets turns control of the plane over to the bombardier and autopilot. A loud radio blip alerts the two accompanying planes that the bomb will drop in two minutes.

0914.17. The Aioi Bridge appears in the Norden bombsight's cross hairs. Ferebee starts the automatic process that will release the bomb.

0915.17. Bomb bay doors open. Little Boy drops free.

Parsons later recalled the *Enola Gay* bolting upward from the release of its four-and-a-half ton cargo. "Now," he said to himself, "it is in the lap of the gods."[16]

Parsons pulled his protective goggles over his eyes. He listened intently for the bomb bay doors to close. If they failed, as had occurred on one test run, the drag would impede the breakaway maneuver. The plane could be caught in the blast. Hearing the doors snap shut, he felt, he said, "intense relief."[17]

With the upward bolt, Tibbets put the *Enola Gay* into the rapid escape maneuver. He had forty-three seconds in which to distance the plane from the blast. At full throttle he went into a 155-degree turn and dive whose centrifugal force pinned the crew in the fore and aft compartments to their seats and gave Caron in the tail what he later described as "better than a Cyclone ride at Coney Island."[18]

A bright purple flash penetrated Parsons' goggles. A heavy shock rocked the plane. Tibbets, as he related in an early published account, thought a Japanese heavy gun battery had found them. He yelled, "Flak!"[19]

"No, no," Parsons responded. "That's not flak. That's it—the shock wave. We're in the clear now."[20]

A second shock wave followed. Parsons pushed back the goggles and looked toward Hiroshima. What he saw shook him. He felt, as he stated later, "completely awestruck by the tremendous mushroom and dust cloud." Boiling dust and debris rose, and "an angry dust cloud" spread over the city.[21]

As the cloud rose, Tibbets extended the escape maneuver into a semicircle rounding the cloud and the scene of devastation below. For a moment there was silence as if the viewers could not comprehend what they were seeing. Then everyone seemed to talk at once, in an outpouring of conflicting emotions that ranged from glee over the mission's success and belief that the war could soon end to sobering reflections on the human consequences. Caron exclaimed, "Holy Moses, what a mess!" A shout came over the intercom: "The war's over!" By one account, "Jeppson felt a kind of numbness, a shock in which there was no joy."[22]

Of all the reactions to the bomb, none have had such diverse interpretations as those of Lewis, the copilot. In the log he was keeping for newsman William Laurence, Lewis' written reaction was an emphatic "My God!"[23] Later Lewis was quoted as saying, "My God, what have we done?" (In this case, "we" meant mankind.) But by some accounts the spontaneous expression of the moment was "My God, look at that son-of-a-bitch go!" In any case Lewis later said, "It was impossible not to be stunned." And what added most to his surprise was "that Captain Parsons, calm, quiet, and knowing more about the bomb than any of us, seemed to be as amazed as we were."[24]

Parsons, having witnessed the fury of Trinity, was probably more awestruck than "amazed." He must have anticipated that the maelstrom from an airburst about two thousand feet above the ground would exceed that from a hundred-foot tower. This time he was experiencing the explosion at a slant range of eleven miles rather than from a plane twenty-five miles away and above the clouds. The awe was mixed with a strong sense of relief, as he said, "that every element of our plan had been carried out successfully."[25]

Caron's voice over the intercom broke into the various emotional responses to Little Boy's performance. "Better turn off, Colonel," the tail gunner said. "That mushroom seems to be coming downwind at us."[26]

Monday, 6 August
   Ca. 0920. The *Enola Gay* heads for Tinian with the observation
   and instrument planes following.

With the plane headed homeward, Jeppson asked Parsons to tell him and the others in the forward compartment about the bomb. Against the steady drone of the engines, Parsons described the basic principles behind nuclear fission.[27] But he soon broke off the discussion in order to encode a message to Farrell. About twenty minutes after the trio of planes left Hiroshima, Parsons sent his coded radio message: "Deak to Farrell: Results in all respects clear-cut and successful. Immediate action to carry out further plans [for second atomic bomb] is recommended. Greater visible effects than at Alamogordo. Target was Hiroshima. Proceeding to Tinian with normal conditions in airplane."[28]

These results were relayed, albeit with some delay, to General Groves in Washington, who had advance agreement from President Truman to release news of the bombing as soon as the results were known. Rather than wait for more specific damage data, Groves approved a press release largely based on Parsons' visual estimate that the power of the Hiroshima bomb was at least as great as that of the Trinity explosion.

Monday, 6 August
   1003. A Japanese fighter appears but does not attack.

   1041. Parsons reports that the mushroom cloud remained visible
   up to 363 miles from Hiroshima.

Haze and clouds finally blotted out the mushroom cloud. By then weariness—and, for some, introspection—had overtaken the emotional rush from the bomb's release. The flight settled down to twelve tired men who had done their job. Tibbets was among those who napped. Lewis remained at the controls, but the autopilot was doing most of the work. With half an ear to the radio, Dick Nelson read a book. Parsons was seen to be withdrawn and meditative.[29] But the haze that obscured the mushroom cloud could not mask its reality from the twelve men, or from the world.

Monday, 6 August
1458. The *Enola Gay* lands at Tinian after a flight of twelve hours and thirteen minutes.

Word of the 509th's true mission had spread rapidly throughout the island after the preflight scene with klieg lights and popping flash bulbs. As a result, the taxiway was lined with servicemen as the *Enola Gay* left the runway and taxied to its coral hardstand. The propellers whined to a stop, and cheers rose up from two hundred or more officers, enlisted men, scientists, and technicians.

The cheering continued as Tibbets led the crew down the hatch. A voice called, "Attention to orders!"[30] Gen. Carl Spaatz, commander of the U.S. Army Strategic Air Forces, strode forward and pinned the Distinguished Service Cross on the breast of Tibbets' coveralls.

Later, in the briefing room, under plainer circumstances, Brig. Gen. John H. Davies awarded Parsons the Silver Star. The inequity rankled many among the Los Alamos overseas team. General Groves had this reaction: "There was never any question on the part of anybody but that Parsons was running the show. The only person who did not get that right was apparently General Spaatz." Later on, when a naval officer expressed resentment over the incident, Parsons responded, "Always remember this, there is no limit to the good a man can do if he doesn't care who gets the credit; I don't care who gets the credit."[31]

While Parsons did not seek personal credit, he did want his record kept straight and his motives understood. First and foremost, he wanted his father to have his own account of the event. On the morning after the bombing, in the quiet of his tent, he wrote:

1st Technical Service Detachment
APO 247, San Francisco, CA
7 Aug. 1945

Dear Dad,

This will be a short note to say that you have lived to see atomic weapons used and that your son was the "weaponeer" and also delivered the first one to the Japanese!

The god Mars was on our side when we took off at a little before 3 a.m. Monday 6 August (east longitude). The engines and everything else purred beautifully as we passed Iwo Jima at sunrise and headed for the Empire. Before we hit the coast we climbed to high altitude and headed in fast hoping for good weather to make absolutely sure of our target. The weather was perfect and Hiroshima stood out in clear detail. The bomb run and release were done with mechanical precision, the same as many times before with test models.

Then the flash, followed seconds later by the shock to the airplane, and when we turned each crew member said "My *God!*" Hiroshima was at the base of a cloud already twenty thousand feet high. The base of the cloud looked like boiling dark colored dust and it covered the city proper.

Right under our bomb was the southern headquarters of the Jap army.[32] Although the cloud was impenetrable throughout the day, I have no doubt that the Jap army headquarters in Hiroshima no longer exists. Also Hiroshima is pretty well blasted to pieces. It *was* about the size of Indianapolis.

Depending on how the Japs felt before there is a definite possibility that this kind of attack may crack them and end the war without an invasion. If so it will save hundreds of thousands of American (and even Japanese) lives.

Of course now that our secret is out we are the focus of attention of the press and military.

I must rush on with the work. I hope Bobs is already home.

Love to you all,
Bill.[33]

·16·

Nagasaki and Peace

If you have to go to war, what a guy to do it with.
Brig. Gen. Thomas Farrell

In their log home among the Los Alamos pines, Peggy and Clare, ten and eight years of age, had just made an early-morning invasion of their mother's bed when the phone rang. Martha Parsons sensed Robert Oppenheimer's excitement as he told her he had just received a call from General Groves. An atomic bomb—a new term to Martha—had been dropped on Japan. Deak was on the plane that made the drop.

She cut in, "Is the plane back?"

"I don't know," he said.

"Well, you just don't call me anymore until you find out if the plane has gotten back!"[1]

Not long afterward, Oppenheimer rang back to confirm: Deak and crew had returned safely to their base.

Martha Parsons and the rest of Los Alamos spent most of Monday, 6 August (7 August in Tinian), listening to radio reports. Jubilation swept the mesa. Scientists congratulated each other. The moral questions being raised at other Manhattan Project laboratories were little evident at Los Alamos during the initial excitement over the professional achievement and prospects for peace.

The one-day backup in the calendar at the International Date Line made it possible for the 6 August evening edition of the *Santa Fe New Mexican* to headline the Tinian-Hiroshima events of 6 August:

LOS ALAMOS SECRET DISCLOSED BY TRUMAN

ATOMIC BOMBS DROP ON JAPAN

The lead story proclaimed that a nuclear bomb equivalent to 20,000 tons of TNT had been released on Hiroshima, "an important Japanese army base." The paper recounted how the Big Three—Truman, Churchill, and Stalin—had warned the Japanese in the 26 July Potsdam ultimatum that utter destruction would follow if they did not concede defeat. "The atomic bomb," Truman said, "is the answer to that rejection."[2]

The *New York Times* on 7 August described stricken Hiroshima as "a city of 318,000, which is—or was—a major quartermaster depot and port of embarkation for the Japanese. In addition to large military supply depots, it manufactured ordnance, mainly larger guns and tanks, and machine tools and aircraft-ordnance parts."[3] The *Times* described the earlier test at Trinity and traced the history of nuclear research. It named major political and scientific leaders involved in the Manhattan Project and identified General Groves as the executive in charge. The three "hidden cities" of Oak Ridge, Richland Village (Hanford), and Los Alamos were revealed. What the *New York Times* and other newspapers of the time did not tell was how the scientific results had been transformed into a practical weapon, how overseas facilities were built and operated for assembly and final bomb rehearsals. They did not describe the work that had gone into assuring that final delivery upon the enemy would go forward flawlessly and on time. What was not told was the story of Deak Parsons.

It appeared that the delivery story might appear under the 8 August *Times* banner headline: "Atomic Bomb Wiped out 68% Hiroshima." Photos of three officers immediately below were captioned, "They Dropped First Atomic Bomb on Japan." The paper identified the officers as Capt. William S. Parsons, Col. Paul W. Tibbets Jr., and Maj. Thomas W. Ferebee. There was only one thing wrong: the first photo was of the navy's Capt. William Seeley Parsons, not Capt. William Sterling Parsons.[4]

When a scientist alerted Martha Parsons of the error, she burst out laughing. When asked what was so funny, she said, "Oh, because

Deak is so sold on the *New York Times*." She added, "I just can't wait to tell him that they got the wrong guy in the picture."[5]

The correction on a back page of the *Times* on 9 August increased the irony. The replacement picture showed the right Capt. William S. Parsons, but the caption identified him merely as a "Navy ordnance expert, who went along as an observer on the flight over Hiroshima."[6]

Radio reports and newspaper accounts of the bombing brought an extra measure of excitement to Fort Sumner. Not since Sheriff Pat Garrett shot Billy the Kid had the town buzzed with so much news about one of the local folks. Harry Parsons' shy, brilliant son had delivered a blow that should make the Japanese surrender. The mild-mannered lawyer and civic leader basked in the town's recognition of his son's achievement. But when the praise escalated from pride to jubilation, the senior Parsons softly told a fellow parishioner at the Episcopal church, "Remember there's another side of this; think how many lives were snuffed out."[7]

When Farrell relayed Parsons' message from the strike plane to Groves, he added a coded message of his own: "Curfew visit to give description to Carve by Judge and Yoke tomorrow."[8] From this we learn that Parsons (Judge) on 7 August (after completing the letter to his father) left with Tibbets (Yoke) for Guam (Curfew) to describe the bombing to Nimitz (Carve).

Upon arriving at Guam, the "Tinian Joint Chiefs" learned that they would be having several meetings with Nimitz, Spaatz, and LeMay. They first reviewed delivery plans for the second bomb, the decision having already been made in Washington that unless the Japanese responded immediately to the call for unconditional surrender, a second bomb would be dropped. The rationale for a rapid follow-up on the first strike was to impress the Japanese that this was not a lone attempt at a knockout blow but the beginning of the steady "rain of ruin" promised by Truman if they did not surrender.[9]

This was not empty rhetoric. As head of Project Alberta, Parsons had planned and organized the Tinian assembly facilities to handle a steady stream of bombs. The plutonium production facilities at Hanford continued to work at capacity. Parsons could report that everything needed for the second bomb was present at Tinian, and essential materials for a third bomb would soon be on their way.

As everyone at the conference knew, the scheduled date for the second bomb was 11 August. However, by 7 August, Parsons and Ramsey realized that they could be ready a day ahead of schedule. When they talked with Tibbets about a possible change of schedule, he expressed regret that the drop could not be advanced two days instead of one, since good weather was forecast for 9 August and bad weather for the following five days. Parsons agreed to compress the assembly time from four days to two.[10]

No one at the Guam meeting questioned the speed-up, nor did the standing instructions from Washington preclude it. For all the scientific analysis that had gone into the bomb, no one had clearly defined how fast the "one-two" punches had to be delivered. No one, so far as we know, asked if three days would give the Japanese enough time to fully comprehend, and respond to, what had happened at Hiroshima. In hindsight it appears that the momentum of the project—the bomb itself—was driving both men and decisions.

The schedule advance meant much for Parsons and Tibbets to do and little time to do it in. Yet before they could return to Tinian they had to meet with the press assembled at Guam. According to one veteran reporter, Parsons and Tibbets "told this, the greatest story of the war, with an air that was almost casual." The reporter added, "They did so without heroics or unnecessary verbiage." The reporter described Parsons as the "naval ordnance expert who designed the bomb" and quoted him as saying the drop was made as quickly as possible "because this weapon is worth so much in terms of shortening the war."[11] Parsons responded to a question as to how he felt upon witnessing the explosion. "At that moment," he said, "I knew what the Japs were in for, but I felt no particular emotion about it."[12]

As the final assembly of Fat Man moved forward on Tinian, Armed Forces Radio warned the Japanese people of atomic destruction and appealed to their government to surrender. The U.S. Office of War Information dropped millions of leaflets over Japanese cities carrying this message:

> America asks that you take immediate heed of what we say on this leaflet. We are in possession of the most destructive explosive ever devised by man. A single one of our newly developed atomic bombs

is actually the equivalent in explosive power to what 2,000 of our giant B-29's can carry on a single mission. . . .

You should take steps now to cease military resistance. Otherwise, we shall resolutely employ this bomb and all our other superior weapons to promptly and forcefully end the war.[13]

On Wednesday, 8 August, as the leaflets fluttered down upon Japan for the second day, the 509th conducted the first full dress rehearsal with an air drop of a Fat Man without a nuclear core.[14] By day's end the Japanese government had made no formal response to the surrender appeals. At 2200 the assembly crew reported that Fat Man— now fully assembled with plutonium core—had been loaded onto the delivery plane and fully checked.[15]

Neither klieg lights nor popping flash bulbs illuminated the aircrew or the naval officer boarding *Bock's Car*, the B-29 selected for the second nuclear mission. This time Maj. Charles Sweeney was the pilot, and Commander Ashworth replaced Parsons as bomb commander. In Groves' mind, Ashworth would be running the second "show" in the same sense that he had seen Parsons as being in charge of the first. In fact, however, the relationship between Ashworth and Sweeney was not the same as that between Parsons and Tibbets. Parsons had stature as the ordnance chief in the design of the bombs and as master planner for the overseas operations; Ashworth, for all his many strengths, did not.[16]

The extent to which the ambiguous command relationship between pilot and bomb commander may have affected the second mission is a subject beyond the scope of this biography.[17] But it should be noted that many of the problems on the Nagasaki run stemmed from causes beyond the control of either officer: the rush to beat an incoming storm over Japan; bad weather over Iwo Jima, which meant that the three primary planes had to rendezvous over the southern tip of Japan instead; the assignment of the observation plane to a 509th staff officer who as a lieutenant colonel was senior in rank to Sweeney and allegedly not responsive to the lead pilot's instructions;[18] inflexible orders requiring visual bombing; and perhaps overconfidence on the part of the "Tinian Joint Chiefs" after the perfect execution of the Hiroshima mission.

The problems on the second run included six hundred gallons of reserve fuel being trapped and rendered unusable before the delivery plane's takeoff; failure of the observation plane to join up at the designated rendezvous; a forty-five-minute delay before the delivery and instrument plane left—without the third plane—for the primary target of Kokura; the weather closing in at Kokura during the delay; fifty additional minutes of fuel burned attempting a bomb drop over Kokura under the required visual conditions; mounting antiaircraft fire at Kokura; and, finally, the decision to move to the secondary target of Nagasaki.

The approach to Nagasaki revealed that it too was obscured by clouds. At this point Sweeney and Ashworth discussed what to do, recognizing that they did not have enough fuel to return with a 9,000-pound bomb aboard. According to Ashworth, they decided together to drop by radar. Sweeney's version makes it more of a decision of his own. A half-century later he tells us, "Ashworth could see that my mind was made up. He perhaps didn't realize that my only reason for any consultation was in the interest of interservice harmony." If that was the case, the relationship between the plane commander and bomb commander on *Bock's Car* was not that of Tibbets and Parsons on the *Enola Gay*—nor was it that intended by Generals Groves and Norstad.[19]

As events transpired, Sweeney and Ashworth need not have anguished so over the decision. The run was set up for radar, but bombardier Capt. Kermit Beahan was able to take advantage of a slight break in the clouds to release the bomb—not precisely on the designated target, but over the Mitsubishi Arms Works.[20] Knowing he did not have enough fuel to return to Tinian, Sweeney headed directly for Okinawa.

The early-afternoon air traffic over Yontan Field was heavy as *Bock's Car*, now critically low on gas, approached Okinawa. Sweeney called repeatedly for landing instructions but could not break through the radio chatter. The right outboard engine quit. Sweeney fired the flares of the day and in desperation yelled over the radio, "Mayday! Mayday!" He broke into the landing pattern so that if he lost power he could still make a dead-stick landing. Still no acknowledgment came from the tower. Sweeney yelled to a crewman to fire more flares.

When the crewman asked, "Which one?" Sweeney responded, "Every goddamn flare we have! Do it now!"[21]

The sky around *Bock's Car* lit up like the Fourth of July with every signal from "aircraft on fire" to "dead aboard." The fireworks cleared the way for the landing, but even so another engine quit immediately after the plane bounced down on the runway. A later dip-sticking showed only seven gallons of fuel left—less than a minute of flight for a B-29.[22] The second nuclear mission ended as it had begun, something less than perfect.

Friday morning, 10 August, brought a more relaxed pace for Parsons and his Alberta team. For the first time since Trinity they did not have an immediate atomic mission facing them. The Washington plan, as Parsons knew, was to have a pause after the first two bombings to give the Japanese a final opportunity to surrender before the complete destruction of their industrial centers by a steady rain of nuclear attacks.

Along with improved prospects of peace came other welcome news for the Alberta team: their military boss was now a commodore. The Los Alamos scientists and technicians viewed Parsons' promotion as recognition for themselves as well. In the absence of an official one-star flag, they fashioned one from available materials and ceremoniously mounted it on the new commodore's jeep. Now they too had flag status.[23]

Parsons had a mixed reaction to the promotion. In the navy, the normal progression from the eagles of a captain is to the two stars of a rear admiral, skipping over the one-star position of commodore. The half measure seemed to reaffirm the traditional view that scientific leadership was no substitute for sea command.

But it was not the promotion of the new commodore but fresh rumors of a Japanese surrender that set Tinian ablaze with gunfire on the evening of 11 August.[24] This was but the first of several false alarms before official news reached Tinian on the morning of the fifteenth that the Japanese had in fact accepted the Potsdam surrender terms. Any proclamation announcing victory over the Japanese, V-J Day, would have to await a formal signing of the peace terms by Japan, but that qualification did not stop Parsons' Alberta group from planning a victory celebration that evening.

"The party took place in and around Commodore Parsons' tent," Harlow Russ explains, "primarily because he had the only table and the few chairs in our camp." Ice cream and fruit juices from the mess hall were put into a large laboratory beaker that served as punch bowl. Into this everyone poured whatever liquor he had, irrespective of kind and brand. Metal canteen cups filled with the mixture were raised in several rounds of toasts by the fifty or so celebrants. The unplanned climax to the evening came with a new version of the game of tag. The object was to catch a designated person and give him a thorough soaking, clothes and all, in the outdoor shower. As Russ tells it, "The game started with considerable enthusiasm, with the chasing going on outside, around the Commodore's tent."[25] At the heart of the celebration were thoughts shared by everyone, including Parsons, of going home to a world at peace.

With the peace process begun, Parsons made plans to send home the first contingent of his Los Alamos team. But Groves quickly interceded. He insisted that everyone stay in order to assure complete readiness to assemble and deliver additional atomic bombs in the event that negotiations with the Japanese broke down. Whether he liked it or not, Parsons' life was on hold until the peace could be formalized.

After being revved up at full throttle for months on end, Parsons found it difficult to stand idly by. If he had to relax he would do so by mixing recreation with work. To this end, he organized a series of fishing parties in which a half-dozen or so of the Alberta team at a time joined a ten-man navy crew aboard a fifty-foot patrol boat equipped with a record player and a large directional loudspeaker. With fishing lines trailing behind, the boat cruised at trolling speed around neighboring Aguijan Island broadcasting a message in Japanese and English that the war was over and urging surrender. In this momentary pause between war and peace, it mattered little to the Los Alamos fishermen that they hooked few fish and netted few, if any, Japanese soldiers.[26]

Among the intertwining exploits in the lives of Deak Parsons and T. B. Hill, T. B. stood among the Allied officers and witnessed the formal signing of the Japanese surrender aboard the USS *Missouri* on 2 September 1945. He participated as a member of Admiral Nimitz's staff, but in a personal sense he was observing the completion of World War II as Deak's representative in the twentieth-century nuclear saga that for these two officers was still far from over.

Back in Tinian on this historic day, Deak wrote a V-mail letter to another old friend, Dr. Thompson. The letter began:

Dear Tommy,

Surrender was signed today. This evening Tokyo Rose ended her broadcast with a quotation from Major George Fielding Elliott and the program then swung into the Mikado! A few more days of this love feast and we'll be able to start home.

In the same note Parsons provided a modest explanation for the clockwork-like overseas success of the Project Alberta: "Once in many centuries you can't shake off the Midas touch. That's what happened to us."[27]

As Parsons wound up his Tinian affairs he received the presidential award of the Distinguished Service Medal. It read in part:

Working with tireless energy, courage and foresight Commodore (then Captain) Parsons applied himself to the tremendous task of transforming the theory of atomic fission into an effective weapon of war capable of being manufactured by American production methods at a time when the task appeared all but impossible. He applied his specialized knowledge in personally directing much of the design and development of many components of the atomic bomb and in formulating and coordinating the plans for disseminating the manufacture of these components. In addition, he also organized much of the procedure required in assembling the components into an effective weapon under conditions of utmost secrecy. He devoted himself fully to these tasks from May 1943 to the initial attack on Hiroshima in which he took part. Commodore Parsons's organizational ability, brilliant professional skill and devotion to duty throughout the development and manufacture of the atomic bomb were outstanding and in keeping with the highest traditions of the United States Naval Service.[28]

·17·

Nuclear Dawn

**He was a scientist, an engineer, and a good naval officer. I think he had
more vision than most of the rest of us ordnance PGs.**
Rear Adm. S. E. Burroughs, USN (Ret.)

Parsons barely had time for a change of clothes at Los Alamos
before heading for the Navy Department in Washington. There,
in early September 1945, he found himself something of a legend in
his own time. With wartime security removed, word of his proximity fuze and atomic bomb achievements had spread throughout the
navy.

By contrast, he received slight recognition in the scientific community except from Oppenheimer and others who had worked directly
with him. One reason for this was the Manhattan Project's official
report, *Atomic Energy for Military Purposes.* Compiled by physicist Henry
DeWolf Smyth of Princeton, this unclassified publication was distributed worldwide within three days of the Nagasaki mission, making it
the largest and promptest military giveaway in history. Never before
had so much information on a former military secret been disclosed
so rapidly. For a world still stunned by the news of the atomic bomb,
the report was a surprisingly full disclosure of the science behind the
bomb and, with one major exception, the project's history.

What the Smyth report did not tell was the ordnance side: the story
of the design, engineering, testing, and fabrication that went into turn-

ing the scientists' nuclear device into a weapon. This omission cannot be attributed solely to Smyth. Parsons himself had objected to the release of information on his division, believing that it could help a potential adversary make an atomic bomb.[1]

When Oppenheimer reviewed the draft of the official report in the spring of 1945, he found the treatment of Parsons' Ordnance Division "critically misleading." He objected to the report's implication that the division had done little more than develop the gun assembly. Oppenheimer wrote, "[The Ordnance Division] had, and still has, the all-important and difficult job of making a weapon of this thing, of fuzing and designing it in such a way that it can be used in combat and can be effective. I take it that you won't be saying much about this aspect of the work but you should certainly know that it is a very large set of problems and will increasingly be so." To overcome Oppenheimer's objections, Smyth took the easy way out; he deleted everything dealing with the weaponization of the bomb—"for reasons of security."[2]

Not only was Parsons ignored in the Smyth report but so too were the vast contributions of the U.S. Navy.

It was the future, not past history, that concerned Commodore Parsons as he met with Admiral Purnell on 13 September at navy headquarters. What he wanted to discuss was the future direction of navy research and development. Purnell had a more urgent task in mind.

Purnell told of proposals bubbling up in the War and Navy Departments to test the effects of atomic bombs against an array of warships. The original proposals were engendered, it seems, by interservice rivalries dating back to Billy Mitchell. Purnell wanted Parsons to evaluate the real value of such tests—that is, to define their scientific and logistical ramifications and to establish what kind of objective information they could provide. Parsons welcomed the task; this was a subject on which he was uniquely qualified. As part of his wartime work he had studied the theoretical effects of atomic weapons on naval vessels and had even pursued the idea of developing a torpedo to deliver an underwater nuclear explosion against ships.[3] These wartime studies were unfinished business, and Parsons did not like loose ends. However, before he could bite into the new challenge, he first had to join Groves, Tolman, and several army engineering officers on another urgent matter.

•

The meeting in Groves' Foggy Bottom office was a pragmatic attempt to save Los Alamos from the uncertainties of the time. Battles raged in Congress over what the nation's nuclear policies and controlling agency should be. With the genie out of the bottle, everyone seemed to have a different idea of how to control it and who should do so. At Los Alamos, most if not all of Project Y's first-string scientists, including Oppenheimer, planned to leave, and the younger physicists were apt to follow if their doubts over the laboratory's future were not resolved.

After the planning meeting, Groves and Parsons departed for Los Alamos, where Groves then addressed the full technical work force. The essence of his message was that the fate of nuclear work and of Los Alamos was in the hands of Congress, but as far as he could see, the Los Alamos laboratory would remain active for a long time. The nation needed their nuclear expertise. He believed that more study was needed on the fundamentals of the bomb. Better solutions were needed to replace shortcuts taken in the development of Fat Man. He assured everyone that a vigorous, immediate effort would be made to select a new director to replace Oppenheimer; he would be a scientist recommended by scientists. With the help of Parsons, the general warded off the immediate crisis. And despite the skepticism of one employee who saw Groves' speech as "a monologue on how great General Groves was," the laboratory did, and does, survive.[4]

After Parsons had done all he could to help put Los Alamos on a forward path, he turned to his navy priorities. First, he reviewed his wartime studies on what might be expected from the use of atomic weapons against naval vessels. He updated his analysis in a paper, "Effects of Large Explosions on Steel Ships," and sent a copy for comment to Johnny von Neumann, then working at Princeton with Einstein.[5] Whether Parsons realized it or not, he was staking out the foundation for what would become the largest military-scientific experiment of the century.

Having moved one priority task forward, Parsons returned to his original postwar objective: going to bat for the most logical navy program to make use of the new technologies, both nuclear and nonnuclear, that came out of the war. He launched this campaign with a well-formulated R&D philosophy that he had defined in a position paper, "Comments on Planning for Army and Navy Research," written back in July 1944, a year before Trinity. At that time he had buttonholed the leading scientists and naval officers, giving them both the paper and his arguments to back it up. He warned that in peacetime, institutional loyalties would again loom larger than national commitment. The disease of cognizance that had stymied early radar would again strangle new ideas. The unity that made the proximity fuze and the atomic bomb possible would no longer exist. And in the absence of war there would be, he wrote, a "temptation to believe our own propaganda and conclude that since we have the best anyway why worry about improving it by expensive research and development."[6]

In his wartime position paper, Parsons stated that the military services needed their own research and development laboratories. He felt it unrealistic "to expect industrial laboratories to concentrate first-class talent on the solution of military development problems whose solution requires years of hard work and has no obvious industrial application." At the same time, he recognized the need within these laboratories to guard against "*dry rot, the curse of peacetime military research.*" He advocated great care in selecting officers to command military research and development establishments, emphasizing the need for youthful officers with flexibility and optimism. "In order to get these characteristics," he said, "these posts should be made stepping stones up rather than berths for those who are over the hump."[7]

Parsons' well-articulated R&D philosophy helped convince Purnell that the time had come to bring him into a policymaking position at naval headquarters. Opening a telephone conversation on 17 October, Purnell told Parsons that Congress was still bogged down in its efforts to create a commission for the control of atomic energy. He then moved to his chief concern: "The thing that is worrying me, with all the scientific development during the war—the guided missiles and robot planes, rockets—and tying in the atomic bomb with them, nobody is doing [coordinating] it, and nobody is setting up to do it, because this other thing [congressional debate] is just dragging on the Hill."[8]

Purnell wanted a coordinating agency within the Navy Department to settle internal squabbles and to establish policy for new technologies, in particular for guided-missile and nuclear matters. Purnell was not certain where this coordinating agency should be located organizationally, but he had a clear idea as to who should be in charge. He said, "My reaction right now is to recommend two stars for you and put you at the head of it." The admiral then asked, "What is your reaction to that?"

Rather than grabbing for the promotional opportunity, Parsons replied, "I'd like to get a little more background on it."

After Purnell clarified the functions of the proposed agency, Parsons again responded with no show of emotion: "Well, I would want to go into the angles and future of it for a little while before I said one way or another on that. Offhand, it might seem logical, but I'd like to go into it."

Purnell: " . . . Suppose that I just recommend that an agency be established and not name you in the recommendations but mention it verbally when I am talking to them [Secretary of the Navy Forrestal and Admiral King]—"

Parsons: "All right."

Purnell: "—that you are a possibility, and a damn good one, see?"[9]

Arriving on Monday, 22 October, at Purnell's office, Parsons learned that the admiral had more on his mind than the proposed coordinating agency. The proposal to test atomic bombs against ships was gaining momentum. Admiral King had proposed to the Joint Chiefs of Staff that the tests be conducted, and he wanted Parsons to prepare tentative plans. That afternoon Parsons wrote Bradbury, "It is quite probable that there will be a Trinity against ships in 1946."[10]

With the help of von Neumann, Parsons had already laid a technical foundation for the nuclear tests. As the next step he formed what he called the Navy Atomic Bomb Group, consisting of himself and Commanders Ashworth and Horacio Rivero.[11] The latter was an early Parsons associate at Dahlgren who suddenly found himself yanked out of a technical assignment and told to report to his former colleague.

Parsons set up a meeting for 25 October in which his Navy Atomic Bomb Group, joined by six other select officers and two civilian scientists, discussed "Possible Tests of Atomic Bombs against Naval Vessels." The group identified four possible tests:

1. An above-water explosion of an atomic bomb suspended from a blimp anchored to a ship located among a representative group of target ships.

2. Explosion of an atomic bomb from within a bathysphere a half-mile below a representative assemblage of ships.
3. A shallow-water explosion within a harbor with an assemblage of moored ships.
4. A second harbor test in which the bomb would be delivered by a B-29 aircraft and the explosion would be above water.

Parsons warned his ad hoc committee of the complexity and difficulty of the proposed tasks.[12] But it is doubtful that even he understood the full magnitude of the undertaking and the dangers that lay ahead.

While Parsons was creating preliminary plans to explode atomic bombs above and below ships, Purnell was setting the stage for Parsons to become the navy's guided-missile and atomic-energy kingpin. Parsons still had his reservations. He finally concluded that the job needed the clout of a three-star admiral a door away from the chief of naval operations. He therefore recommended that the organization be not directly under himself but under Vice Adm. "Spike" Blandy.[13]

Admiral King approved the suggestion and on 13 November 1945 issued a directive establishing a deputy chief of naval operations/special weapons (Op06) in the Office of the Chief of Naval Operations to coordinate within the Navy Department all matters relating to research, testing, and development for atomic energy, guided missiles, and related devices.[14] No one from Forrestal to Purnell was under any illusions as to how this organization would work: Spike Blandy would give it clout; Deak Parsons would give it technical substance.

After watching Deak yo-yo between West and East for two months, Martha was prepared for his mid-November announcement that within the week they would be moving from Los Alamos to Washington.

Los Alamos well-wishers interrupted Deak and Martha's packing with a going-away party at Fuller Lodge on 19 November. Tributes to Martha rang with phrases of "community service," "good neighbor," and "queen of horsemanship." The most meaningful kudo for Deak was an ornate "diploma" signed by the scientists "on the hill." Given with highball toasts in an atmosphere of frivolity, the document nonetheless expressed the serious attachment the scientists had developed for this naval officer among them:

DIPLOMA
Know all men by these present
that
COMMODORE W. S. PARSONS
is a Scientist, Gentleman, and
above all an Officer of the
Highest Caliber, and it is with
deep and profound regret
that we see him leave our midst.[15]

Thus Deak Parsons "graduated" from the most intensive course of nuclear physics ever undergone by a naval officer.

On 29 November 1945 the Los Alamos "graduate" moved into the entirely different world of Main Navy, the wooden hive on Washington's Constitution Avenue. As assistant chief of special weapons, Parsons was to formulate and coordinate the navy's nuclear and guided-missile policies.

Admiral Blandy's arrival in December only strengthened Parsons' position as the navy's chief navigator for new technology. According to Parsons' closest colleagues, he was recognized as the fount of the navy's nuclear knowledge by Secretary of the Navy James Forrestal, and by the chief of naval operations—Adm. Ernest King at the time and, soon after, Adm. Chester Nimitz.[16] Blandy had no objections to these officials going directly to Parsons with their nuclear concerns. This trust and confidence worked both ways. Parsons saw Blandy as one of several officers "who did not develop acute inferiority complexes when they started playing ball in the scientific major league."[17]

Parsons filled the core positions of his Special Weapons Office overnight with Ashworth and Rivero, who were already working for him in the Navy Atomic Bomb Group planning the bomb-versus-ship test. Now he persuaded Hazel Greenbacker to come on loan from Los Alamos to help him organize the office.[18]

The original Special Weapons team of Blandy, Parsons, Ashworth, and Rivero was a tight-knit group of brilliant, savvy officers. As individuals, they were well received throughout the navy's corridors of power. But the Special Weapons Office they represented was not. Traditionalists resented this organizational newcomer being placed at the top level of the navy.[19] On the nuclear front, Special Weapons was caught in the cross fire between those who saw only a limited role for atomic energy in the navy and those who saw it as a panacea for all the navy's tactical and strategic needs. To the former, nuclear energy meant superbombs dropped from large bombers, hence a weapon of concern for the air forces and not the navy. As Ashworth recalled, "All the nuclear stuff was a complete mystery to many [naval] officers, a kind of stepchild. Most of these people felt it was not our business."[20]

Parsons and Blandy defended the need to give atomic energy and guided missiles special high-level treatment, predicting that these would be the dynamic new elements in the navy. They foresaw "a groping period" ahead while these technologies crystallized. The Special Weapons Office was needed as a kind of "naval chairman" for all matters except basic research in these new technologies.[21] By "all matters," they meant not only weapons but nuclear power for ships and submarines as well.

Deak Parsons was advocating atomic energy to power naval ships and submarines well before his classmate Hyman Rickover entered the nuclear scene.[22] This statement would stand on its own were it not that in his later years Rickover claimed that the navy had from the beginning opposed nuclear power.[23] The oddity of this allegation becomes evident in the light of the historical facts.

It was Parsons' former civilian scientific partner at the Naval Research Laboratory, Ross Gunn, who first envisioned using nuclear energy to power ships. In June 1939 Gunn proposed uranium as the fuel for "submarine submerged propulsion," declaring that this "would enormously increase the range and military effectiveness of a submarine."[24] Work begun at NRL toward this objective had been diverted during the war to the more immediate and urgent work of completing the atomic bomb.[25] However, in May 1945, following the defeat of Germany, Rear Adm. E. W. Mills, deputy chief of the Bureau of Ships, picked up on the NRL work. He issued a secret report that accentuated the logistical advantages of nuclear-powered ships.[26] Following the nuclear climax of World War II, Mills again advocated research and experimentation leading to ship propulsion.

On 27 November 1945 Mills personally presented his case to Purnell and Groves, and there is little doubt but that Parsons was made aware of it two days later when he reported for his new assignment in Washington. In any case, Parsons became an active supporter of nuclear power for ships and submarines in the early months of the Special Weapons Office. In a March memo to Blandy, Parsons stated, "The naval application of atomic power for ship propulsion is the obvious first feasible use of this phenomenon."[27]

During this time Rickover was still an undistinguished, little-known captain doing the routine work of mothballing excess navy ships in the Pacific. Months would elapse before he found his way into the nuclear field. By then research on nuclear power for ships was already under way within Groves' Manhattan Project. Parsons' close relations with Groves help explain the readiness of the general to undertake this research.[28]

As the chief nuclear adviser to Forrestal and Nimitz, Parsons helped promote nuclear power for ships as a high navy priority. Forrestal enunciated this position in a letter to the secretary of war on 14 March 1946. Indicative of the unanimity that existed on this issue, Secretary of War Robert P. Patterson responded promptly, assuring a "cooperative approach by the War and Navy Departments on a program of engineering development of atomic power."[29]

The only damper to the navy program for nuclear power was the limited access that Groves then allowed to the Manhattan District. Better than his navy colleagues, Parsons understood Groves' insistence on tight controls over nuclear information. To the consternation of some fellow officers, Parsons opposed attempts by the navy to create its own nuclear laboratories.

To keep a tight lid on nuclear secrets and yet open the way for the development of navy nuclear reactors, Parsons proposed in March 1946 that "several of our brightest and most imaginative and most creative young engineering officers" be selected for transfer to the Manhattan Project full-time.[30] This proposal received Blandy's and Nimitz's approval as well as acceptance by Groves. It provided the opening through which a cadre of officers and navy department civilians, including Rickover, gained the nuclear experience to later supervise the engineering development of nuclear reactors for submarines and ships. Far from opposing nuclear propulsion for naval vessels, as Rickover alleged, the navy, through Deak Parsons' nuclear leadership, opened the door for Rickover's eventual success.

•

The support Parsons received on nuclear-power research stands in marked contrast to the opposition he faced on other nuclear and guided-missile issues. And while the opponents varied, the chief antagonist was Rear Adm. Harold Bowen, former director of the Naval Research Laboratory and now head of the navy's Office of Research and Invention.

The outer civility of the correspondence between Parsons' and Bowen's offices belies the intensity of the personal enmity. For a person who normally withheld criticism of others, especially fellow officers, Parsons pulled no punches when it came to alerting Admiral Blandy of Bowen's "churlish, selfish, credit-grabbing, small-time attitude."[31] In Parsons' view, this attitude had isolated the Naval Research Laboratory during the war from the Office of Scientific Research and Development's mainstream advances in radar and thereby denied the laboratory its rightful place at the forefront of radar development. Now Parsons saw this same attitude threatening a wide spectrum of postwar research and development. After identifying Bowen as the subject of his memo "Naval Research and Development as Affected by Personality," Parsons wrote:

> I feel it is most important that the navy should preserve its major-league style and should avoid as the plague the kind of dirty political infighting which a second rater with an inferiority complex adopts when he encounters a first class group (of super scientists and super industrial engineers) that is not overly interested in him or his personal problems.[32]

A quick look at the two main issues in the Parsons-Bowen feud can give the impression that Parsons was acting contrary to his own advocacy of limited controls over naval research. He opposed Bowen's argument that the Office of Research and Invention should have "full freedom and initiative" to conduct applied as well as basic research for guided missiles and atomic energy, without regard to the Special Weapons Office.[33]

Parsons and Blandy argued that special circumstances existed for both atomic energy and guided missiles in the immediate postwar period. In the case of atomic energy, they believed that it was important to hold the line until Congress established a national policy and a new commission for its control. With respect to guided missiles, they were concerned with "the numerous semi-autonomous projects . . . inherited from the war period."[34] Neither logic nor the budget could support all these projects. On the other hand, it would be undesirable to stop programs that were fundamentally sound and could fill a future gap in national defense. In short, the war was over, and the time had come to establish a missile policy.

Bowen's attempts to embroil the Navy Department in a fight with General Groves demanded Parsons' early attention. In a call to battle Bowen had said, "The Navy is not doing its duty to itself or to the country" in failing "to break the monopoly of the Manhattan Project."[35] Bowen resented that access to atomic energy information by the navy's officers and scientists had to be endorsed by Parsons' Special Weapons Office.[36]

As the navy's gatekeeper to the Manhattan Project, Parsons limited security clearances to the people assigned to full-time nuclear work. He wanted no revolving door into and out of the nuclear vault. He viewed the security standards of the postwar army and navy as not on a par with the Manhattan District's tight controls. Keeping a tight lid on security was more important than unhampered exploitation of atomic energy.

Parsons strongly opposed "the violent attack" Bowen was trying to provoke against the Manhattan Project. Not only was it unwarranted, it was unwinnable. Groves operated under a presidential directive, and neither the secretary of war nor the secretary of the navy could override him. In exasperation, Parsons commented on Bowen's call to arms: "What this would accomplish beyond stirring up a bitter battle I do not know."[37]

The promotion of Deak Parsons to rear admiral on 9 January 1946 more nearly leveled the field for his jousts with Rear Admiral Bowen. According to Rivero, it was Admiral Nimitz who did the masterful engineering required to promote Parsons, a commodore who had once been in command of a bomb, but never a ship. As Rivero explains, "People were very hard-nosed in those days as to the need for operational experience as a requirement for admiral." There was the likelihood, Rivero added, that "some crusty old admirals on the board might have said he wasn't a sailor."[38]

To avoid this type of opposition, Nimitz required that one rear admiral position in the navy should be filled by an officer with extensive nuclear engineering experience. There was only one naval officer who could fill the bill. At forty-four years of age, the once-shy boy from the dry plains of New Mexico became Rear Adm. William S. Parsons.

Upon reading the announcement in the *Washington Post*, Critchell Parsons wrote a "Dear Dad" letter telling the elder Parsons, "Bill has done it again." He added, "I believe he is the navy's youngest rear admiral and am fairly sure he is the only one of his rank in his Academy Class." At the office, Hazel Greenbacker found herself surprised by the changes that came with her boss's promotion. "I never knew," she said, "that the rank of admiral brought everybody to his feet immediately if not sooner." Recalling the informality of Los Alamos, Hazel reacted to all this "snapping to" with the thought "Well, that's nice. It's about time for some respect."[39]

Deak and Martha had a second reason to celebrate. The home of their choice became available in Chevy Chase, an upscale neighborhood on the edge of Washington. Martha liked the spaciousness of the two-story house with it large screened porch. Although she may have missed the big yards they had enjoyed at Dahlgren and Los Alamos, there was something to be said for a small yard when married to a man who did little work around the place.

Martha and Deak had the new home to themselves during their first months in Washington while Peggy and Clare finished the school year at Worcester, where they stayed with their Cluverius grandparents. It was a time of renewal for Deak and Martha, with leisurely evenings together at home and at the Chevy Chase and Army-Navy Clubs. Deak worked Saturday mornings and brought reports home to read, but he came closer to leaving his work at the office than had ever been possible at Dahlgren or Los Alamos, where fellow workers and neighbors had been one and the same.

Like most American families of the time, Deak and Martha Parsons were limited to one car. Until Deak organized a "driving team," he rode the public bus on the days Martha needed the car. He must have presented a striking but anomalous figure on the capital city transit system in his winter blues, a chest full of military ribbons, sleeves with star (denoting an officer of the line) and one broad and one half-inch stripe, and peaked hat with broad visor—as described by his daughter Clare—with "all those scrambled eggs."[40]

Once at Main Navy, Parsons blended into a sea of uniforms, and that is the way he liked it. He worked best when least conspicuous. Persuasion, not rank or position, was his most effective tool in resolving issues. But when he needed high-level support, he had it. As in Project Y, he maintained direct links to the power hitters above him: Nimitz, Blandy, Purnell, and Hussey in the navy; Groves and Col. Kenneth Nichols in the Manhattan District; Bush, Conant, Oppenheimer, and Arthur Compton among the nation's leading scientists.

Parsons both served and drew upon these heavy hitters in defining lines of responsibility for what were called guided missiles in one instance and pilotless aircraft in another. The distinction was important. If a guided missile, the item under development was a weapon and therefore belonged in the navy's Bureau of Ordnance; if a pilotless aircraft, it belonged in the Bureau of Aeronautics. Well before Parsons entered the scene, a vigorous rivalry existed between the two bureaus over this issue. As Rear Adm. Frederic Withington, a Parsons colleague, observed, "We had a group of highly dedicated and able naval aviators on duty in the Bureau of Ordnance. There was an equally dedicated and able group in the Bureau of Aeronautics, and they fought sometimes like cats and dogs. It was purely and simply disgraceful."[41]

In the face of the willy-nilly burgeoning of missile projects, Parsons had mixed reactions to a planned review by the director of the budget. While the review could be useful in closing some poor bets, it might also eliminate, he said, "some programs which may have been prepared with great care and represent fundamentally sound and crystallized thought."[42] Instead of clearing the forest of all new growth, Parsons advocated preservation of the status quo for a transition period during which ideas could be tested and technology itself could point the way to the future.

One reason Parsons and Blandy pushed to settle the differences within navy between BuOrd and BuAer was to protect the navy's flanks from an expected offensive by the Army Air Forces to obtain control of all guided-missile projects. According to Parsons, that offensive became a reality on 19 March 1946. On that day he informed colleagues in Special Weapons that "AAF wants primary and overall cognizance of guided missiles and is starting open warfare in this field beginning today."[43]

Although Parsons' alert may have helped slow the AAF attack, there was no way of stopping it. Certainly it would not be stemmed by the Special Weapons Office. There a lean staff was increasingly being sucked away from policy issues into preparations for a nuclear rerun of the Billy Mitchell shootout with the navy.

·18·

Operation Crossroads

**Parsons was the one who worked both sides of the fence
[military and scientific]. . . . He was listened to by everyone.**
Vice Adm. Horacio Rivero, USN (Ret.)

In December 1945 Parsons became the senior navy member of a special army-navy subcommittee formed by the Joint Chiefs' Planning Staff to plan the proposed nuclear tests against ships. In addition to his technical responsibilities, Parsons had the burden of defending the navy's interests against the subcommittee's chairman, Maj. Gen. Curtis LeMay.

LeMay wanted to put control of the tests under the Strategic Air Force inasmuch as it had the only airplane large enough to deliver an atomic bomb. Parsons defended the navy position that the ships and most of the personnel and material would be navy. Moreover, the navy had officers with nuclear experience at a scientific level; Parsons' own Navy Atomic Bomb Group had laid the groundwork for the tests. Rather than concede the leadership to the navy, LeMay proposed that General Groves be put in charge. The Joint Chiefs decided instead that the task force commander should be a naval officer. Acting on a recommendation originated by Parsons, the Joint Chiefs agreed on Blandy as their choice.[1]

On 11 January 1946 President Truman announced the formation of Joint Task Force One under Vice Adm. William P. Blandy. In his public acceptance, Blandy coined the name Operation Crossroads because, as he said, "sea power, air power, and perhaps humanity itself . . . are at the crossroads."[2]

Blandy appointed Parsons as deputy commander for technical direction and Maj. Gen. William Kepner as deputy commander for air operations. Operation Crossroads soon became many things to many people, but to Deak Parsons it was a vital experiment, not a contest. He cautioned associates not to let the tests "become the football in the . . . airplane versus battleship argument."[3] He saw Crossroads as providing information that defense planners needed in facing the realities of a nuclear world. And he believed that the tests would reveal the future direction of ship design and fleet deployments.

As task force deputy commander, Parsons headed an organization that consisted of two divisions. The first, Ship Material, was under Rear Adm. Thorvald Solberg, whose job was to prepare the target ships and other military equipment for exposure to the atomic explosions, to make damaged ships safe for boarding, and to perform damage assessment. For this task Solberg had about two hundred naval, military, and civilian engineers in addition to ships crews totaling nearly ten thousand men. The deployment of the target ships remained under Parsons in his additional role as commander, Task Group One.

Parsons' second division, Instrumentation, was headed by Ralph Sawyer, a former scientific colleague at Dahlgren. Sawyer's division consisted of about five hundred scientists and engineers from a variety of government and university laboratories. These professionals were assisted by an equal number of civilian workmen, cameramen, and technicians. At Parsons' insistence, the lead laboratory was Los Alamos. Marshall Holloway headed the Los Alamos contingent, and Roger Warner had responsibility for bomb assembly.[4]

Besides the target ships, the task force required a hundred other ships as well as three hundred airplanes. These were the makings of what Parsons described as "the largest laboratory experiment in history, conducted by a Task Force of 40,000 men, 4,000 miles west of the West Coast."[5]

The four tests originally contemplated by Parsons' Navy Atomic Bomb Group were now pared down to three. The test eliminated was of an atomic bomb suspended from a blimp over a harbor filled with ships. The tests still planned included Able, an airburst of an atomic bomb dropped by a B-29 over an array of ships; Baker, an underwater nuclear explosion at low depth against an assemblage of moored ships; and Charlie, the explosion of an atomic bomb from within a bathysphere at a depth of about a half-mile below an assemblage of ships.

Parsons' arrival in Bikini Lagoon in early May 1946 renewed his long-standing partnership with Admiral Blandy, but in an environment far different from Washington. To those on Blandy's flagship, the USS *Mount McKinley,* it appeared that Parsons had the worst of this partnership. According to Comdr. Curtis Youngblood of Blandy's staff, Parsons seemed to be working twenty-four hours a day, whereas "Admiral Blandy would go fishing two or three times a week. And at noontime he'd come up on top of the ship where us young squirts were taking sun baths and horsing around, and Blandy's boy would bring a cot up there, and Old Spike would lay there and read a Whiz Bang magazine. . . . And then at night Blandy would have a bridge game." While Blandy relaxed, Parsons worked and participated in meetings. "He had his finger on everything," Youngblood says, "and he kept Blandy informed."[6]

From Deak Parsons' point of view, Spike Blandy had the worst part of it. Blandy had to bring diverse military groups together in a truly joint operation. He had to be the front man in relations with higher military echelons, politicians, foreign observers, the press, and two scientific evaluation groups—one representing the president and the other the Joint Chiefs. It was Blandy who had to respond to the wild speculations that the atomic bomb explosions would kill half the fish in the ocean and poison the other half, blow out the bottom of the sea, trigger worldwide climate changes, and create a tidal wave that would swamp all the ships at sea.

A well-defined command line ran from Blandy as task force commander to every Operation Crossroads activity. Organization charts showed who was responsible—whether army, navy, or civilian—for everything from the nuclear countdown to recreational swimming. This applied as well to the delegation of tasks under Parsons. But the military format no longer applied when it came to actual performance of the technical work. As reported by Rivero, Parsons' chief aide at

Crossroads, "On the science side there was none of this 'who reports to whom?'"[7] Civilians and military worked side by side with little regard for protocol. Parsons outlined the objectives, and the scientists took the initiative in accomplishing them. When they ran into obstacles, the civilians turned to Parsons, who in radio communications carried the code name Wet Nurse, since he was the officer who came when the scientists cried.[8]

Sawyer's code name was Between, based on his being the link between the scientists and the military. In practice that was also Parsons' role. When Sawyer could not get enough small boats to send his work forces out to install cameras and recording instruments on ships in the lagoon, he turned to Parsons, telling him, "I can't get things done this way. I need a chief of staff." "Good," replied Parsons, "We'll get one." Within forty-eight hours a navy captain, the eighth ranking in the lagoon, arrived, saying, "I am reporting as your chief of staff."[9]

Thereafter, Sawyer had no trouble getting small boats. But that did not end his calls on "Wet Nurse." Soon afterward he told Parsons, "People [on the target ships] think my boats don't take precedence and my instrumentation can go on depending on whether they are chipping paint or whatever." By the next day Parsons had an order issued over Blandy's signature: "The requirements of the technical operation will take precedence over everything except health and safety."[10]

The 24 June full-dress "Queen Day" rehearsal for the Able shot fit the pattern of a Parsons operation. Nothing was assumed until tried. Like most rehearsals, Queen Day had its share of misfortunes. Timing signals went out prematurely to some cameras and instruments; an Army Air Forces captain walked in front of a propeller of the bomb plane and was killed; the bomb plane's radar failed after takeoff; and two photography planes developed engine trouble. But to Parsons it was a success. The rehearsal bomb containing a token charge of high explosives hit right on target, the USS *Nevada,* and gouged holes in her wooden deck. Most instruments were triggered on time.[11]

Parsons wrote his father, "We held a full rehearsal which went much better than we could have hoped for. If we can do that well in early July then the bomb and the ships will really be set up for a performance." He extended the metaphor:

In about one day our "audience" arrives. There are three ships bringing them, the *Appalachian* with the press and radio, the *Blue Ridge* with the senior military and naval observers and the *Panamint* with the scientists and congressmen and foreigners.

James Forrestal is due here tomorrow and will be a guest in our flag mess.

With all these people arriving it is lucky that the stage is set.[12]

Blandy flashed the word to all ship and land stations: "One July is Able Day. HOW hour is zero eight thirty."[13] The announcement turned Bikini Lagoon into a hive of activity. Parsons watched support ships file southward to their designated positions in the open sea, leaving behind the cluster of ninety-five target ships in front of the now abandoned beaches of Bikini. He could see the interlacing wakes of patrol boats as they rushed scientists and technicians back and forth among the target ships. Scientists could be seen making final adjustments to pressure gauges, electronic instruments, and cameras of every description, from Bowen ribbon frames to Askania cinetheodolites. The USS *Appalachian* filled with the newsmen steamed out of the lagoon, leaving the target ships behind to their uncertain fate.

Parsons was among those on the *Mount McKinley* on the morning of 1 July who scanned the sky for the appearance of *Dave's Dream*, the B-29 with the atomic bomb. He could hardly have avoided comparing the *Dave's Dream* mission with that of the *Enola Gay*. Here at Bikini there was no concern over enemy fire. The flight to the target was relatively close, and ships lined the route as navigational aids. A radar beacon emitted signals from the target ship, and radio reports provided the bombing team with up-to-the-minute wind data. Bright red paint and a flashing light clearly distinguished the *Nevada* as the target in the center of the ship array.

After two practice runs under these ideal conditions, the crew of *Dave's Dream* began their final run at 0850 from a distance of fifty miles. Visibility was excellent. A few seconds after 0900, the bomb was released.

Below was the most gigantic test target array ever assembled. Clustered around the *Nevada* were seventy or more ships—battleships, carriers, cruisers, destroyers, barges, amphibious ships, landing craft, and submarines. A wide variety of army weapons and equipment were also exposed on the island and aboard the ships.

At distances of ten to fifteen miles from target center, forty-two thousand men lined the rails of their ships, waiting to be told when to pull down their darkened glasses or to face away from the initial blast. Both manned and drone airplanes operated aloft, ready for their various photographic and radiation-monitoring missions.

The Nagasaki-type implosion bomb fell to the prescribed 515 feet above the lagoon and exploded. The amount of energy released was roughly equivalent to the detonation of 20,000 tons of TNT.[14] But to many newsmen on the *Appalachian* fifteen miles away, the event did not measure up to expectations. No devastating tidal wave. No hole that would drain the ocean. Not only did the earth survive, so too did most of the target fleet. Most surprising of all, the proud battleship *Nevada* could be seen through binoculars still floating proudly, resplendent in the bright red paint job that identified her as the bull's-eye. As a press spectacle, Able was a flop. To one congressman, the explosion was just a "giant firecracker."[15] Simon Alexandrov, a Russian among the twenty-two foreign observers, summed up his reaction by pointing to the distant mushroom cloud and saying, "Not so much."[16] If this had been a demonstration bomb, as argued for toward the end of World War II, it is unlikely that it would have persuaded anyone to surrender.

Even Parsons, upon witnessing his first atomic explosion from the earth's surface, said that the Able bomb seemed less powerful than those dropped on Japan.[17] This was before the scientists examined the results and determined the blast to be equivalent to that of the earlier atomic bombs. And it was before Parsons learned that the bomb had not gone off over the *Nevada*. After months of practice bombings and an abundance of navigational aids, the bombing team on *Dave's Dream* missed the target by a half-mile. Instead of bursting over the *Nevada*, the bomb went off close to the attack transport USS *Gilliam*, which carried many of the scientists' most important instruments. Thousands of feet of film ran through high-speed cameras set up on Bikini and various ships, but they were focused on the *Nevada* and her immediate area. The limited metric photography of the blast itself made it difficult to determine where the bomb had gone off—critical information in evaluating its effects.

Nonetheless, Blandy publicly declared Able "a complete and unqualified success." And Kepner commended all Army Air Forces personnel "for one of the most outstanding air operations in history."[18]

Kepner later acknowledged a gross error requiring further study. AAF officers were inclined to blame the poor ballistics of the bomb, calling it a "wobbler." Scientists and naval officers tended to place the fault upon the bombing crew or upon the criteria by which the crew had been selected.[19] Parsons characteristically did not engage in faultfinding.

At 1430 the *Mount McKinley* led the support ships back into the lagoon. Parsons' organization then began to piece together a picture of where the bomb had exploded. Clearly it was near the *Gilliam,* which sank within a minute of the blast, and also near the transport USS *Carlisle,* which had been thrown 150 yards and sank forty minutes later. Four minutes after the blast, the destroyer USS *Anderson* stood on end, then sank. The destroyer USS *Lamson* lasted hours before going under. The Japanese cruiser *Sakawa* burned fiercely but remained afloat until afternoon, when, as if on cue, she slid beneath the deep as Blandy watched from a patrol boat fifty yards away.

The carrier *Independence* still floated, but her superstructure was torn and twisted, her flight deck destroyed, her twenty-five planes tossed overboard like toys. Fires burned on the wooden deck of the Japanese battleship *Nagato.* The structures of the *Arkansas* and heavy cruiser *Pensacola* were twisted and their smokestacks crumpled. The superstructure of the submarine *Skate* was twisted and torn.[20]

The destructive power was not in explosive force alone; as Crossroads would eventually make clear, the radiation effects of an atomic explosion could be at least as deadly. Parsons and the scientists had recognized the danger of radiation in the early work at Los Alamos, but they had greatly underestimated its persistence.

To learn about the effects of radiation, Parsons' scientists at Crossroads had brought with them 204 goats, 200 pigs, and 5,000 rats for use in Able, Baker, and Charlie. About seven hours after *Dave's Dream* made its drop, the gathering of the test animals from the target ships began, but months passed before all the effects on the animals became known. By late September 1946, 10 percent of the Able Day animals had died from the blast, 15 percent had died from radioactivity, and 10 percent had been killed for study.[21]

In covering Able, the press paid less attention to radiation than to the continuing controversies of bombs versus ships and air forces versus naval forces. Air power advocates claimed that the whole array of ships would have been wiped out of action had this been combat. At the same time, naval officers emphasized that only five ships sank, of which none were capital ships.[22] Amplifying this view, Blandy said, "We had carriers and destroyers sunk in the war with Japan, but we didn't stop building them."[23]

Blandy called a staff meeting a few hours after Able. He made it clear that he wanted the Baker underwater test to occur soon because of the problems of holding the scientific staff together. He asked how soon the task force could be ready. Solberg said it would take six weeks to prepare the target ships. Speaking for the scientists, Sawyer said, "I'll be ready in three weeks." Parsons agreed that three weeks was reasonable. Blandy concluded, "We'll have it in three weeks." According to Sawyer, "Solberg went off muttering."[24]

For Parsons, the tight schedule meant completing the test reports on Able and preparing for Baker Test at the same time. He managed, he later recalled, "by working throughout the day and writing throughout the night."[25] The voluminous first set of technical reports on Able was released within five days, the second set in twenty days. Parsons reported to Blandy that scientific preparations for Baker would be completed in time for the test to be conducted on 24 July.

All during the preparations there were concerns as to just how violently the bomb would react from under ninety feet of water. As early as October 1945, Stafford Warren, Groves' radiological adviser, had warned against underwater tests. Even though Los Alamos leaders thought that Warren represented an "extreme view," his concerns were not taken lightly.[26] Parsons understood Warren's worries and had taken the position that an underwater test should await proof that the information to be gained was "absolutely vital and obtainable in no other manner."[27] That had been judged to be the case in late 1945. That 1945 decision did not eliminate concerns as to what would happen in an underwater nuclear explosion: how many tons of water would be thrown into the air, how high would it go, how great the underwater pressures, how great the radiation, what surprises lay in store. The answers lay with the test, and that was the point of it.

Parsons scheduled the Baker final dress rehearsal for 19 July. All went well except that as Sawyer's team prepared to leave the lagoon, the magnesium flare representing the bomb ignited. Floating on a raft in the middle of the lagoon, it had been prematurely triggered by a stray signal, probably from a news broadcast of the event. While no harm was done, the mishap created a morale problem with some of Sawyer's technicians. As he later reported, "Some of the boys thought they didn't want to wait around the next time until the real bomb went off."[28]

After Sawyer and Parsons established that this was not something that could happen at the main event, Blandy confirmed 25 July as Baker Day. The remaining ships from Able and a few additional were positioned in the lagoon, a total of forty vessels within a mile of the bomb. Instruments were set up, test animals put in place.

Support ships began evacuating on the twenty-fourth. By evening the lagoon was a harbor of ghost ships, except for one small boat carrying Parsons, Holloway, Warner, and at least one other scientist to LSM-60, a modified amphibious landing ship. LSM-60 stood out among the big carriers and battleships because of an exceptionally high antenna that permitted line-of-sight transmission of the coded radio signal that would fire the bomb. Parsons and the civilians boarded LSM-60 for the night. As with the Little Boy combat mission, Parsons wanted to be there to correct any unforeseen problem. Ninety feet below him and the civilians lay the implosion-type atomic bomb waiting in its watertight caisson for the radio signal that would trigger nuclear violence.

By 0530 on Baker Day, Parsons and the scientists were bustling about the decks of the condemned LSM-60 making final checks of the radio links.[29] By clearing the transmission path for the coded signal, they were in effect arming the bomb. This was not Parsons in the role of admiral and deputy task force commander, but rather Deak Parsons as hands-on experimental officer and master of critical details. As on the *Enola Gay,* he demonstrated that unusual combination of courage and confidence that it took to remain calm, steady, and thorough in the face of the dragon.

Assured that every detail was exactly right, he and the civilians left LSM-60 at 0607 for the USS *Cumberland Sound* moored at the entrance of the lagoon. During the *Cumberland Sound*'s passage to her position fifteen miles from LSM-60, Holloway took his position at the control console, which he described as a "glorified alarm clock."[30]

Again, the decks of the support ships were lined with watching scientists, technicians, foreign observers, politicians, newsmen, and servicemen. But this time they needed no darkened goggles. Over the intercom they heard the countdown, as did the world through radio broadcasts. At precisely 59.7 seconds after 0834 on 25 July, the world's fifth atomic bomb detonated.

Although the energy released was about the same as that for Able Test, the results were far different. Even from fifteen miles, Baker was a spectacle. The underwater shock wave was by the scientists' accounts the most severe ever produced, measuring 10,000 pounds per square inch near the center. Ninety-foot waves struck the target ships. A gas bubble rose from the surface to create an illuminated dome. For a brief moment the LSM rode phantomlike atop the dome; then the dome burst, and a fireball and water column leaped skyward. Within fifteen seconds the column reached an altitude of one mile. Within a minute it reached its peak of one and a half miles, a tower of water resembling Niagara Falls flowing in reverse. When the column collapsed, millions of tons of water thundered back into the lagoon, creating a surge of radioactive spray and mist. This surge, as described by Shurcliff, "left a kiss of death on the majority of [the] target vessels."[31]

However, on 25 July it was not the radiation death kiss but the physical damage that shocked observers. Only a few fragments of LSM-60 were recovered. The *Arkansas,* YO-160, and LCT-1114 sank immediately, and the *Saratoga* seven and a half hours later. Three of the submerged submarines sank. The Japanese battleship *Nagato* lasted four and half days before going under. Many ships were seriously damaged, including the German cruiser *Prinz Eugen,* which sank months later in shallow waters off Kwajalein. With time it became evident that the physical damage was only part of the devastation. Over 90 percent of the target vessels fell victim to radiation, contamination all the more sinister because it could not be seen, smelled, or tasted.

Some test animals died from radiation before the ships could be reboarded. All twenty-six pigs died within two weeks. The animal victims and the radiological studies left a lesson that became increasingly clear with time: even if ships in the vicinity of a submerged nuclear explosion survived the blast, their crews would be dead or dying.

The scientific half of Parsons' organization had carried the brunt of test preparations. In the aftermath of Baker, it was the engineering half under Admiral Solberg that had to decontaminate the ships so that they could be safely reboarded. In desperation, Solberg's crews tried everything from soap powder to diesel fuel. Old-fashioned scrubbing failed to do the job. Seawater washdowns from fireboats helped, but they did not solve the problem. Crews facing this invisible enemy worked against the clock, the danger to each sailor increasing with exposure time.

According to Parsons, the amount of residual radioactivity from the Baker bomb had been predicted; however, he added, "we hardly realized all the ramifications and implications of this persistent radioactivity."[32]

While Parsons saw cause for concern, Warren saw disaster. As radiological adviser, Warren urged Blandy to end the operation and to beach the contaminated ships. Solberg disagreed, believing that his crews could successfully decontaminate the ships. Blandy sided with Solberg.[33]

As others debated the issue, Parsons sent sample materials from the ships and fish specimens to Los Alamos for evaluation. He knew that their laboratory equipment was designed to detect plutonium particles that Geiger counters would not register. He received the results on 10 August, the day he and Blandy were scheduled to return home. Parsons wasted no time in showing the results to Warren. "This," Parsons said, "stops us cold!"[34]

At the time, Parsons and Warren were on their way to the Blandy-Parsons farewell luncheon on the *Mount McKinley*. At the end of lunch, Warren again presented his case, this time with the laboratory results from Los Alamos—and Parsons' full backing. Blandy, always high in his respect for Parsons, responded, "If that is it, then we call it all to a halt."[35]

Decontamination was stopped. Support vessels began leaving for Hawaii. Target ships were towed to Kwajalein, where nature was supposed to help reduce their radioactivity before their next planned use as targets for Charlie, the ultimate underwater test with an atomic bomb a half-mile below the ships.

Although Blandy announced before departing Bikini that Charlie Test would occur in April 1947, there is a question of whether or not he really believed that it would occur at all. As reported by Rivero, Blandy set up a meeting that included himself, Parsons, Kepner, and Ashworth among others to discuss plans for Charlie. In his usual style, Blandy systematically asked for everyone to identify the problems and to present his views and arguments. The group aired numerous technical problems, including the physical problems of precisely positioning an atomic bomb at a depth of a thousand feet below the ocean surface and of keeping target ships in fixed positions by means of cables extended out from islands, as well as the radiation problems still unresolved at Baker Test. After all views had been examined, according to Rivero's account, Blandy decided against going ahead with Charlie Test.[36]

Why, then, did Blandy afterward announce that the test would take place the following spring? The answer, it seems, lies in a memo he wrote Nimitz shortly after leaving Bikini, which said, "If [Charlie] is canceled, it should be over the protest of the navy. Otherwise the navy will be essentially accused of dodging the 'most decisive test.'"[37]

While Blandy's true position on Charlie was clouded, there was no doubt about where General Groves stood. With the nuclear spotlight on Blandy and Crossroads, it is easy to forget that Groves still held extraordinary powers as the director of the Manhattan Engineering District and that it was through him that Los Alamos had provided the atomic bombs and most of the scientific manpower for the Able and Baker tests.

Although Groves, with some reluctance, had supported the first two Crossroads tests, he became determined to stop the third. The new director of Los Alamos, Norris Bradbury, gave the general the ammunition he needed. Bradbury wrote that the accuracy of the hydrodynamic predictions for Baker Test made it possible to determine the effects of a deep-water atomic explosion without having to make an actual nuclear test. As Bradbury saw it, Charlie would be an extremely difficult way of proving what was already known: that "an atomic bomb will destroy at least one capital ship no matter how delivered, within a radius of 500 yards." In taking Bradbury's argument to the Joint Chiefs of Staff, Groves added a concern of his own: the test would consume another of the atomic bombs in the nation's limited stockpile, then—as only a few officials knew—numbering seven.[38]

On 7 September 1946 Truman announced that the deep-water test was indefinitely postponed. Parsons, who did not expect Charlie to be revived, called upon all sections of Joint Task Force One to send their Charlie documents to the central files for preservation. Several months later, on 1 November 1946, Joint Task Force One was officially dissolved, and the Joint Crossroads Committee was set up under Parsons to complete the data gathering and to assist the Joint Chiefs' evaluation board in completing its task.

A year passed before the Joint Chiefs' evaluation board completed its final report on Crossroads, and nearly two decades before its disturbing contents on the severity of the radiation problem were released.

Upon his return to Washington, Parsons found himself besieged with requests to address both large and small groups on the Crossroads tests. According to one listener, "He carried an aura of conviction and moral integrity, and of character."[39] His messages were frank. He believed that any major war would end up with both sides using atomic weapons. Man, not the atomic bomb, was the danger. The Able and Baker tests established beyond doubt, he said, "that atomic energy can be controlled if man has the skill and will to do it."[40] To him the first step in control was knowledge of the kind provided by the Able and Baker tests.

Parsons' messages addressed the growing public hysteria over the atomic bomb. He defined his objective as "substituting a healthy fear of the known for an unhealthy fear of the unknown in the mind of humanity."[41] His messages had a positive spin. He described Able Test as being valuable because it confirmed the expected; Baker Test became even more important by producing the unexpected. Successes were successes, and most failures were learning experiences. In elaborating on the Baker experience he said, "The paralyzing radioactivity of the second bomb had to be experienced to be believed. It was difficult and dangerous to carry it out, but in the long run it would have been much more dangerous not to carry it out, since without it we would have had only incomplete and unconvincing theory to guide us in our preparations and plans for the future."[42]

What Parsons' messages did not reveal was the effect of Crossroads upon himself. The radiation problems revealed by Baker Test brought Parsons to a crossroads of his own. Although he wanted to make the public aware of the bomb's dangers and the need for national and international controls, he also wanted to avoid feeding public hysteria. On the journey ahead, it would not always be clear which road to take.

·19·

Atomic Admiral

Everything he touched felt his vivifying influence.
Rear Adm. Malcolm Schoeffel, USN (Ret.)

In September 1947, after seven years with no vacation, Deak Parsons flew to Hancock Point, Maine, where he spent two weeks at the old Cluverius place with Martha and the girls.

At Crossroads, Deak had seen firsthand the evanescence of man's creations: battleships floating one moment, sinking the next. By contrast, Hancock Point lay calm, seemingly changeless, firmly anchored to the past. True, the wooden icebox at the Cluverius place had finally given way to an electric refrigerator, but the cast-iron cookstove still dominated the kitchen as it had in Admiral Sampson's day.

Upon arrival Deak pledged that this would be a family vacation; he would not be talking before groups about the bomb. The commitment was one he could not keep. As he explained in a letter to his father, "There is so much interest in the atomic business that informal discussions take place at every picnic and party." Deak provided his father with the essence of his message: "In spite of emotional thinking and shouting by self-styled experts a fairly satisfactory law [the Atomic Energy Act of 1 August 1946] has been enacted and a decent proposal for international control of atomic energy has been put forward by some *real* experts, and adopted by [Bernard] Baruch as the U.S. proposal."[1]

Parsons supported the Baruch plan, by which the United States would turn over its nuclear advantage if a program of international control could be established under the United Nations. He favored this even though he saw little chance of the existing Russian regime agreeing to the international inspections that were a key provision. Until adequate international safeguards were in force, Parsons advocated an aggressive U.S. nuclear program. He believed that communist Russia was committed to official hostility toward democracies. To change this, he said, "would involve suicide for the ruling group."[2]

Martha would have preferred a vacation without the bomb, but there was consolation in family folklore. Her grandfather had similarly regaled Point Hancock friends with tales of the Spanish-American War. Sharing of experiences and philosophies was a custom at the Point.

While Parsons and Blandy had been busy testing nuclear bombs in the Pacific, opponents in Main Navy were busy undermining the Special Weapons Office.[3] Spearheaded by Vice Adm. Arthur Radford, the opposing forces had persuaded Admiral Nimitz to reorganize. There was no need, they maintained, for guided-missile and nuclear matters to be represented at the deputy chief level; there was no need for special nurturing of infant technologies, especially the nuclear brat. Blandy and Parsons returned to a *fait accompli.*

Blandy received a new command at sea, and on 12 November 1946 the Special Weapons Office was disestablished. The guided-missile function became part of Admiral Radford's office of Deputy Chief of Naval Operations (Air). Parsons and his nuclear functions were moved under the deputy chief of operational readiness. Parsons suggested the name "director of atomic warfare" for his new position, but this was opposed. Instead, as he informed a friend, "I assumed the imposing title of Director of Atomic Defense, Navy Department. This title seems a little odd in view of the fact the scientists agree that there is no such thing as atomic defense, but this seemed a little less warlike than any other."[4]

What remained unchanged within the new organization was Parsons' stature as the navy's foremost expert and spokesman on nuclear matters, both scientific and tactical. The position gave new meaning to the title of Atomic Admiral that had been used to describe Parsons in Crossroads newspaper accounts.[5] As expressed by Vice Adm. Edwin Hooper, a Parsons contemporary in navy R&D and later director of Naval History, "Everything to do with atomic energy had him in the act. . . . Certainly many, probably most, of the navy's policies in the atomic energy field were originated by Deak Parsons."[6]

As the navy's point man on nuclear issues, Parsons had the dual challenges of protecting the navy's interests and implementing the Atomic Energy Act of 1946. This act, which created the Atomic Energy Commission (AEC), had been argued in Congress for a full year before passage. One divisive issue centered on what role, if any, the military should have within the commission—in particular, should there be military or civilian control of the weapon aspects of nuclear energy. The eventual compromise, introduced by Senator Arthur Vandenberg, provided for a Military Liaison Committee (MLC) to the Atomic Energy Commission. By law, the AEC would inform the MLC of deliberations and actions affecting national defense, and the MLC in turn would report nuclear-related military plans to the commission. The objective of the Vandenberg amendment was civilian control with military guidance. It would be easier to state in principle than to achieve.

The presence of both Parsons and Groves among the six-member MLC, three each for the army and navy, meant that the committee began with a core of nuclear-savvy officers. Parsons' own position was enhanced by his military and science networks. One of his closest supporters was Captain Ashworth, who became executive secretary of the MLC. Another disciple, Captain Rivero, worked half-time for the AEC while spending the remaining half in Parsons' Office of Atomic Defense. As Rivero later acknowledged, he often found himself "coordinating with himself."[7]

Parsons' strong ties with leading scientists included Oppenheimer, then chairman of the AEC's General Advisory Committee, and Vannevar Bush, who was actively involved in postwar research and development planning. On any nuclear forum involving military issues, the same familiar faces—particularly Groves', Oppenheimer's, Bush's, and Parsons'—were likely to appear.

The Military Liaison Committee provided the policy link between the Atomic Energy Commission and the War and Navy Departments (and the U.S. Air Force, when it became an independent service). The MLC did not provide the operational means by which the armed services could fight a nuclear war. The task of devising an organization for that purpose had been given to General Groves, who was to remain head of the Manhattan Project until the AEC took over nuclear affairs on 1 January 1947. In the interim, Groves had to produce a plan for the military services to manage their nuclear resources. As in the old days, Groves turned to Parsons for help.

In the fall of 1946 Groves and Parsons, along with their respective workhorses, Brig. Gen. Kenneth Nichols and Capt. Horacio Rivero, spent long hours together drawing up what eventually became the Armed Forces Special Weapons Project (AFSWP). Usually it was Groves at the blackboard drawing organization charts and Parsons applying various scenarios to test the latest stratagem.[8]

Under the circumstances, it is not surprising that Groves became the head of AFSWP and Parsons became the deputy representing the navy. Anticipating armed forces unification and an independent air force, Col. Roscoe Wilson of the Army Air Forces was also named a deputy. Thus, three officers of the MLC also directed the new AFSWP, a joint agency reporting to the secretaries of war and navy. Coordination was no problem!

The immediate responsibility of the AFSWP as of 1 January 1947 was to take over all the military service functions of the then disbanded Manhattan Project. The long-range task was to see that the military had the nuclear weaponry and expertise to respond offensively and defensively in time of national crisis.

As director of atomic defense, senior navy member MLC, and deputy director AFSWP, Parsons was indeed the Atomic Admiral. And it is in this light that his actions and positions on nuclear matters from late 1945 to May 1949 are summarized here.

Among the nuclear opportunities facing the navy, Parsons considered the development of nuclear energy as a power source for ships and submarines to be of utmost importance.[9] According to Ashworth, Parsons recognized that nuclear energy would ultimately be more important for power than for weapons, and he did so well before Rickover came upon the scene. Parsons saw it as a superior power source for ships and "concluded that the possibility of nuclear power made it possible to build the true submarine." Rivero, the other officer closest to Parsons in this period, similarly attests to Parsons' early advocacy of nuclear power for ships and submarines.[10]

Although Parsons advocated development of nuclear reactors for power, he opposed the navy's creating a nuclear laboratory for that, or any, purpose. He believed that "maximum progress for the United States, including the navy, can be made by friendly collaboration with the scientists and engineers who have so far proved themselves pre-eminent in the world in the field of applied physics."[11] That meant the scientists of the Manhattan Project and, after 1 January 1947, of the AEC laboratories.

Parsons supported the assignment of Rickover along with four other officers and three civilians to the Oak Ridge Laboratory in June 1946. He brought in Lt. Comdr. Edward L. "Ned" Beach, whom he described as "a bright young submarine officer," as assistant for submarine applications to support the nuclear propulsion work by the Office of Atomic Defense.[12]

Parsons did not have the same enthusiasm for the idea of nuclear-powered aircraft as he did for naval vessels. He believed a nuclear bomber feasible but highly improbable. Despite reservations, he joined Groves on the Military Liaison Committee in approving an ambitious Army Air Forces plan for a project called Nuclear Energy for the Propulsion of Aircraft (NEPA). Contracts went out to aircraft industry giants, but many years and many millions of dollars later neither NEPA nor its dream project had made it off the ground. Parsons blamed the failure on project leaders "of great enthusiasm and little qualification in nuclear matters."[13]

Parsons' views on the American nuclear stockpile need to be viewed in the context of the time. Then there was no cause for the kind of alarm later expressed by Ashworth: "I have never understood the numbers that were built. Ten thousand, twenty thousand, however many we have. It's ridiculous."[14] In the summer of 1947, one of the best-kept secrets about nuclear weapons was that the United States, then relying on the atomic bomb as the cornerstone of national defense, had only thirteen of them.[15] Parsons, one of the few officials who knew the exact number, pressed for expanded production. Among other actions, he pushed continued support for the Salt Well Pilot Plant that he had started during the war at the Naval Ordnance Test Station, China Lake (formerly NOTS Inyokern). The processes developed at Salt Well for precision casting and machining of the high-explosive lenses for implosion bombs helped open the way for post-war large-scale manufacture of these critical and unique elements of implosion bombs.[16]

Parsons played a major role in making Sandia Base at Albuquerque the principal field installation of the Armed Forces Special Weapons Project (AFSWP). At the end of World War II, Sandia had consisted of a dozen ramshackle buildings left over from a wartime air depot. These were taken over by Los Alamos Z-Division, the remnant of Parsons' wartime Ordnance Division.[17] The transfer of Z-Division to Sandia was a step in Norris Bradbury's plan to take weapons engineering out of the Los Alamos mission so that the laboratory could center its efforts on research. With the formation of the MLC and AFSWP, Parsons was among those responsible for expanding Z-Division's operations at Sandia to cover design of non-nuclear components of atomic bombs, testing these components, and training bomb assembly teams for nuclear missions.

Parsons insisted on turning Sandia into a first-class engineering and development establishment. He and Groves corrected a leadership problem there by bringing in Paul Larsen as director. By the spring of 1948, Larsen with Parsons' backing had transformed Sandia from a makeshift, unwanted branch of Los Alamos to a full-fledged laboratory in its own right. A later study of the expanded production and research functions of Sandia Base led to its management being turned over to Sandia Corporation in November 1949.[18]

Parsons believed in the national strategy of nuclear deterrence. He wrote the Navy General Board, "I would favor creating the impression that we have a 'doomed city' list and that our blows are as inevitable as Fate."[19] In the summer of 1946, seeking a navy role in deterrence, Parsons asked Ashworth to determine what was needed to open the way for delivering atomic weapons by carrier-based naval aircraft. Based on Ashworth's spadework, Parsons joined with the navy's Bureau of Aeronautics to have the AJ-1 Savage modified to carry an atomic bomb. While awaiting the modified AJ, a nuclear aircraft squadron began operations at Sandia with the P2V-3C Neptune. The AJ-1 entered service with composite squadron (VC)5 in September 1949. The squadron commander, Chick Hayward, and executive officer, Dick Ashworth, were personally selected by Parsons.[20] The assignment of Hayward and

Ashworth was not cronyism but common sense. They were naval aviators with nuclear experience and they had the kind of leadership drive required to introduce nuclear capabilities into the fleet.

In the summer of 1947 Parsons pushed the research and engineering for the Mark IV bomb as an improved design of the Mark III implosion bomb of the type used at Nagasaki and Crossroads. The earlier bomb had been produced by cut-and-try methods under wartime conditions and was more a laboratory device than a production weapon. The Mark IV was designed to exact specifications and production standards. A team of scientists would not be required to assemble it.[21]

Parsons' interest in bomb design went beyond improvements in quality and ease of production. He played a key managerial role in bringing the diameter of the implosion bombs down from the sixty inches of the Mark III to thirty-five inches, and ultimately less.[22] The smaller bombs strengthened the navy's nuclear mission. Diminished weight increased the range of carrier aircraft and freed designers from the old problem of shaping an aerodynamically stable bomb around a monstrous globe.

Deak Parsons played a prominent role in the conduct of the first eight atomic explosions and was the only person to witness seven of them.[23] The most powerful, and least known, are those he participated in during Operation Sandstone.

The dissimilarities between Crossroads and Sandstone are significant. Highly publicized, Crossroads was shared with the world; Sandstone was all but hidden. In the summer of 1946, hopes for international control of the atomic genie had been high; by the spring of 1948, when Sandstone took place, they had all but vanished. The primary objective of Crossroads was to test the effects of atomic bombs against ships; the Sandstone objective to test components going into the latest bomb designs. The armed services conducted Crossroads with the scientific help of the Manhattan Engineering District; the Atomic Energy Commission conducted Sandstone with the logistical support of the armed services.

Some things remained the same. Sandstone occurred at a remote atoll in the Pacific, in this case Eniwetok in the Marshall Islands. For both operations, Los Alamos served as the lead laboratory. Most of the technical procedures followed at Sandstone were those Parsons and his scientific team had established at Crossroads.

Military support for Sandstone came through Joint Task Force Seven with Lt. Gen. John E. Hull as task commander. Parsons and Major General Kepner again served as deputy commanders. Navy captain James Russell served as the AEC test director.

Whatever drama the tests may have had has been lost because of predigested press releases and the exclusion of reporters from the tests. The pacing and rapidity of the tests reflect the task force's no-nonsense approach: Test One, 15 April 1948; Test Two, 1 May; Test Three, 15 May; closing of the site, 22 May.[24]

If reporters and broadcasters had had access to the millions of feet of photographic and electronic records made during Sandstone's three nuclear events, they might well have summed up the results as "stunning!" The explosive yield of Test One registered as equivalent to 37,000 tons of TNT, compared with something less than 20,000 tons for the previous bombs. Most important to Parsons and colleagues, the tests verified the new design of the bomb's components.

Although the Sandstone results opened the way for increased bomb production, there was little public reaction, partly because of the controlled press coverage and partly because atomic tests in the far-off Pacific were now old stuff. By then, the public was more easily stirred by imaginative speculations on push-button warfare. In that regard, Parsons took a cautious view of what the future might bring. As Thompson tells us, "Deak had a remarkable capacity to see to the horizon of his time." He might have added, "but not beyond." Parsons limited his projections to weapons systems that did not depend on yet-to-be-discovered technology. The trouble in going beyond the proven, he believed, "is that it rationalizes wishes into discoveries."[25]

Based on the technology of 1947, Parsons foresaw new designs of carriers, aircraft, and bombs that would allow tactical nuclear missions from ships. He believed that missiles with nuclear warheads could be fired from submarines. He cautioned against optimism on the idea of anti-guided missiles shooting down incoming missiles with atomic warheads. And he agreed with Rivero that "the mention of long-range, accurate guided missiles at this time [late 1940s] can serve no useful purpose."[26]

Parsons' view of the future reveals him again at a crossroads. On the one hand, he tried to allay fears over "push-button warfare" as sensationalized in the press. This treatment, he said, "immediately conjures up a magazine picture of huge V-2 rockets crossing oceans and plunging into cities." On the other hand, he wanted "to avoid any tendency toward Maginot Line psychology." Parsons wrote, "In planning for the future, one has the disagreeable choice of two crystal balls, neither of them uncolored."[27] Rather than using the rose-colored ball, which rationalized new discoveries, Parsons took what he described as the bluish ball, which limited his forecasts to those based on verifiable advances.

Deak Parsons' horizon moved forward with the technological advances of his time. He maintained a strikingly clear view up to five years ahead, far enough to make necessary corrections in course—as long as he was among those at the helm.

Parsons understood why the navy wanted to keep him in assignments where he could respond, as he said, to "the chronic state of atomic emergency." But he believed that no officer should be indispensable. Under this reasoning, he brought in a navy captain to groom as his successor: T. B. Hill, his academy roommate, shipmate on the *Idaho*, colleague in the Marianas. With Hill's selection to flag rank in late 1948, Parsons made his next move. He reminded the chief of naval personnel that his own last "official" sea duty—not counting short stints as additional duty—had ended in June 1939. He added, "I now have a relief fully qualified in all respects."[28]

In May 1949 Parsons did receive new orders, but rather than sending him to sea these orders sent him across the Potomac River to the Pentagon. There he became a member of the Weapon Systems Evaluation Group (WSEG), a select group of military officers and civilian scientists brought together within the National Military Establishment (later, the Department of Defense) to examine the effectiveness of present and future weapons from a scientific perspective. Even though this operational research assignment further postponed a sea command, he did not object. The WSEG was a new concept that met one of his own philosophical objectives, that of bringing scientists of stature into defense problems. The range of WSEG's mission is seen in the studies it undertook during Parsons' stint. These included a review of Strategic Air Command procedures, army tank requirements, antisubmarine warfare, the nation's air defense, and a special project on nuclear submarines. Parsons had high hopes for WSEG as a means of subjecting weapons systems and plans "to careful scrutiny based on real data and technically enlightened common sense."[29]

These hopes for improving military decision making were somewhat dashed by a string of calamitous events in the spring of 1949. These started with Secretary of Defense James Forrestal's resignation in March 1949 for reasons of failing health. Forrestal's replacement, Louis A. Johnson, came into the job swinging a two-bladed ax. In trimming the budget, he chopped heavy chunks out of the navy's air arm and its long-range atomic-bombing capability.

Parsons was disturbed, and not just by Johnson's undercutting of the navy's nuclear capability. He saw in Johnson the return of the pinch-penny mentality that had traditionally followed American wars. This had been costly policy in the past; for meeting a future nuclear threat, it could be catastrophic. In World War III there would be no time for a technological buildup. Johnson became an exception to Deak Parsons' longstanding rule about not criticizing his superiors. When among friends, he lambasted the new secretary of defense as an untrustworthy third-caliber person in a position demanding the best.[30]

Parsons' distress reached new bounds with the shocking news that circulated instantaneously through the ramps and corridors of the Pentagon on 22 May: the former boss of this sprawling empire, James Forrestal, had plunged to his death from a window of the Bethesda Medical Center.

Forrestal had been more than Deak Parsons' tennis companion and boss. Like Parsons, he was a man fully committed to mission. If Parsons attributed any part of Forrestal's tragedy to an unrelenting preoccupation with work, he never applied the lesson to himself. Even in his new position with WSEG, Parsons drove himself as if the nation's defense depended solely on him.

Although the WSEG assignment was not a nuclear post, Parsons' reputation tied him to atomic affairs. No matter what his title, he remained the Atomic Admiral. Thus, he was summoned in early September 1949 to serve on an urgent, secret panel with Vannevar Bush, Robert Oppenheimer, and Robert Bacher. Traces of radioactivity had been picked up by a weather reconnaissance plane on patrol in the northern Pacific. The question: Had the Russians exploded an atomic bomb?

The answer required highly sophisticated interpretation of the facts. After examining the evidence, the panel concluded that "an atomic bomb had exploded on August 29."[31] The United States no longer had a monopoly. Russian nuclear technology was more advanced than Parsons and his scientist friends had realized. However, although recognizing the increased danger of nuclear war, Parsons did not believe that such a war was likely. He wrote his father:

> As I see it the Russians should go full out to produce the atomic bomb for two reasons, neither of them looking toward actual use of the bomb. The first reason is that it is intolerable, in their materialistic scheme of things, to have their group unable to produce something defined as important. The second is that they probably consider the atomic bomb as a propaganda weapon of first-class importance against England and any other countries not directly threatened by their armies.[32]

Parsons' political forecasts were often the results of his philosophical interchanges with Oppenheimer. Besides the frequent crossing of work paths, they periodically visited each other's homes with their wives. The visits of the Parsons family to Olden Manor at Princeton left lasting impressions on Peggy and Clare Parsons. Clare later recalled, "We would go on these picnics on their grounds which were lovely with brooks running through." But Clare did not care for the food. She said, "They had champagne and wine and they would get out the rye toast and the eggs and the caviar and the cheeses, and I kept waiting for the peanut butter sandwiches." The highlight of these weekend visits was neither setting nor drink nor food but the unfettered sharing and testing of ideas between a mild-mannered, conservative officer whose wife was steeped in military tradition and a tense, freethinking scientist with a liberal wife. After one visit Deak wrote, "Dear Oppy, As always our weekend with you and Kitty was the event of the season for us. Our little affairs and even the world problems seem more nearly soluble in such an atmosphere."[33]

The world problem in June 1950 was the North Korean invasion of South Korea. The United States under the banner of the United Nations sent troops to repel the attack. After initial success, the U.N. forces were pushed back when the Chinese joined the North Koreans. With the possibility of a humiliating American defeat, cries rang out to use the atomic bomb.

This public reaction alarmed some scientists, including Norman Ramsey, now back at Harvard. He expressed his concerns in a letter to Parsons: "I presume that in any decision on the use of atomic bombs much attention will be given to the humanitarian and moral aspects of the problem as well as the military ones."[34]

Parsons assured Ramsey that the military thinking on the subject was "sober and practical" and took into account "emotional repercussions." He added, "On the other hand it would be the height of folly for the military to make a unilateral negative decision in advance by failing to prepare for strategic and tactical use." As for public clamor to pull the nuclear trigger, Parsons wrote, "Since 1945, Americans have shown an unhealthy tendency to feel that atoms and electrons—gadgets—can do their fighting and even their thinking." Alluding to calls to use the bomb to stem U.N. reverses in Korea, he commented, "It would not be impossible to find the 'MILITARY' of 1951 resisting a popular and Congressional demand to use the bomb in some desperate situation."[35] Parsons' principal worry was not, he said, "whether the United States would have any qualms about using [atomic bombs], but that our own people have an unjustifiable belief that our bombs would have an overwhelming decisive effect in the initial stages of a war."[36]

From this same letter to Ramsey we also learn that Parsons had reopened his campaign for sea duty. He confided, "As promised deadlines passed with no orders I finally threatened to call myself 'Former Naval Person.'"[37] The threat worked. After twenty-eight years of naval service, Deak Parsons received orders to take command not of a single ship but of Cruiser Division Six.

On 2 February 1951 aboard his flagship, the USS *Macon*, in Guantánamo Bay, Deak Parsons entered a world far apart from the Washington bureaucracy. He was back in a ritualistic culture with clear lines of authority, salutes, bells, side boys, and precedence lists. The new life began at 1610 with the "breaking" of Parsons' two-star flag and the firing of a thirteen-gun salute.[38]

After five months of routine operations along the Atlantic coast and in the Caribbean, the *Macon* rendezvoused at sea with other ships of

Cruiser Division Six and headed for the Mediterranean. On arrival in Gibraltar, 5,015 men from ships of Parsons' command went on leave. The dictates of diplomacy and protocol filled Parsons' social calendar: 23 September, a cocktail party hosted by Lord and Lady Ashbourne for flag officers and unit commanders; 24 September, a cocktail party hosted by the U.S. consul for flag officers; 25 September, Commander Cruiser Division Four requests Rear Admiral Parsons' presence for dinner on the USS *Worcester;* and so it went. As Parsons had always suspected, flag-rank sea duty had its merits.[39]

Life became even better as the *Macon* made her rounds of Mediterranean ports. On 20 October, Martha joined Deak in Augusta Bay, Sicily. A week later they treated themselves to a tour of Naples, including a romantic gondola "cruise." As in her younger years in California, Martha followed the ships and met up with Deak in Trieste and Valetta before returning home via London in time to share Christmas with Clare and Peggy.[40]

As part of his operational duties Parsons planned and conducted joint exercises of the U.S. Navy and the Royal Hellenic Air Forces. But most of his duties called on his diplomatic talents more than his operational skills. Whether greeting a high government official of Greece or the mayor of some port of call, he did so with grace and quiet charm. And wherever he went, he arrived well versed in local history and customs.

After showing the flag in Izmir, Tripoli, and Palma de Mallorca, the *Macon* returned to Gibraltar where Parsons left by military air for home on 26 January 1952. At Pier Seven, Norfolk, on 1 March 1952, Rear Admiral Parsons was relieved as commander of Cruiser Division Six.[41] His dream of a sea command had been fulfilled.

The Mediterranean assignment insulated Parsons from most atomic matters. One exception centered on Metro-Goldwyn-Mayer Studio's production of a film based on the life of Col. Paul Tibbets and the atomic bomb. The studio informed Parsons that it had paid Tibbets for the story and now needed releases from Parsons and other principal figures who would be portrayed. An air force public-relations colonel assured Parsons that the filming would be done under the Department of Defense and air force headquarters supervision.

Parsons refused to sign a release. "My first reaction was negative," he informed the navy chief of information, "not because the Air Force might intend to distort history and present the 509th Composite as the whole show, but because Metro-Goldwyn-Mayer made such a complete mess of their 1947 attempt at the same thing." Parsons had found the 1947 film, *The Beginning or the End*, to be sloppy, slushy, and generally distorted. But what irritated him most was, in his words, "MGM's attempt to inject phony drama into the Hiroshima delivery by picturing it as haywire, unplanned, and always on the brink of disaster."[42] Parsons stood fast. He would sign off on the film only if he could review the script and if he then found it acceptable.

The first draft confirmed his worst fears. He qualified his return comments by saying that he had "great admiration for [Tibbets'] courage, judgment, and skill as a pilot." He also credited him for a good job of "getting together a very fine group of airplanes and crews." However, Parsons was concerned with the impression left by the script that Tibbets had been in the program back in January 1944, when the flight testing began at Muroc, and that Tibbets had had a voice in the Los Alamos technical work on the bomb, neither of which was true. And, as with the earlier film, Parsons strenuously objected to depictions suggesting "that most of the Los Alamos scientists were irresponsible, scatterbrained childish types only to be trusted when under military supervision."[43] Parsons wrote a separate letter to Maj. Gen. Thomas Farrell, who had been General Groves' personal representative at Tinian. He suggested that Farrell should get a copy of the script if he wanted "to be amused, amazed, and annoyed." He alerted Farrell, "One thing they have done is to cut *you* out completely. Your questions to me after take-off are attributed to Spaatz!"[44]

A second draft of the script failed to address Parsons' objections. It had Tibbets making judgments on bomb design and performing technical functions that, in Parsons' words, were not "primarily Tibbets' worries." When an air force colonel suggested that Parsons might be overly modest about his own role, Parsons responded, "It is not a desire on my part to 'hide my light' under a bushel when I object to being pictured as MGM's 'push-button atomic hero.'" To him the treatment was "offensive" because it portrayed actions being done on impulse when in reality "every technical and operational decision of the Manhattan Project was thoroughly studied and discussed in advance."[45]

•

Immediately upon his return from the Mediterranean, Parsons laid the groundwork for his next assignment. He revealed his strategy in a letter to his brother Critchell: "I knew the boys in Washington would be plotting to get me ashore and probably in that [nuclear] snake pit again."[46]

To stave off a purely atomic job, he argued that it would be more advantageous to the navy's nuclear interests to make him deputy chief of the Bureau of Ordnance. That way, he could "inject a shot of atomic energy in the weapons center of the navy." The strategy worked. Deak wrote Critchell, "It now appears that my nibble inspired them [BuOrd] to hook me."[47] In fact, Rear Adm. Malcolm Schoeffel, the successor to Hussey as chief of BuOrd, leaped at the opportunity to bring Parsons into the bureau as his own alter ego. He saw Parsons as "very palsy-walsy with the big physicist brains of the country" and believed he could strengthen the bureau's ties with the nation's top scientists. Beyond that, Schoeffel considered Parsons a first-rate ordnance officer with "a great personality, a man of tremendous personal magnetism."[48]

Parsons became deputy chief of BuOrd in March 1952. Though it could have been a sinecure by virtue of his ordnance expertise, he chose instead to work with his usual intensity. He extended his agenda to cover the full range of the navy's scientific interests. His door was open to the nation's scientists, and his mind to new ideas.

One of Parsons' objectives was to chart a middle course for the navy in nuclear weaponry. On the one hand, he objected to the military being put into the position, as he said, "of sharecroppers" who had to take the jobs the Atomic Energy Commission parceled out.[49] On the other hand, he believed it unwise for the navy to try to set up a full-fledged atomic weapon development organization of its own. In his bureau position, Parsons achieved what he considered a practical level of BuOrd involvement in nuclear weapon development by working with the AEC. Under his leadership the way was opened for the navy to develop "Betty" as a nuclear depth charge and bombs of the "Elsie" program for hard-target and underground penetration.[50]

As deputy chief of BuOrd, Parsons promoted management of the navy's ordnance laboratories by military-civilian partnerships wherein the commanding officer provided overall administrative control and the civilian director provided technical leadership. Parsons' strongest influence on a particular navy laboratory occurred through his support of Thompson's efforts to make NOTS China Lake the consummation of their early dream. In 1946 Parsons had helped Thompson overcome China Lake's first major management crisis, that of a commanding officer, Capt. James Sykes, who was determined to run the laboratory like a ship.[51] In 1953 China Lake faced the opposite problem, a civilian technical director, Fred Brown, seeking full civilian control and alienating his military partners. Neither extreme was acceptable to Parsons. After his attempts to soften Brown's management style failed, he pressed for Brown's resignation.[52]

Parsons also lent China Lake a helping hand in the development of the revolutionary guided-missile Sidewinder. Invented by China Lake physicist William B. McLean, this missile with an infrared sensor could lock onto the heat of a target aircraft and follow it to intercept. By March 1952, when Parsons became deputy chief of BuOrd, Sidewinder prototypes had not as yet come near any drone target. Still unproved, the missile became vulnerable to the ax of K. T. Keller, the Chrysler Corporation executive brought in by the secretary of defense to serve as director of guided missiles.

During a December 1952 business luncheon, Ralph Sawyer learned of Keller's intentions to eliminate Sidewinder, calling it "a boondoggle which had been oversold . . . not enough better than an ordinary rocket to make it worthwhile." Sawyer wrote Thompson, "You are no doubt familiar with his general attitude, which is that weapon development should be done only by experienced industrial companies and that government and university laboratories are quite incompetent to do this." Sawyer advised, "I think that you or Deak Parsons ought to get into the picture."[53]

Parsons did not hesitate. He knew that Sidewinder was based on sound, although still unproved, technology. Through influence and bootleg funding, he helped keep Sidewinder alive until it could prove itself. In September 1953 Parsons read a telegram from China Lake: a Sidewinder had passed within six inches of a target drone. This was but the beginning. Direct hits followed. In time Sidewinder became one of the most effective weapons to come out of the weapons revolution. It was a product not only of inventive genius and China Lake teamwork but also of Parsons' managerial faith and creative financing.

•

Officials collaborating with Deak Parsons in the bootleg financing of Sidewinder might have been more concerned had they been familiar with his management of family finances. He never had a will and carried little life insurance—a peculiar position for a man who did not hesitate to put his life at risk. Aside from the Washington home, his only significant investments were the oil ventures of Critchell, now an up-again, down-again millionaire.[54]

In early 1952 Parsons had hopes that his oil investments were growing. He wrote Critch, "I hear from Clarissa that you had a nice visit there and surprised her with your Cadillac. That means to me your oil business is booming. Give me the news."[55] But there was no good news. The absence of family financial records makes it impossible to establish what amounts Deak may have lost on Critchell's ventures, but Deak's comments in letters about money invested are not matched by reports of returns.

In the fall of 1953, during a visit to Sandia, Deak spent several hours with his sister, Clarissa. While on a leisurely drive together, Clarissa expressed her concerns about the cold war with Russia. Deak assured her that there was no iron curtain that could keep ideas from getting through to the Russian people. He said that when the Russians learned about American ideals and aspirations, the two countries would be friends.[56]

"What ideals and aspirations?" Clarissa asked. Deak then described his own dream for the future: the use of atomic energy to desalt seawater for arid countries, allowing new farms to feed starving people; a sharing of medical knowledge in the battle against diseases; educational and cultural exchanges among all nations; and other ways in which the future could open the way for peace. He told Clarissa that if these positive changes came about there need be no more wars. But, he emphasized, until such a time came, the United States had to keep as defensively strong as possible. He said, "It would be dangerous to have it any other way."[57]

Deak's optimism rose even higher that fall, when he thought he saw a break in the clouds of suspicion created by Senator Joseph McCarthy's anticommunism crusade. Unaware that Oppenheimer would soon become a target of the McCarthy hysteria, Parsons commented in a "Dear Oppy" letter, "The anti-intellectualism of recent months may have passed its peak. It is hard to judge here [in Washington]. We might be in the eye of the hurricane."[58]

On 4 December, Parsons learned that they had indeed been in the eye of the hurricane. As the calm passed, it left Oppenheimer exposed to the full fury of the storm. Early that Friday afternoon Parsons learned that President Eisenhower had ordered a "blank wall" placed between Oppenheimer and any sensitive security information. The restriction was to remain in place until a full hearing had been conducted into the scientist's loyalty. Later that afternoon, Deak joined Martha at a cocktail party. He went directly to her, distress showing in his face as he told her the news.[59]

Like General Groves, Parsons had known of Oppenheimer's association with communists at Berkeley before joining the Manhattan Project. But that was past history that Groves had investigated to his satisfaction. Parsons also knew that Oppenheimer had created enemies through his early opposition to the hydrogen bomb and with his sometimes sharp tongue. But these were not reasons for challenging his loyalty and denying him security clearance. Parsons had no doubts about Oppenheimer's loyalty. He understood the man's unique brilliance and the dedication with which he had served the nation both during and after World War II.[60]

That evening at home Deak became, according to his wife, "extremely upset" about the Oppenheimer news. Throwing off his usual calm, Deak exclaimed, "This is the biggest mistake the United States could make!" He would take the matter up with secretary of the navy the next day to see what could be done. Martha said, "Deak, you're an admiral, why can't you go to the President?" "No," Deak said, "the Secretary of the Navy is my boss. I can't go around him."[61]

Later that evening Deak complained of pains in his chest. Martha said, "Oh, you've got a cold. I'll go make you some hot lemonade." When she returned with the lemonade, Deak was reading about heart attacks in the encyclopedia. He decided that this was not the problem, because he did not have any pain in his left arm. On Saturday morning, after a restless night, he still had the chest pains. He looked pale. Martha persuaded him to go the naval hospital to be checked over.

And even though he usually worked on Saturday mornings, he said, "And I won't work today; we'll just play golf." They put the golf clubs in the car trunk.[62]

Doctors at Bethesda Naval Hospital took Parsons into the examining room immediately upon his arrival. But before they could complete their examination, Deak Parsons, naval officer extraordinary, was dead.

Epilogue

During the war there was created a professional partnership between military men and scientific men in this country. . . . Admiral Parsons was the great exemplar in our minds of this relationship. We all regarded him as a friend, we admired him as a naval officer, we respected him as a man.
Dr. Vannevar Bush

The odyssey that took Deak Parsons to the USS *Helena,* Los Alamos, the *Enola Gay,* and Crossroads began in his boyhood home of Fort Sumner, New Mexico. The modest ranch house still guards a rise on the edge of town, but the outbuildings are now mere weathered shells. The old Eclipse windmill stands, but without vanes to turn or water to pump. These and the surrounding barren land are all that remain of Harry Parsons Sr.'s dream of orchards and prosperity.

In 1909, when Harry Parsons arrived at Fort Sumner in a freight car with furniture and carriage horse, the town's population was four thousand; now it has half that number. The proud old Fort Sumner Railroad Station still stands, but the trains no longer stop; the interstate passes miles to the north. Except for a historical mural Bob Parsons painted on an aging downtown brick building, nothing reveals that this place was once the home of the navy's Atomic Admiral.

Brought home from college by the news of her father's death, Peggy Parsons, then nineteen, wrote her grandfather, "Only for a second or two do I realize what has happened. He was so completely alive that none of the words associated with death seem fitting."[1]

Admiral Schoeffel felt a "horrible shock" the morning he arrived at the office and learned that "this man who seemed so healthy the afternoon before was dead."[2] In thirty-five years with the navy, Deak Parsons had not missed a day of duty since the flu epidemic of 1918 invaded the Naval Academy. Despite long hours and intense work, he had always appeared fit and healthy. Just a few months before, a physical examination had shown him to be in good health.[3]

Those closest to Parsons at home and at work concluded that stress was a major factor in his death. He had always kept his problems to himself; he constantly extended himself. Vice Admiral Ashworth believes that the navy would have done well to give Parsons the same support in his BuOrd position that it had given him in the postwar atomic work and in the Weapons Systems Evaluation Group—that is, a Captain Rivero to follow through on the many administrative and technical details Deak heaped upon himself.[4] Whatever the other stresses, Martha Parsons saw the event precipitating the heart attack as his frustration over the accusations against Oppenheimer.[5]

The funeral occurred on a crisp, clear winter day. As Clarissa Fuller recalled, "The navy was out with all its finest pageantry." The procession wound slowly through historic Arlington National Cemetery with the band playing the marching hymns "The Son of Man goes forth to war" and "Eternal Father, strong to save, whose arm hath bound the restless wave." The procession ended at the flower-covered grave on the side of a hill overlooking the Potomac. Nearby tombstones marked the graves of Admiral Sampson, Admiral Cluverius, and little Hannah Parsons. A short religious service was followed by the final gun salute and taps.[6]

Martha found some consolation in the outpouring of sentiment from government officials, officers of all the services, scientists, former shipmates, and the press. Of these, she most treasured the summation from the *Durham (N.C.) Morning Herald:*

> Rear Admiral Parsons was as kindly as he was outstandingly able. Despite his position as one of the greatest scientists in the Military Services, he remained to the last as an approachable, genial, yet surprisingly efficient human being. All those who ever worked with him will feel his passing as the sharpest of personal losses. It is the nation as a whole that has suffered most greatly. It has been

deprived of an able military servant and a great man. It is certain that the example he set will remain part of the finest tradition in the long, illustrious Naval history of this land.[7]

The various honors Deak Parsons received in his lifetime, including a doctor of science degree, are listed in the Appendix. Additional recognition has been given posthumously. On 16 October 1954, prominent leaders of government, science, education, and the military honored him at the dedication of Johns Hopkins' new Applied Physics Laboratory Building and its new William S. Parsons Auditorium. In a speech at the dedication ceremony, Vannevar Bush summarized Parsons' roles in early radar and the proximity fuze. He called attention to Parsons' invaluable service in the development of the atomic bomb and "as officer in charge of the technical group which carried the principal burden of first utilization." Admiral Schoeffel added his own tribute: "[Deak] threw himself into all the problems of his work with imagination, keen intelligence, great energy—with real fire. Everything he touched felt his vivifying influence."[8]

Deak Parsons' scientific contributions to the navy caused many to forget that he was at heart an officer of the line. The navy of the 1950s did not forget. On 19 August 1958 a new destroyer was launched as the USS *Parsons,* with Martha Parsons doing the christening. By Clarissa Fuller's account, "Martha not only sent the ship's hull out into the deep water, but drenched the assembled crowd with champagne."[9]

Originally commissioned as a conventional destroyer, DD-949, the *Parsons* was later converted into a guided-missile destroyer, DDG-33, accommodating the Tartar guided missile aft and an antisubmarine rocket (ASROC) amidships. The conversion was appropriate inasmuch as the ship's namesake had been at the heart of the weapons revolution that produced Tartar, ASROC, and other new-generation weapons that were transforming the striking power of the U.S. Navy.[10] Although brought up in the battleship navy, Parsons, through technological leadership, hastened the navy's transition from big guns to jet-propelled guided missiles and rockets. The rechristening of the *Parsons* occurred on 3 November 1967 with Clare Parsons, by then a naval officer herself, representing the family.

In May 1979 the navy acknowledged that Parsons had pioneered naval training in the handling, assembly, and deployment of nuclear weapons. It did so by dedicating the Nuclear Weapons Training Center, Atlantic, at Norfolk as the Deak Parsons Center. In choosing to use "Deak" rather than "William," officials showed that they understood the essence of the man.[11]

The Deak Parsons legacy goes beyond military decorations, honorary science degrees, street names, ships, buildings. It lives on in the advanced weaponry and technology of the American armed forces, rigorous standards in nuclear weapons training, and a philosophy of military-scientific cooperation for military research and development.

Deak Parsons' legacy rose out of the unique brand of leadership he exerted at a time of great national peril and unparalleled scientific advances. He built teams spanning diverse cultures: the military and the scientific, the fleet and the laboratory. He put his own career on the line to serve the national interests: as lieutenant he fought the bureaucracy for what would become radar; as commander he not only provided military leadership in the development of the first mass-produced smart weapon but also took responsibility for the millions of dollars bet on this technological gamble; as captain he not only took on the ordnance development of the most revolutionary weapon of the ages but also took technical responsibility and command of the weapon in its first combat delivery.

The same dedication and brilliance that made Parsons a pivotal figure during the war also established him as the navy's nuclear leader in peace. At Operation Crossroads he took technical responsibility for the largest naval experiment of the century. As the Atomic Admiral he became the voice of experience in the formulation of navy nuclear policy at the dawn of the nuclear age.

Parsons participated in many of the great technical advances of his time. He witnessed great progress, but he hoped for more, including strong international controls of nuclear weaponry; nuclear-powered ships and submarines; a lasting bond between American science and the military; elimination of autocratic and bureaucratic controls over military R&D; and scientific developments capable of offsetting the economic and material causes of war. His dreams went beyond the subjects of weaponry and war. Those dreams included friendly relations between the Soviet Union and the United States, broad medical and educational exchanges among nations in the fight against disease and ignorance, and even massive seawater desalinization projects to wipe out famine in arid nations.[12]

An optimist to the end—the Oppenheimer episode excepted—Deak Parsons believed all these objectives possible. He saw unlimited possibilities deriving from the process found so effective during the war— that is, the nation's best minds working together, without concern for personal credit, on the most vital problems of the time. Of the future he said, "While the problems [of the atomic age] are as colossal as the concept of atomic energy, they are primarily human and man will be inspired to solve them."[13]

Time has left its mark on the Parsons family. Martha became the Washington Junior League's office manager and later married Robert Burroughs, brother of Rear Adm. S. E. "Ev" Burroughs. They lived in Manchester, New Hampshire, until her death in January 1988. Daughter Peggy (formally Margaret) Parsons graduated from Vassar. She studied horticulture at Temple University and is active in horticultural activities. She married a Philadelphia banker, Nathaniel Bowditch, the great-great-grandson of the American navigation pioneer bearing that name. Daughter Clare (formally Clara) graduated from the University of New Mexico, obtained a master's degree from the University of Rhode Island, received a commission in the U.S. Navy, and served twelve years on active duty and fourteen as a drilling reservist. She is now a sales representative in the Norfolk area for Prudential Insurance Company of America. Harry Parsons Sr. died in 1961 at age eighty-nine. Deak's sister Clarissa at ninety-plus years is a respected historical scholar living in Albuquerque. After an active career in the oil industry, Critchell Parsons died in January 1984 at age seventy-six. Deak's younger brother Bob (formally Harry Jr.) taught history to generations of Fort Sumner High School students. Now retired, he still lives in Fort Sumner with his wife, Eileen. Like his father, Bob Parsons has applied his many talents, including writing and painting, in the service of the community.

Appendix

William S. Parsons' Honors

CAREER

Silver Star, 6 August 1945, for gallantry in action during aerial flight against Japanese Empire. Tasks included in-flight loading of the powder charge on first atomic bomb, ensuring correct use of the bomb, and approving release. Awarded by Headquarters, Army Strategic Air Forces.

Distinguished Service Medal, September 1945, for exceptionally meritorious service in transforming the theory of atomic fusion into an effective weapon. The citation notes his personal direction of much of the design and development of the atomic bomb's components. Navy Department award.

Legion of Merit, August 1947, for sound judgment, broad vision, and initiative in organizing and directing the activities of the Technical Staff and the Technical Task Group during Operations Crossroads. Presidential award.

Doctor of science honorary degree, 13 June 1948, presented by Board of Trustees, Union College, Schenectady, New York.

In addition to the Silver Star, Distinguished Service Medal, and Legion of Merit, Rear Admiral Parsons had the Victory Medal, American Defense Service Medal, Asiatic-Pacific Campaign Medal, American Campaign Medal, World War II Victory Medal, and National Defense Service Medal.

POSTHUMOUS

William S. Parsons Auditorium dedicated 16 October 1954. Postwar scientific and naval leaders paid tribute to Parsons at the dedication

of this new building at the Applied Physics Laboratory, the Johns
Hopkins University.

USS *Parsons* (DD-949) christened August 1958 by Martha Parsons in
honor of her husband. The destroyer operated with the U.S. First
and Seventh Fleets in the Pacific.

USS *Parsons* recommissioned November 1967 as a *Decatur*-class
destroyer (DDG), following a conversion in which 90 percent of the
ship's existing superstructure was removed and the latest antiair and
antisubmarine weapon systems were added.

Deak Parsons Center, Norfolk, Virginia, dedicated 30 May 1979. This
center served as the principal nuclear training facility for the U.S.
Atlantic Fleet until April 1997, when the Nuclear Weapons Training Center Detachment–Atlantic was decommissioned and its functions transferred to Submarine Force Atlantic Fleet. The building
still retains the name Deak Parsons Center.

Notes

ABBREVIATIONS

LAM   Los Alamos Historical Museum, Los Alamos, N.Mex.

LANL   Los Alamos National Laboratory, Los Alamos, N.Mex.

LC   Manuscript Division, Library of Congress, Washington, D.C.

NA   National Archives, Washington, D.C.

NHC   Operational Archives, Naval Historical Center, Washington, D.C.

NI   United States Naval Institute, Annapolis, Md.

NLCG   Navy Laboratories/Center Coordinating Group collection held by
        Naval Historical Center, Washington, D.C.

Sources cited in abbreviated form at first reference appear in full in the Bibliography.

Chapter 1. A New Kind of Warrior

Epigraph: Hayward to author, 3 May 1993.

1. Thomas and Witts, *Enola Gay,* 227.
2. Ibid., 228.
3. Parsons to Col. W. C. Lindley, USAF, 20 Aug. 1951, Parsons papers, LC.
4. Groves, *Now It Can Be Told,* 282, says thirty-seven in Parsons' overseas group; Ramsey, who was there, names fifty-one in his "History of Project A."
5. Accounts vary as to the number of crashes; Laurence, *Dawn over Zero,* 205, and Tibbets, *Tibbets Story,* 199, say four.
6. Laurence, *Dawn over Zero,* 205.
7. Groves, *Now It Can Be Told,* 317.
8. Parsons to Lt. Col. Walter Ott, 14 Dec. 1951, Parsons papers, LC.
9. Laurence, *Dawn over Zero,* 206.
10. Knebel and Bailey, *No High Ground,* 152.
11. The press also dubbed Rear Adm. W. H. P. Blandy, commander of Operation Crossroads, the Atomic Admiral. However, Blandy never claimed to have either the nuclear expertise or the experience of Parsons. See Waldo Drake, "Parsons, the Atomic Admiral," *Los Angeles Times,* 24 July 1946.

Chapter 2. Cow Town to Crab Town

Epigraph: Naval Academy class of 1922, *Lucky Bag,* 220.

1. Harry Parsons Jr. interview, Feb. 1967, 5.
2. Mid-Pecos, *Living Water,* 187.
3. Bob (Harry Jr.) Parsons, "Ghosts, Black Holes, and Pecos Diamonds," *DeBaca County News* (Fort Sumner, N.Mex.), 5 Apr. 1980.
4. Mid-Pecos, *Living Water,* 190.
5. Ibid.
6. Ibid., 188.
7. Harry Parsons Jr. interview, Feb. 1967, 6–7; Fuller interview, 4.
8. Fuller interview, 3.
9. Bob Parsons, in *DeBaca County News,* 5 Apr. 1990.
10. Fuller interview, 6.
11. Harry Parsons Jr. interview, Sept. 1992.
12. Mid-Pecos, *Living Water,* 191.
13. Fuller to author, 20 Jan. 1967.
14. Stearns interview, 5.
15. Mid-Pecos, *Living Water,* 191.
16. Fuller interview, 14.
17. Stearns interview, 18–19.
18. By historical coincidence, William S. Parsons' grandfather, Senator James R. Doolittle, visited Fort Sumner and the Bosque Redondo Indian Reservation in 1865 as the head of a presidential commission on Indian affairs. The commission contributed to the abandonment of the reservation and helped open the way for the treaty establishing the Navajo homeland. For early history of the area, see articles by Harry "Bob" Parsons Jr.: "Ghosts, Black Holes, and Pecos Diamonds," *DeBaca County News,* 23 June 1988, 1 Dec. 1988, 5 Apr. 1990, 17 Jan. 1991, 10 Oct. 1991, and 14 Nov. 1991.
19. Mid-Pecos, *Living Water,* 188.
20. Fuller interview, 103–4.
21. Ibid., 15–17, 24.
22. Mid-Pecos, *Living Water,* 192.
23. Fuller interview, 22.
24. Margaret Bowditch interview, index 2-1.
25. Stearns interview, 4.
26. Fort Sumner High School, *El Tepocate,* 49.
27. Fuller interview, 28.
28. Ibid., 29.
29. Margaret Bowditch interview, index 2-1.
30. Midshipman Personnel Jackets on microfilm, U.S. Naval Academy; A. A. Jones, U.S. Senate, to H. R. Parsons Sr., 29 June 1918, Harry Parsons Jr. papers.
31. Naval Academy class of 1922, *Lucky Bag,* 357, 356.
32. Mid-Pecos, *Living Water,* 192. Parsons signed his personal correspondence

"Deak"; however, some of his close associates have used "Deke" and other forms.

33. Naval Academy class of 1922, *Lucky Bag*, 7.
34. Ibid., 358.
35. Livingston, *Master of Light*, 36.
36. Description of cruise based on Naval Academy class of 1922, *Lucky Bag*, 362–80.
37. Ibid.
38. Mid-Pecos, *Living Water*, 192.
39. Scores from Midshipman Jackets, William S. Parsons and Hyman Rickover; "premier ordnance expert" from Ashworth, "Parsons and the Atomic Bomb," 24–26.
40. Midshipman Jackets, William S. Parsons and Hyman Rickover.
41. Naval Academy class of 1922, *Lucky Bag*, 220; Mid-Pecos, *Living Water*, 192.
42. Naval Academy class of 1922, *Lucky Bag*, 194; Effie Cottman, "Navy Nag: Rickover No Academy Fan," 9 July 1986, article file, U.S. Naval Academy Alumni Association.
43. Naval Academy class of 1922, *Lucky Bag*, 220.
44. Ibid.
45. Ibid., 181, 220.
46. Martha Parsons Burroughs interviews, 33, 37.
47. Naval Academy Register, 1921–22.
48. Ibid.; Martha Parsons Burroughs interviews, 26.
49. Naval Academy class of 1922, *Lucky Bag*, 46.
50. Margaret Bowditch interview, index 2-70; Martha Parsons Burroughs interviews, 26.
51. Mid-Pecos, *Living Water*, 192.

Chapter 3. Battleship Navy

Epigraph: Granum interview, 1.
1. *Idaho* log, 1 Jan.–31 Dec. 1922.
2. Ibid; Naval History Division, *Dictionary of Naval Ships*, USS *Idaho*.
3. Granum interview, 8.
4. *Idaho* log, 28 Aug. 1922.
5. Ibid., 1 Jan.–31 Dec. 1922.
6. Fuller to author, 5 Feb. 1992.
7. Martha Parsons Burroughs interviews, 90.
8. Fuller interview, 60, 94.
9. Ibid., 93.
10. Granum interview, 4–6.
11. Ibid., 1.
12. Ibid., 7.
13. Ibid., 5.

14. Ibid., 6. Allusions to the significance of Parsons' 14-inch gun-dispersion study are made in Ashworth, "Parsons and the Atomic Bomb," 24, and Hooper interview, 6–7.
15. Mid-Pecos, *Living Water,* 192.
16. Harry Parsons Sr. to Miss Olsen, 24 Nov. 1925, Harry Parsons Jr. papers.
17. Stearns interview, 13; Fuller interview, 90.
18. Mid-Pecos, *Living Water,* 185–86.

Chapter 4. Romance and Weapons

Epigraph: Bramble interview, 7.

1. Martha Parsons Burroughs, in Apr. 1966 interviews, speaks of six ordnance PG students in the class with Deak Parsons; Bramble, in May 1969 interview, says ten or fewer.
2. Bramble interview, 1, 2.
3. Parsons to Professor Bramble, 3 Apr. 1930, attachment to Bramble interview.
4. Harry Parsons (Sr.) to Agnes Cornell, 24 Dec. 1928, Harry Parsons Jr. papers.
5. Ibid.
6. Martha Parsons Burroughs interviews, 33.
7. Harral and Swartz, *Service Etiquette,* 362–69.
8. Martha Parsons Burroughs interviews, 88.
9. Ibid., 34–35.
10. Ibid.
11. Harry Parsons (Sr.) to Agnes Cornell, 21 Aug. 1929.
12. Ibid.
13. Martha Parsons Burroughs interviews, 22–23, 135–36, 137–39.
14. Ibid., 22–23.
15. John Dahlgren background from Christman, *Naval Innovators.*
16. There was a 15-inch Dahlgren gun, but it had problems.
17. McCollum, *Dahlgren,* provides a history of Naval Proving Ground, Dahlgren, through oral histories.
18. Until purchased by the U.S. Navy in 1917, the *Grampus* was the *Boothbay* of the Eastern Steam Ship Line. The proving ground had a second passenger ship, the *Porpoise,* providing transportation between Washington and Dahlgren.
19. History of early proving grounds from Van Auken, *Notes on Naval Ordnance,* and Christman, *Naval Innovators.*
20. Van Auken, *Notes on Naval Ordnance,* 9.
21. Naval Ordnance Station, *1890,* 38; McCollum, *Dahlgren,* 1.
22. Thompson speech, "After Forty Years," 3.
23. Martha Parsons Burroughs interviews, 141.
24. Thompson speech, "After Forty Years," 3.
25. Thompson interview, Nov. 1965, 37–53, provides Thompson's background relative to Parsons.

26. Hussey and Thompson interview, 89–90.
27. Thompson interview, Nov. 1965, 1.
28. Waldo Drake, "Parsons, the Atomic Admiral," *Los Angeles Times,* 24 July 1946.
29. Thompson interview, Nov. 1965, 4–5; Thompson interview, May 1966, 28–29.
30. Thompson interview, May 1966, 28–29.

Chapter 5. Fighting for Radar

Epigraph: Gunn interview, 3.
1. Naval History Division, *Dictionary of Naval Ships,* USS *Texas; Texas* log.
2. *Texas* log, Nov. 1930 entry.
3. Martha Parsons Burroughs interviews, 90.
4. Ibid., 44.
5. Examples include Parsons to Bramble, 3 Apr. 1930; and Parsons to Thompson, 13 Nov. 1930, 10 June 1931, and 26 Aug. 1931.
6. Parsons to Thompson, 13 Nov. 1930.
7. Martha Parsons Burroughs interviews, 36.
8. Fiske, *From Midshipman,* 86, 128.
9. Paul Stillwell to author, 21 Apr. 1993.
10. Martha Parsons Burroughs interviews, 132.
11. Margaret Bowditch interview, index 2-141–49.
12. Martha Parsons Burroughs interviews, 97.
13. Mid-Pecos, *Living Water,* 186.
14. Ibid., 193.
15. Fuller interview, 45.
16. Mid-Pecos, *Living Water,* 192–93.
17. Major sources on NRL and early radar: Taylor, *First Twenty-five Years,* and Allison, *New Eye.*
18. Parsons to Capt. E. B. Taylor, "Comments on NRL Situation in 1933," 6 Nov. 1945, box 3, WSP file, RG 38, NHC.
19. Allison, *New Eye,* 113–14.
20. Secretary of War to Secretary of Navy, "Radio—Use of Echo Signals to Detect Moving Objects," 9 Jan. 1932, RG 38, NHC.
21. Ibid.; Allison, *New Eye,* 63–64.
22. Parsons to E. B. Taylor, 6 Nov. 1945.
23. Ibid.; Gunn interview, 3.
24. Director, NRL, to Chief, BuOrd, "Super-High Frequency Radio: Possible Use of Reflected Waves in Airplane Detection and Fire Control," 2 Aug. 1933, box 3, RG 38, NHC; see also Allison, *New Eye,* p. 115 n. 6, regarding copy in BuOrd files, RG 74.
25. Allison, *New Eye,* 115.
26. Parsons to E. B. Taylor, 6 Nov. 1945.
27. Director, NRL, to Chief, Ord, via Chief, BuEng, "Fire Control Possibilities of Radio Micro Rays," 15 Sept. 1933, box 3, WSP file, RG 38, NHC.

28. Parsons to Bush, 26 May 1951, box 2, RG 38, NHC.
29. Director, NRL, to Chief, BuOrd, "Fire Control Possibilities of Radio Micro Rays," 15 Sept. 1933.
30. Allison, *New Eye*, 116.
31. Parsons to E. B. Taylor, 6 Nov. 1945.
32. Bush speech, Parsons Auditorium dedication.
33. Parsons to Arthur Compton, "Cognizance," 10 Feb. 1949, Parsons papers, LC.
34. Parsons to Blandy, "Naval Research and Development as Affected by Personalities," 9 Mar. 1946, box 24, RG 38, NHC.
35. Gunn interview, 7; Martha Parsons Burroughs interviews, 43.
36. Parsons to Compton, 10 Feb. 1949.
37. Ibid.
38. Gunn interview, 3.
39. Ibid.
40. For NRL organization, see Taylor, *First Twenty-five Years*.
41. Gunn interview, 3.
42. Ibid., 4.
43. Bush speech, Parsons Auditorium dedication.
44. Allison, *New Eye*, 78.
45. Parsons to E. B. Taylor, 6 Nov. 1945.
46. Ibid.
47. Martha Parsons Burroughs interviews, 44.
48. Ibid., 78.
49. Ibid., 115, 117.
50. Fuller interview, 65; Margaret Bowditch interview, index 2-141.
51. Fuller telecon, 2 Mar. 1997.
52. Margaret Bowditch interview, index 2-141.
53. Bush speech, Parsons Auditorium dedication.
54. Taylor, *First Twenty-five Years*, 40.
55. Parsons to Bush, 26 May 1951, Parsons papers, LC.
56. Parsons to Blandy, 9 Mar. 1946.
57. For a history of the Radiation Laboratory, see Buderi, *Invention That Changed the World;* for a confirming view of Bowen, see 143.
58. Entwistle interview, 5.
59. Ibid.
60. Parsons to Compton, 10 Feb. 1949.

Chapter 6. Breaking Storm

Epigraph: Capt. Ward F. Hardman, Los Altos, Calif., telecon with author, 19 Apr. 1996.
1. For *Aylwin*, see *Aylwin* log and Naval History Division, *Dictionary of Naval Ships*.
2. Hardman telecon, 19 Apr. 1996.
3. Ibid.

4. *Aylwin* log.

5. Hardman telecon, 19 Apr. 1996.

6. Keith oral history, NI.

7. Martha Parsons Burroughs interviews, 35.

8. Ibid., 139.

9. Ibid.

10. Ibid., 27.

11. Parsons to Bush, 26 May 1951, box 2, RG 38, NHC; Parsons to Capt. E. B. Taylor, "Comments on NRL Situation in 1933," 6 Nov. 1945, box 3, RG 38, NHC.

12. Margaret Bowditch interview, index 2-203; Clara Parsons interview, index 1-600, 2-164.

13. Parsons to H. R. Parsons Sr., 7 Sept. 1946, Harry Parsons Jr. papers; Clara Parsons interview, index 2-164.

14. Martha Parsons Burroughs interviews, 60.

15. McCollum, *Dahlgren*, 8.

16. Sawyer interview, 12.

17. Martha Parsons Burroughs interviews, 59.

18. McCollum, *Dahlgren*, 61.

19. Director, NRL, to Chief, BuOrd, 30 July 1940, Thompson papers, NLCG.

20. Martha Parsons Burroughs interviews, 58–59.

21. Thompson interview, Nov. 1965, 44; Youngblood interview, 6–7.

22. Hooper, "Over the Span," 21.

23. Thompson and Goddard joined Webster in forming the Ballistics Institute, a pioneering effort at the start of World War I to improve American guns through ballistics science. See Christman, *Sailors, Scientists, and Rockets.*

24. Esther Goddard and Pendray, eds., *Papers of Robert H. Goddard,* 126–27; Christman, *Sailors, Scientists, and Rockets,* 2–3.

25. Christman, *Sailors, Scientists, and Rockets,* 36–41.

26. Thompson interview, Nov. 1965, 46–47. Proposed design of rocket device: Esther Goddard and Pendray, eds., *Papers of Robert H. Goddard,* 1307–8, and R. H. Goddard to Thompson, 9 May 1940, Thompson papers, NLCG.

27. Christman, *Sailors, Scientists, and Rockets,* 97.

28. Esther Goddard and Pendray, eds., *Papers of Robert H. Goddard,* 1310 (diary entry for 25 May 1940).

29. Thompson interview, Nov. 1965, 46–47.

30. Esther Goddard and Pendray, eds., *Papers of Robert H. Goddard,* 1315 (R. H. Goddard to Hickman, 9 June 1940); R. H. Goddard to Thompson, 18 July 1940, Thompson papers, NLCG.

31. Schuyler interview, 23–24.

32. Esther Goddard and Pendray, eds., *Papers of Robert H. Goddard,* 1312–13 (Hickman to R. H. Goddard, 5 June 1940); ibid., 1314 (R. H. Goddard to Hickman, 9 June 1940).

33. S. E. Burroughs interview. Rear Admiral Burroughs describes the concept of the Naval Ordnance Test Station, Inyokern, Calif., as an American Peenemunde.

Chapter 7. Sparking a Weapons Revolution

Epigraph: Loeb interview, 51.

1. Christman, *Sailors, Scientists, and Rockets*, 15, 85.
2. Baxter, *Scientists against Time*, 222.
3. Ibid., 14.
4. Bowen, *Ships, Machinery, and Mossbacks*, 178.
5. Thompson interview, Nov. 1965, 47.
6. Ibid.
7. Tolman to Thompson, 12 July 1940, Thompson papers, NLCG.
8. Tuve interview, 4.
9. Parsons, "Summer 1939–Summer 1949."
10. Tuve interview, 2.
11. Baldwin, *Deadly Fuze*, 25; Henderson and Ashworth interview, 1.
12. Henderson and Ashworth interview, 6.
13. Baldwin, *Deadly Fuze*, 62, 66.
14. Hafstad interview, 5.
15. Lauritsen interview, 6.
16. "Transcript of Meeting on VT Fuze," 66; Baldwin, *Deadly Fuze*, 61.
17. Martha Parsons Burroughs interviews, 135.
18. Ibid., 36–37.
19. Margaret Bowditch interview, index 2-355.
20. Clara Parsons interview, index 398.
21. Margaret Bowditch interview, index 1-627; Clara Parsons interview, 1-58, 69.
22. Clara Parsons interview, index 398.
23. Thompson interview, Nov. 1965, 44.
24. Loeb interview, 4, 5.
25. Youngblood interview, 9–10.
26. Loeb interview, 6.
27. Ibid.
28. Ibid., 4, 5, 8.
29. Hafstad interview, 11; Baxter, *Scientists against Time*, 224.
30. Hafstad interview, 7–21.
31. Tuve interview, 6–7.
32. Baldwin, *Deadly Fuze*, 77.
33. Baxter, *Scientists against Time*, 225; Baldwin, *Deadly Fuze*, 95.
34. Baldwin, *Deadly Fuze*, 87–88.
35. Tuve to Section T files, 9 Sept. 1941, RG 227, NA.
36. Margaret Bowditch interview, index 2-548.
37. Parsons to Arthur Compton, 10 Feb. 1949, Parsons papers, LC.
38. George Raynor Thompson et al., *The Signal Corps: The Test* (Washington, D.C.: Department of the Army, 1957), 3–10, cited by Allison, *New Eye*, 180; Buderi, *Invention That Changed the World*, 126.
39. Parsons to Compton, 10 Feb. 1949.

Chapter 8. Into Battle with the Smart Fuze

Epigraph: Tuve interview, 17.

1. Goss and Porter interview, 10.
2. Hafstad interview, 4.
3. Ibid., 10.
4. Ibid., 11; Baxter, *Scientists against Time,* 229.
5. Goss and Porter interview, 11.
6. Ibid.
7. Ibid.
8. Herbert Trotter Jr. reminiscence in "Transcript of Meeting on VT Fuze," 57.
9. The Office of Scientific Research and Development was created in June 1941. The change gave the scientists' organization recognition by Congress and cleared the way for funding beyond that possible for NDRC through the president. See Baxter, *Scientists against Time.*
10. Bush, *Pieces of the Action,* 56. Bush directs his compliment to both Parsons and Capt. Carroll L. Tyler ("two of the finest men I ever worked with"), but through error the order in which these officers served Bush is reversed.
11. Bush to Richard Tolman, 31 Mar. 1942, RG 227, NA. For additional documentation of Parsons' managerial role in Section T and the fuze program, see Tolman to Cleveland Norcross, 1 Apr. 1942, RG 227, NA; Applied Physics Laboratory, "Senior Staff Assignments, Section T, OSRD, and Associated Laboratories as of Sept. 21, 1942," RG 227, NA; and Baxter, *Scientists against Time,* 229, 230. For Tuve's view of the relationship, see Tuve interview, 34, 35.
12. Edward Moreland to Warren Weaver, 5 Aug. 1942, RG 227, NA; Goss and Porter interview, 29; Hafstad interview, 9.
13. Bush to Conant, 16 Mar. 1942, box 66, RG 227, NA; Michael Aaron Dennis, "A Change of State: The Political Cultures of Technical Practice at the MIT Instrumentation Laboratory and the Johns Hopkins University Applied Physics Laboratory, 1930–1945" (Ph.D. diss., Johns Hopkins Univ., Baltimore, Md., 1990), 313, 314.
14. Baxter, *Scientists against Time,* 230.
15. Tuve interview, 8–9.
16. Booz-Allen & Hamilton, Inc., "Review of Navy R and D Management, 1946–1973, Summary" (1976), 59–60, cited in Allard, "Development of the Radio Proximity Fuze," 359.
17. Hafstad interview, 14, 27.
18. Baldwin, *Deadly Fuze,* 80–81.
19. Mid-Pecos, *Living Water,* 186.
20. Martha Parsons Burroughs interviews, 51.
21. Loeb to Parsons, 10 Feb. 1942, Thompson papers, NLCG.
22. When Thompson joined Norden, the company placed him with its new subsidiary, Lukas-Harold Corporation, which provided management for

BuOrd's Naval Ordnance Plant, Indianapolis. As technical director of this plant, Thompson was available for future BuOrd tasks.

23. Ralph Sawyer reminiscence in McCollum, *Dahlgren*, 72.
24. Hafstad interview, 14, 83.
25. Goss and Porter interview, 2–3; Baldwin, *Deadly Fuze*, 144.
26. Baldwin, *Deadly Fuze*, 146.
27. Hafstad interview, 14.
28. Ibid.
29. S. E. Burroughs interview, 16; S. E. Burroughs to author, 3 June 1989.
30. Burke reminiscence in "Transcript of Meeting on VT Fuze," 38. Burke recalled this incident occurring on the USS *Conway*. As his memory was admittedly hazy on the incident, there is a possibility that the incident may have occurred after, rather than before, Parsons was on the *Helena*.
31. Smith interview, 5.
32. Chief of Naval Personnel to Parsons, 17 May 1951, Parsons papers, LC.
33. Commanding Officer, USS *Helena*, to Commander in Chief, U.S. Pacific Fleet, 8 Jan. 1943, NHC.
34. Baldwin, *Deadly Fuze*, 234.
35. Commanding Officer, USS *Helena*, to Commander in Chief, U.S. Pacific Fleet, 8 Jan. 1943.
36. Chew oral history, NI, 70; Smith interview, 6.
37. Commanding Officer, USS *Helena*, to Commander in Chief, U.S. Pacific Fleet, 8 Jan. 1943.
38. Goss and Porter interview, 37–38.
39. Mid-Pecos, *Living Water*, 193.
40. Enclosure A, Commanding Officer, USS *Helena*, to Commander in Chief, U.S. Pacific Fleet, 8 Jan. 1943.
41. Chief of Naval Personnel to Parsons, 17 May 1951.
42. Commanding Officer, USS *Cleveland*, to Chief, Bureau of Ordnance, 11 Mar. 1943, NHC.
43. Baldwin, *Deadly Fuze*, 56.
44. Burke reminiscence in "Transcript of Meeting on VT Fuze," 39.
45. Baldwin, *Deadly Fuze*, 280–81.
46. Ibid.
47. Personal experience of author as combat engineer, Ninety-ninth Infantry Division, at Elsenborn Ridge in Battle of the Bulge, Dec. 1944.
48. Baldwin, *Deadly Fuze*, 279–80.

Chapter 9. Into the Secret World of "Y"

Epigraph: Hirschfelder in Badash et al., eds., *Reminiscences of Los Alamos*, 82.
1. Parsons to Vice Adm. D. L. Cochrane, 5 Oct. 1950, Parsons papers, LC, confirms that Parsons had no knowledge of the atomic bomb project before 5 May 1943.

2. Goldberg, "Inventing a Climate of Opinion," 434.
3. Ibid., 430; Hewlett and Anderson, *New World,* 19–24.
4. Powers, *Heisenberg's War,* 478.
5. Goldberg, "Inventing a Climate of Opinion," 429.
6. V. Bush to the President, 9 Mar. 1942, RG 227, NA.
7. Parsons to Op06 (Blandy), "Nuclear Energy for the Navy," box 1, RG 38, NHC.
8. Groves, *Now It Can Be Told,* 20.
9. Martha Parsons Burroughs interviews, 50.
10. Youngblood interview, 10–12.
11. Martha Parsons Burroughs interviews, 145, 146.
12. Hoddeson et al., *Critical Assembly,* 59; Goodchild, *Robert Oppenheimer,* 73.
13. Conant and Groves to Oppenheimer, 25 Feb. 1943, RG 227, NA.
14. Hoddeson et al., *Critical Assembly,* 82.
15. "Los Alamos Project" organization chart, ca. Apr. 1943, lists Oppenheimer as director and E. U. Condon as associate director; work was divided into Administration plus two groups, Research and Applications. The first of the five Applications units was ordnance, headed by Richard Tolman. Oppenheimer papers, LC.
16. Groves interview, 4.
17. Groves, *Now It Can Be Told,* 159.
18. Ibid.
19. Groves interview, 4. The inference that Bush consciously maneuvered the selection of Parsons cannot be proved. But it would be consistent with the concerns he then had about Groves and the advantages of having an officer he knew and trusted at the center of Los Alamos technical operations.
20. Parsons to Cochrane, 5 Oct. 1950.
21. Ibid.
22. Fleet Adm. E. J. King to Chief of Naval Personnel, 28 Mar. 1946, Parsons papers, LC.
23. Ibid.
24. Parsons to Cochrane, 5 Oct. 1950.
25. Groves interview, 1.
26. Groves, *Now It Can Be Told,* 160.
27. Groves interview, 5.
28. In Parsons to Frank Fallowfield, "Corrections to History of Los Alamos," 14 Apr. 1947, unique doc. SAO 200109490000, box 29, file "Operation Crossroads," RG 38, NHC, Parsons says he was committed to the ordnance position before he ever visited Los Alamos. This corrects previous accounts by author.
29. Ibid.; Paul C. Fine minutes of "Meeting in Board Room at Academy on May 15, 1943, at 1:45 P.M.," RG 227, NA.
30. Parsons to Cochrane, 5 Oct. 1950.
31. Ibid.; Parsons to Fallowfield, 14 Apr. 1947.

32. Parsons to Cochrane, 5 Oct. 1950.
33. Ibid.
34. John H. Dudley, "Ranch House to Secret City," in Badash et al., eds., *Reminiscences of Los Alamos,* 3, 4.
35. Hewlett and Anderson, *New World,* 236.
36. Joseph O. Hirschfelder, "The Scientific and Technological Miracle at Los Alamos," in Badash et al., eds., *Reminiscences of Los Alamos,* 71.
37. Hewlett and Anderson, *New World,* 236.
38. Parsons and Oppenheimer to Groves, 21 May 1943, doc. 34-11, A-84-019, LANL.
39. Martha Parsons Burroughs interviews, 78.
40. Ibid., 141.
41. Parsons, typed response to questions about *Enola Gay* flight, attached to Raymond E. Leis Jr. to Parsons, 26 Jan. 1948, Parsons papers, LC.
42. Groves in his interview, 15, says a firm decision was not made at this time to have Parsons accompany the bomb on the first mission, as he did not know then if this would be necessary.
43. Martha Parsons Burroughs interviews, 85.
44. Parsons described the ComInCh assignment in his letter to Oppenheimer, 1 June 1943, doc. 35-8, A-84-019, LANL.
45. Ibid.; Parsons to Oppenheimer, 4 June 1943, doc. 34-12, A-84-019, LANL.
46. Parsons to Oppenheimer, 4 June 1943.
47. Ibid.

Chapter 10. In a Nest of Scientists

Epigraph: Bainbridge interview, 21.
1. To be less conspicuous, Parsons had the maroon Mercury painted dark green. It is uncertain whether the change occurred just before or right after he arrived at Los Alamos. Clara Parsons note to author, 21 July 1993.
2. Clara Parsons interview, index 69, 249.
3. Clara Parsons to author, 6 Mar. 1997.
4. Margaret Bowditch interview, index 3-195, 3-691.
5. Stearns interview, 5.
6. Clara Parsons interview, index 128.
7. Groves, *Now It Can Be Told,* 160, 161.
8. McKibben interview, 1, 2; Margaret Bowditch interview, index 1-586.
9. Ibid.
10. Critchfield interview, index 1-190.
11. Parsons to Edwin L. Rose, 23 June 1943, Tolman files, box 15, RG 227, NA.
12. Ibid.

13. Lawren, *General and the Bomb,* 128.
14. Groves interview, 9, 10.
15. Parsons' extraordinary powers are set forth by Joseph Hirschfelder in Badash et al., eds., *Reminiscences of Los Alamos;* and Lawren, *General and the Bomb,* 128–29.
16. Critchfield interview, index 1-1.
17. For views of Neddermeyer, see Groves interview, 8; Birch interview, 26; Critchfield interview, index 1-292; Carmondy interview, 14; Rhodes, *Making of the Atomic Bomb,* 479.
18. Hoddeson et al., *Critical Assembly,* 55.
19. Critchfield interview, index 1-190.
20. Hoddeson et al., *Critical Assembly,* 117.
21. Critchfield interview, index 1-475.
22. John Hittel to Oppenheimer, 27 Nov. 1943, doc. 35-1, A-84-019, LANL.
23. Hawkins, ed., "Manhattan District History, Project Y," vol. 1, paras. 7.5, 7.11.
24. Parsons to Oppenheimer, 20 June 1943, doc. 36-12, A-84-019, LANL.
25. Ibid.
26. Critchfield interview, index 1-292; Carmondy interview, 14.
27. Thompson to Neddermeyer, 23 June 1943, doc. 4-1, A-84-019, LANL; Rhodes, *Making of the Atomic Bomb,* 479.
28. Thompson to Neddermeyer, 23 June 1943.
29. Hoddeson et al., *Critical Assembly,* 88; Critchfield interview, index 1-291.
30. Critchfield interview, index 1-291.
31. Oppenheimer to Groves, 21 June 1943, Oppenheimer papers, LC.
32. Oppenheimer and Tolman to Conant, 14 Sept. 1943, doc. 35-8, A-84-019, LANL.
33. Ibid.; Edward L. Bowles to Maj. Gen. Styer, 23 Sept. 1943, doc. 66-4, A-84-019, LANL.
34. Ramsey, "History of Project A," 2.
35. Ibid., 3.
36. Ibid.; Parsons log, 14 Aug. 1943 entry.
37. Parsons log, 23 July 1943 entry.
38. Ibid., 24 July entry.
39. Parsons to Thompson, 4 Aug. 1943, Tolman files, RG 227, NA.
40. Oppenheimer to von Neumann, 27 July 1943, doc. 35-8, A-84-019, LANL.
41. Ibid.
42. Parsons log, 17 and 23 Aug. 1943 entries; Parsons to Purnell, 23 Aug. 1943, doc. 35-8, A-84-019, LANL.
43. Parsons to A. L. Hughes, "Personnel of Ordnance Division, Present and Prospective," 8 Sept. 1943, doc. 35-8, A-84-019, LANL.
44. Carmondy interview, 5.

Chapter 11. Thin Man versus Fat Man

Epigraph: Bradbury interview, Jan. 1967, 1.

1. Hawkins, *Project Y: The Los Alamos Story,* 484; Norris Bradbury in Badash et al., eds., *Reminiscences of Los Alamos,* 162.
2. Newkirk to Larkin, "List of all USNR Officers at This Station," 18 Aug. 1945, doc. 36-8, A-84-019, LANL.
3. Elsie McMillan in Badash et al., eds., *Reminiscences of Los Alamos,* 43; Joseph Hirschfelder in ibid., 83.
4. Elsie McMillan in ibid., 43.
5. Martha Parsons Burroughs interviews, 127; Clara Parsons interview, index 1-398.
6. Martha Parsons Burroughs interviews, 68, 69; Clara Parsons interview, index 1-165.
7. Clara Parsons interview, index 1-165.
8. Margaret Bowditch interview, index 3-87.
9. Martha Parsons Burroughs interviews, 126.
10. Ramsey interview, 8.
11. Bradbury interview, Jan. 1967, 4.
12. Parsons log, 29 Oct.–17 Nov. 1943 entries; Parsons, "Activities for Week 17–23 October," 17 Oct. 1943, doc. 37-1, A-84-019, LANL; Parsons to Oppenheimer, 29 Oct. 1943, doc. 40-1, A-84-019, LANL; W. S. Parsons to Group Leaders, 24 Dec. 1943, doc. 66-6, A-84-019, LANL.
13. Ashworth, "Parsons and the Atomic Bomb," 24.
14. Kistiakowsky to Conant, 1 Nov. 1943, RG 227, NA.
15. Ibid.
16. Kistiakowsky interview, 3–4.
17. Parsons log, 3 Nov. 1943 entry.
18. Kistiakowsky interview, 4.
19. Ibid., 6; Hoddeson et al., *Critical Assembly,* 167.
20. Kistiakowsky interview, 2; Kistiakowsky to Conant, 1 Nov. 1943.
21. Kistiakowsky interview, 16.
22. Bradbury interview, Jan. 1967, 3.
23. Martha Parsons Burroughs interviews, 50.
24. Ramsey, "History of Project A," 3.
25. Parsons log, 29 Nov. 1943 entry.
26. Ibid.
27. Ibid., 11, 18, 20 Dec. 1943, 4 Jan. 1944 entries.
28. Ibid., 22 Jan. 1944 entry.
29. Ibid., 23–25 Feb. 1944 entries.
30. Ibid., 20 Mar. 1944 entry.
31. Ramsey, "History of Project A," 4.
32. Ibid.; Parsons log, 4 Mar. 1944 entry.
33. Groves to Chief of Staff, War Department, 23 July 1943, RG 77, NA; Parsons log, 11 Feb. 1944 entry.

34. Parsons to Vice Adm. B. L. Cochrane, 5 Oct. 1950, Parsons papers, LC.

35. Parsons to Purnell, 23 July 1943, doc. 35-8, A-84-019, LANL.

36. Birch interview, 5, 2–4.

37. Parsons log, 3 Nov. 1943 entry; Capt. R. A. Larkin to Col. L. E. Seeman, 26 Aug. 1946, doc. 36-12, A-84-019, LANL.

38. Parsons log, 16 Oct. 1943 entry.

39. Ibid., 25 Aug. 1943 entry.

40. Hoddeson et al., *Critical Assembly,* 128.

41. Hewlett and Anderson, *New World,* 168.

42. Navy Department press release, "Naval Research Laboratory Pioneered in Research That Led to Development of the Atomic Bomb," 11 Aug. 1945, NHC.

Chapter 12. Common Sense and Hypotheticals

Epigraph: Oppenheimer to Groves, 10 Jan. 1945, Oppenheimer papers, LC.

1. Hawkins, *Project Y: The Los Alamos Story,* 155, 156; Hoddeson et al., *Critical Assembly,* 245–47.

2. Parsons to Bradbury, 30 Oct. 1945, doc. 40-18, A-84-019, LANL.

3. Oppenheimer to Bacher, "Organization of Gadget Division," 14 Aug. 1944; Oppenheimer to Kistiakowsky, "Organization of Explosives Division," 14 Aug. 1944, doc. 35-6, A-84-019, LANL.

4. Kistiakowsky interview, 5; Ramsey interview, 8; Bradbury interview, Jan. 1967, 3.

5. Bradbury interview, Jan. 1967, 2; Lauritsen at Weapons Exhibit dedication, Naval Weapons Center, China Lake, Calif., 4 Nov. 1964; Ramsey interview, 8; Oppenheimer to Groves, 10 Jan. 1945.

6. Ramsey, "History of Project A," 5, describes the tail as Ramsey's creation; Ashworth, "Parsons and the Atomic Bomb," 24–25, attributes the idea to Parsons.

7. Parsons log, 20–21 June 1944 entries.

8. Christman, *Sailors, Scientists, and Rockets,* 99–104.

9. Birch interview, 7; Hayward interview, 9–10.

10. Parsons quoted in Oppenheimer to Groves, 30 June 1944, doc. 34-11, A-84-019, LANL.

11. Ramsey to file, "Conferences in Oppenheimer's Office Aug. 12 and 14, 1944 on Air Forces Organization for Our Project," 18 Aug. 1944, doc. 66-6, A-84-019, LANL.

12. The fourteen aircraft discussed in Ramsey's 18 Aug. memo later became fifteen aircraft; see Ramsey, "History of Project A."

13. Tibbets, *Tibbets Story,* 152–54.

14. Ibid., 157.

15. Ibid., 158.

16. Ashworth interview, Apr. 1969, 2.

17. Ibid., 2, 3; Ramsey, "History of Project A," 7.
18. Ashworth interview, Apr. 1969, 8.
19. Groves, *Now It Can Be Told,* 271–72.
20. Ashworth interview, Apr. 1969, 3.
21. Bainbridge interview, 21.
22. Carmondy interview, 13.
23. Officer's Fitness Report, Ens. Cordelia Louise Newkirk, navy file 417381, Newkirk papers, LAM.
24. Parsons to Purnell, "Port Chicago Disaster, Preliminary Data," 24 July 1944, NHC.
25. Badash and Hewlett, "Story Too Good to Kill." The conclusions of Badash and Hewlett are fully supported by the present study. Nothing in the author's search of the Parsons records at the Los Alamos archives, National Archives, Library of Congress, and Naval Historical Center gives credence to claims regarding any nuclear explosion before Trinity.
26. Parsons, "Comments on Planning for Army and Navy Research: Difficulties in Peacetime," 8 July 1944, Thompson papers, NLCG.
27. Deak Parsons to Tommy (L. T. E. Thompson), 11 Sept. 1944, Thompson papers, NLCG.
28. Christman, *Sailors, Scientists, and Rockets,* 176–80.
29. Thompson to Deak, 18 Sept. 1944, Thompson papers, NLCG.
30. Ibid.
31. Parsons to Thompson, 21 Nov. 1944, doc. 38-4, A-84-019, LANL.
32. Fuller interview, 33, 40.
33. Oppenheimer to Parsons, 8 Aug. 1944, Oppenheimer papers, LC.
34. Parsons to Oppenheimer (handwritten), "Organization," 7 Sept. 1944, Oppenheimer papers, LC; Oppenheimer to Parsons, "Organization," 15 Sept. 1944, doc. 34-12, A-84-019, LANL.
35. Oppenheimer to Parsons, "Organization," 15 Sept. 1944.
36. Parsons to Groves via Oppenheimer, "Special Report of Ordnance and Engineering Activities of Project Y," 25 Sept. 1944, Parsons papers, LC.
37. Ibid.
38. Ibid.
39. Ibid.
40. Ibid.
41. Ibid.

Chapter 13. Homestretch

Epigraph: Ashworth oral history, NI, 2-308.
1. Parsons to Oppenheimer, "Home Stretch Measures," 19 Feb. 1945, doc. 13-3, A-84-019, LANL; Hoddeson et al., *Critical Assembly,* 300.
2. Parsons to Oppenheimer, "Home Stretch Measures," 19 Feb. 1945. Parsons' candidates for the "ruthless band" included Lauritsen, Kistiakowsky, Bainbridge, Brode, Warner, Samuel Allison, Bacher, Joseph Kennedy, Oppenheimer, and himself.

3. Hoddeson et al., *Critical Assembly,* 312.
4. Ibid., 248; Parsons to Vice Adm. B. L. Cochrane, 5 Oct. 1950, Parsons papers, LC.
5. Ramsey, "History of Project A," 8. Many reassignments occurred as the project progressed.
6. Parsons to Groves, 26 Dec. 1944, memos to Parsons, RG 77, NA.
7. Ramsey interview, 12–14; Hoddeson et al., *Critical Assembly,* 388.
8. Parsons to Groves, "Special Operational Research Group for Gadget Delivery," 19 Mar. 1945, doc. 34-11, A-84-019, LANL.
9. Ibid.
10. Ibid.
11. Hoddeson et al., *Critical Assembly,* 388.
12. Goldberg videohistory, session 17 (with Norman Ramsey), 8–9; Hoddeson et al., *Critical Assembly,* 260–61; Ashworth interview, Sept. 1992, index 4-71.
13. Ashworth interview, Apr. 1969, 9.
14. Parsons to Ashworth, transcribed telephone conversation, 24 May 1945, doc. 41-24, A-84-019, LANL.
15. Groves interview, 11.
16. Parsons memorandum for file, "Negotiations in San Francisco Area," 9 May 1945, doc. 66-6, A-84-019, LANL.
17. Groves interview, 12.
18. "History of 509th Composite Group," 2.
19. Ibid., attachment.
20. Parsons to Cochrane, 5 Oct. 1950.
21. Ibid.
22. Lamont, *Day of Trinity,* 192.
23. Ibid., 198–99; Alvarez interview, 5.
24. Alvarez, *Alvarez: Adventures of a Physicist,* 141.
25. L. W. Alvarez, "An Eye-Witness Account of the Trinity Shot on Monday Morning at 5:30 AM—16 July 1945," one-page signed account with sketch, RG 77, NA.
26. Ibid.
27. Ibid.
28. Lamont, *Day of Trinity,* 242.
29. Ibid.
30. Ibid., 167, 243.

Chapter 14. Tinian

Epigraph: Groves to Brig. Gen. Thomas Farrell, quoted in Knebel and Bailey, *No High Ground,* 145.
1. Hewlett and Anderson, *New World,* 2.
2. Fuller interview, 31.
3. Harry Parsons Jr. interview, Sept. 1992, 3–4.
4. Parsons, "Summer 1939–Summer 1949."

5. Parsons to Chairman, Military Liaison Committee, 19 Apr. 1948, enclosure A, file 600.12, box 77, MED Dec files, NA; manuscript "History of Atomic Bomb—Design, Assembly, Delivery," file A23, box 6, RG 38, NHC.

6. "History of 509th Composite Group," 58–62.

7. Ramsey interview, 8–9.

8. Groves, *Now It Can Be Told,* 282, gives the size of the Alberta overseas group as thirty-seven; Ramsey, "History of Project A," 11, lists fifty-one by name.

9. Russ, *Project Alberta,* 40.

10. Knebel and Bailey, *No High Ground,* 145.

11. Groves, *Now It Can Be Told,* 311.

12. Ashworth interview, Apr. 1969, 12.

13. Groves, *Now It Can Be Told,* 310–11; Norstad to Commanding General, XXI Bomber Command, 29 May 1945, microfilm M1109, RG 77, "Correspondence MED, 1942–1946," NA.

14. Groves to Norstad, 6 Mar. 1945, microfilm M1108, RG 77, Harrison-Bundy files, 1942–46, reel 1, file 8, "Manhattan District Project," NA.

15. Jones, *Manhattan: The Army and the Atomic Bomb,* 527.

16. Parsons identifies later distortions in Parsons to Lt. Col. Walter Ott, 14 Dec. 1951, Parsons papers, LC.

17. Ramsey, "History of Project A," 11; Hawkins, ed., "Manhattan District History, Project Y," vol. 1, 252, states that the Los Alamos group was part of the First Technical Service Detachment, an army administrative organization for security, housing, and various other services.

18. The "master log" is based largely on Ramsey, "History of Project A," which includes Captain Parsons' flight log for the Hiroshima mission and Commander Ashworth's log for the Nagasaki mission. Other sources include Marx, *Seven Hours to Zero,* and Thomas and Witts, *Enola Gay.*

19. Parsons to Ott, 14 Dec. 1951.

20. Tibbets, *Tibbets Story,* 186–88.

21. Groves, *Now It Can Be Told,* 283–84.

22. Maj. Gen. Lauris Norstad, Chief of Staff, Twentieth Air Force, to Maj. Gen. Curtis LeMay, Commanding General, Twenty-first Bomber Command, June 1945, quoted in Farrell to Groves, "Status of Project Officer in Combat Airplane—Atomic Bomb Operations," 22 Oct. 1945, box 5, RG 38, NHC.

23. Ibid.

24. Parsons, "Summer 1939–Summer 1949."

25. Parsons to Col. W. C. Lindley, USAF, 20 Aug. 1951, Parsons papers, LC.

26. Ibid.

27. Ibid.

28. Laurence, *Dawn over Zero,* 205.

29. Ibid., 205–6.

30. Parsons to Ott, 14 Dec. 1951.

31. Accounts vary as to the time Little Boy was taken to the *Enola Gay* and loaded. Thomas and Witts, *Enola Gay,* 232, show the events starting at 1530.

32. Some accounts have Parsons briefing the crews on the bomb at this pre-flight meeting. This could not be the case, in view of Parsons' documented statement that he wanted the crews informed ahead of time so that they could think things through before takeoff.

33. Russ, *Project Alberta,* 62.

34. Thomas and Witts, *Enola Gay,* 241.

35. Parsons, typed response to questions about *Enola Gay* flight, attached to Raymond E. Leis Jr. to Parsons, 26 Jan. 1948, answer 25, Parsons papers, LC.

36. Ibid., answer 26.

37. Ibid., answer 36.

38. Parsons, "Summer 1939–Summer 1949."

Chapter 15. Hiroshima

Epigraph: Ramsey interview, 11.

1. Thomas and Witts, *Enola Gay,* 245.

2. "Check list for loading charge with special breech plug," attachment to Jeppson interview.

3. Parsons to Col. Walter Ott, 14 Dec. 1951, Parsons papers, LC.

4. Parsons, typed response to questions about *Enola Gay* flight, attached to Raymond E. Leis Jr. to Parsons, 26 Jan. 1948, answer 38, Parsons papers, LC.

5. Groves, *Now It Can Be Told,* 310.

6. Parsons response to Leis, 26 Jan. 1948, answer 36.

7. Parsons to Chairman, Military Liaison Committee, 19 Apr. 1948, enclosure A, file 600.12, box 77, MED Dec files, NA.

8. Marx, *Seven Hours to Zero,* 118.

9. Ibid.

10. Parsons response to Leis, 26 Jan. 1948, answer 38.

11. Tuve interview, 39–40.

12. Parsons to Groves, "Special Report of Ordnance and Engineering Activities of Project Y," 25 Sept. 1944, Parsons papers, LC.

13. Groves, *Now It Can Be Told,* 324.

14. Naval History Division, *Dictionary of Naval Ships,* second *Helena* (CL-50).

15. Knebel and Bailey, *No High Ground,* 149.

16. Parsons response to Leis, 26 Jan. 1948, answer 39.

17. Ibid.

18. Marx, *Seven Hours to Zero,* 173, 191.

19. Tibbets yelled, "It's flak," according to his own June 1946 account in "How to Drop an Atomic Bomb," 136, and in a United Press interview

reported in the *Chicago Daily News,* 8 Aug. 1945. Knebel and Bailey, *No High Ground,* 204, quote Tibbets as yelling "It's flak." Three decades later in his biography, *Tibbets Story,* 226, Tibbets says it was Parsons who shouted, "It's flak."

20. Knebel and Bailey, *No High Ground,* 204.
21. Parsons, "Summer 1939–Summer 1949"; "Airman Tells of Havoc: Town Vanishes in Smoke Cloud," *Chicago Daily News,* 12 Aug. 1945.
22. Knebel and Bailey, *No High Ground,* 206.
23. Laurence, *Dawn over Zero,* 221.
24. Marx, *Seven Hours to Zero,* 172.
25. Parsons, "Summer 1939–Summer 1949."
26. Knebel and Bailey, *No High Ground,* 207.
27. Jeppson interview, 9.
28. Parsons response to Leis, 26 Jan. 1948, answer 41.
29. Marx, *Seven Hours to Zero,* 193.
30. Knebel and Bailey, *No High Ground,* 212.
31. Groves interview, 33; Hayward interview, 14–15.
32. Like most servicemen in the Pacific, Parsons sometimes used derogatory terms for the enemy.
33. Bill (W. S. Parsons) to Dad (Harry Parsons Sr.), 7 Aug. 1945, Harry Parsons Jr. papers.

Chapter 16. Nagasaki and Peace

Epigraph: Farrell quoted in Marx, *Seven Hours to Zero,* 77.
1. Martha Parsons Burroughs interviews, 73–74.
2. *Santa Fe New Mexican,* 6 Aug. 1945.
3. *New York Times,* 7 Aug. 1945.
4. Ibid., 8 Aug. 1945.
5. Martha Parsons Burroughs interviews, 75–76.
6. *New York Times,* 9 Aug. 1945.
7. Stearns interview, 12.
8. Teletype Washington Liaison Office (Groves) to Commanding Officer, Clear Creek, N.Mex. (Los Alamos) (dateline not clear; probably 5 Aug. Washington time), NHC.
9. *New York Times,* 7 Aug. 1945.
10. Ramsey, "History of Project A," 15.
11. William Laurence press release, "Navy Captain Designed Bomb," 8 Aug. 1945, to *New York Times,* as reprinted in New York Times, *Hiroshima Plus Twenty,* 157–58.
12. United Press press release, "Airman Tells of Havoc," *Chicago Daily News,* 8 Aug. 1945.
13. Translation printed in Knebel and Bailey, *No High Ground,* 222.
14. Ashworth oral history draft, "Postwar Washington," NI, 129.
15. Ramsey, "History of Project A," 15.

16. Groves interview, 32, 33.

17. Alvarez to Groves, 5 May 1965, criticizes the Nagasaki flight; Ashworth to Dr. Frank H. Shelton, 20 May 1992, responds to the criticism. Both documents in Ashworth personal papers.

18. Goldberg videohistory, combined transcript sessions 17–18, 77; Sweeney, *War's End*, 199.

19. Ashworth interview, Apr. 1969, 30–31; Sweeney, *War's End*, 217.

20. Ashworth interview, Apr. 1969, 31.

21. Sweeney, *War's End*, 225; Ashworth speech, B-29 display dedication, National Atomic Museum.

22. Sweeney, *War's End*, 229.

23. Russ, *Project Alberta*, 64.

24. Ibid., 73–75.

25. Ibid.

26. Ibid., 76.

27. Deak to Tommy (L. T. E. Thompson), V-mail, 2 Sept. 1945, Thompson papers, NLCG.

28. Distinguished Service Medal citation printed in Navy Department press and radio release, 4 Sept. 1945, NHC.

Chapter 17. Nuclear Dawn

Epigraph: S. E. Burroughs interview, 17.

1. Parsons to Bradbury, "Declassification Implosion," 30 Oct. 1945, doc. 40-18, A-84-019, LANL.

2. Oppenheimer to Smyth, 14 Apr. 1945, Groves files, MED, NA; Smyth, *Atomic Energy for Military Purposes*, 222.

3. Parsons to Ordnance Group Leaders, 22 Nov. 1943, doc. 40-4, A-84-019, LANL.

4. Furman, *Sandia National Laboratories*, 125; Hawkins, ed., "Manhattan District History, Project Y," vol. 2, 13.

5. Parsons study referenced in von Neumann to Parsons, 27 Sept. 1945, RG 227, NA, and Parsons to Bradbury, "Possible Tests of Atomic Bombs against Naval Vessels," 26 Oct. 1945, doc. 36-7, A-84-019, LANL.

6. Parsons, "Comments on Planning for Army and Navy Research: Difficulties in Peacetime," 8 July 1944, Thompson papers, NLCG.

7. Ibid.

8. Parsons to Purnell, transcribed telephone conversation, 17 Oct. 1945, doc. 43-14, A-84-019, LANL.

9. Ibid.

10. Parsons to Bradbury, "Reines Visit to Hiroshima and Nagasaki," 22 Oct. 1945, doc. 39-2, A-84-019, LANL.

11. Parsons to Bradbury, "Possible Tests of Atomic Bombs against Naval Vessels," 26 Oct. 1945, doc. 36-7, A-84-019, LANL.

12. Ibid.

13. Rivero interview, Oct. 1994, index 539, 568.
14. CNO to all Navy Departments, 13 Nov. 1945, RG 38, NHC.
15. Photograph of "diploma," Clara Parsons papers.
16. Ashworth interview, Sept. 1992; Ashworth oral history, NI, 2-376.
17. Parsons to Blandy, "Naval Research and Development as Affected by Personality," 9 Mar. 1946, box 24, RG 38, NHC.
18. Carmondy interview, 37.
19. Ashworth interview, Sept. 1992, index 144.
20. Ibid.
21. Blandy to CNO, "Functions of Op06 and ORI Regarding Atomic Energy, Guided Missiles, and Related Devices," 10 Jan. 1946, box 6, RG 38, NHC.
22. Ashworth interview, Sept. 1992, index 200; Rivero interview, Oct. 1994, index 646.
23. Polmar and Allen in *Rickover*, 661–63, refute Rickover's claims of navy opposition to nuclear-powered naval vessels.
24. Gunn to Director, NRL, "Submarine Submerged Propulsion—Uranium Power Source," 1 June 1939, attachment to Gunn interview.
25. Op60 (Parsons) to Op06 (Blandy), "Nuclear Energy for the Navy," 28 Mar. 1946, box 1, A23-14, RG 38, NHC.
26. Mills, "Probable Advantages of the Use of a Substitute of Fuel Oil as a Power Source."
27. Op60 to Op06, 28 Mar. 1946.
28. Ibid.
29. Secretary of Navy to Secretary of War, 14 Mar. 1946, and Secretary of War to Secretary of Navy, undated reply, RG 38, NHC.
30. Op60 to Op61, "Utilization of Nuclear Energy for Ship Propulsion," 26 Mar. 1946, and Blandy's attached 1 Apr. note of approval, box 1, A23-14, RG 38, NHC.
31. Parsons to Blandy, 9 Mar. 1946.
32. Ibid.
33. Bowen to Rear Adm. DeWitt Ramsey, "Functions of Op06 and ORI regarding Atomic Energy, Guided Missiles, and Related Devices," 23 Jan. 1946, RG 38, NHC.
34. Parsons to Capts. Teller and Klakring, "Guided Missile Coordination," 24 Jan. 1946; Blandy to CNO, 10 Jan. 1946, box 6, RG 38, NHC.
35. Bowen to DeWitt Ramsey, 23 Jan. 1946.
36. Ibid.; Op60 to Op61, 26 Mar. 1946.
37. Op60 to Op61, 26 Mar. 1946.
38. Rivero interview, Oct. 1994, index 602.
39. Critch to Dad (Harry Parsons Sr.), 10 Jan. 1946, Harry Parsons Jr. papers; Carmondy interview, 39. Parsons promoted to rear admiral, temporary service, Jan. 1946 and again Nov. 1947; assigned permanent rank rear admiral (register 5) on 1 July 1948.
40. Clara Parsons interview, index 2-585.

41. Withington oral history, NI.
42. Parsons to Teller and Klakring, 24 Jan. 1946.
43. Op60 to Op06, "AAF Action Regarding Guided Missiles," 19 Mar. 1946, RG 38, NHC.

Chapter 18. Operation Crossroads

Epigraph: Rivero interview, May 1967, 12, 22.
1. Weisgall, *Operation Crossroads*, 31.
2. *New York Times*, 25 Jan. 1946, 1.
3. Parsons to Bradbury, 26 Oct. 1945, quoted in Weisgall, *Operation Crossroads*, 134.
4. Parsons speech, "Results of Operation Crossroads," 27 Dec. 1946; Sawyer speech, "Technical Side of Crossroads," 16 Dec. 1946.
5. Parsons speech, "Results of Operation Crossroads," 27 Dec. 1946.
6. Youngblood interview, 25.
7. Rivero interview, Oct. 1994, index 606.
8. Sawyer interview, 29; Shurcliff, *Bombs at Bikini*, 36.
9. Sawyer interview, 26, 29.
10. Ibid., 27.
11. Weisgall, *Operation Crossroads*, 174.
12. Bill (W. S. Parsons) to Dad (Harry Parsons Sr.), 28 June 1946, Harry Parsons Jr. papers.
13. Shurcliff, *Bombs at Bikini*, 103.
14. Ibid., 107–8.
15. Weisgall, *Operation Crossroads*, 187.
16. *New York Times*, 1 July 1946, 3.
17. Weisgall, *Operation Crossroads*, 188.
18. Ibid., 189.
19. For a navy perspective of the criteria used in selecting the bombing crew, see Riley oral history, NI.
20. Shurcliff, *Bombs at Bikini*, 125–35.
21. Ibid., 140–41.
22. Ashworth, "Back to Washington" chapter, life history, 5.
23. Weisgall, *Operation Crossroads*, 196.
24. Sawyer interview, 37–38.
25. Parsons speech, "Results of Operation Crossroads," 27 Dec. 1946.
26. Bradbury to "Marshall, Roger, et al.," 20 May 1946, doc. 22-15, A-84-019, LANL.
27. Parsons to Blandy, "Underwater Tests of Atomic Bombs against Naval Vessels," 3 Dec. 1945, microfilm M1109, RG 77, file 8, NA.
28. Sawyer interview, 38.
29. Shurcliff, *Bombs at Bikini*, 150.
30. Weisgall, *Operation Crossroads*, 221.

31. Shurcliff, *Bombs at Bikini,* 153, 159.

32. Parsons speech, "Results of Operation Crossroads," 27 Dec. 1946.

33. Weisgall, *Operation Crossroads,* 240.

34. Stafford Warren to Viola Warren, 11 Aug. 1946, quoted in Weisgall, *Operation Crossroads,* 242.

35. Ibid.

36. Rivero oral history, NI, 2-171.

37. Weisgall, *Operation Crossroads,* 259.

38. Bradbury to Groves, undated (ca. Aug. 1946), MED Dec files, NA; Rosenberg, "U.S. Nuclear Stockpile," 26.

39. Root interview, index 4-97.

40. Parsons speech, "Atomic Energy," 5 June 1947.

41. Parsons speech before Science Talent Institute, 3 Mar. 1947.

42. Parsons speech before Reader's Digest Forum, 20 Mar. 1947.

Chapter 19. Atomic Admiral

Epigraph: Schoeffel speech, Parsons Auditorium dedication.

1. Bill (W. S. Parsons) to Dad (Harry Parsons Sr.), 7 Sept. 1947, Harry Parsons Jr. papers.

2. Ibid.

3. Jerauld Wright to Blandy, 2 Aug. 1946, shows Blandy alerted to Radford's efforts to absorb the Special Weapons Office; file A23, box 6, unique doc. SAC 20010947000, RG 38, NHC.

4. Parsons to Loeb, 20 Nov. 1946, Parsons papers, LC.

5. Waldo Drake, "Parsons, the Atomic Admiral," *Los Angeles Times,* 24 July 1946.

6. Hooper interview, 10–14.

7. Rivero oral history, NI, 2-187.

8. Ibid., 2-185.

9. Ashworth interview, Sept. 1992, index 200; Rivero interview, Oct. 1994, index 646.

10. Ashworth oral history draft, "Postwar Washington," NI, 180; Rivero interview, Oct. 1994, index 1-646.

11. Op60 (Parsons) to Op06 (Blandy), "Nuclear Energy for the Navy," 28 Mar. 1946, A23-14, box 1, RG 38, NHC.

12. Rivero oral history, NI, 2-182.

13. Parsons to Cal Fitzhugh, "Status NEPA," 21 Jan. 1948, box 29, RG 38, NHC.

14. Ashworth interview, Sept. 1992, index 4-89.

15. Rosenberg, "U.S. Nuclear Stockpile," 26.

16. Robinson, "Salt Wells," 3, 16, 33.

17. For evolution of the Los Alamos Ordnance Division into Sandia Base, see Furman, *Sandia National Laboratories.*

18. Parsons to Chairman, MLC, "Engineering and Development of Atomic

Weapons," 27 Jan. 1947, file MLC, box 5, RG 38; Hewlett and Duncan, *Atomic Shield,* 175; Furman, *Sandia National Laboratories,* 357.

19. Parsons to Chairman, General Board, 23 Apr. 1948, A23-9, box 18, unique doc. SAC 2001099480000, RG 38, NHC.
20. Ashworth, "Back to Washington" chapter, life history, 10–13.
21. Hewlett and Duncan, *Atomic Shield,* 151.
22. Hayward interview, 25; Hooper interview, 12.
23. Parsons, "Summer 1939–Summer 1949."
24. Hewlett and Duncan, *Atomic Shield,* 163.
25. Thompson to author, 7 Nov. 1965; Parsons to files, 1 Apr. 1947, WSP file, box 12, RG 38, NHC.
26. Rivero to Op60 (Parsons), 24 Sept. 1946, box 3, RG 38, NHC.
27. Parsons to files, 1 Apr. 1947.
28. Parsons to Vice Adm. A. D. Strubble, "Sea Duty," 22 Dec. 1948, WSP file, box 12, RG 38, NHC.
29. Parsons to Bill (W. J. Horvath), 29 Dec. 1951, Parsons papers, LC.
30. Root interview, index 4-276; Margaret Bowditch interview, index 3-284.
31. Carroll Wilson diary, 19 Sept. 1949, AEC, quoted in Hewlett and Duncan, *Atomic Shield,* 366.
32. Bill (W. S. Parsons) to Harry Parsons Sr., ca. Sept. 1949 (first page with date missing), Harry Parsons Jr. papers.
33. Clara Parsons interview, index 428; Deak to Oppy, 26 Sept. 1950, Parsons papers, LC.
34. Ramsey to Parsons, 1 Dec. 1950, Parsons papers, LC.
35. Parsons to Ramsey, 11 Dec. 1950, Parsons papers, LC.
36. Parsons to Chairman, General Board, 23 Apr. 1948.
37. Parsons to Ramsey, 11 Dec. 1950.
38. "1951, Journal of All Dates, Visitations, Cruiser Division Six," 2 Feb. 1951 entry, Parsons papers, LC.
39. Cruiser Division Six, serial for Aug.–Dec. 1951, 22–25 Sept. and 5 Oct. 1951 entries, NHC.
40. Bill (W. S. Parsons) to Dad (Harry Parsons Sr.), 4 Dec. 1951, Harry Parsons Jr. papers.
41. Cruiser Division Six, serial for Aug.–Dec. 1951, 8 Dec. 1951 entry; Bill (W. S. Parsons) to Dad (Harry Parsons Sr.), 2 Mar. 1952, Harry Parsons Jr. papers.
42. Parsons to Rear Adm. R. F. Hickey, 13 July 1951, Parsons papers, LC.
43. Parsons to Col. W. C. Lindley, USAF, 20 Aug. 1951, Parsons papers, LC.
44. Parsons to Farrell, 20 Aug. 1951, Parsons papers, LC.
45. Parsons to Col. Walter Ott, USAF, 26 Dec. 1951, Parsons papers, LC.
46. Bill (W. S. Parsons) to Critch, 14 Feb. 1952, Harry Parsons Jr. papers.
47. Ibid.
48. Schoeffel interview, 6.
49. Parsons to Schoeffel, 10 Feb. 1952, Parsons papers, LC.
50. McCollum, *Dahlgren,* 99; Smaldone, *History of the White Oak Laboratory,* 36.

51. Gerard-Gough and Christman, *Grand Experiment,* 232; Thompson interview, May 1966, 50.
52. Thompson interview, May 1966, 50–51; Entwistle interview, 16, 32.
53. Sawyer to Thompson, 22 Dec. 1952, attachment to Sawyer interview.
54. Martha Parsons Burroughs interviews, 82, 90; Margaret Bowditch interview, index 1-273.
55. Bill to Critch, 14 Feb. 1952.
56. Mid-Pecos, *Living Water,* 195.
57. Ibid.
58. Deak to Oppy, 25 Sept. 1953, Parsons papers, LC.
59. Stern, *Oppenheimer Case,* 222.
60. Martha Parsons Burroughs interviews, 149–50.
61. Ibid., 13–14.
62. Ibid., 15.

Epilogue

Epigraph: Bush speech, Parsons Auditorium dedication.
1. Peggy (Parsons) to Granddaddy Parsons, Monday (7 Dec. 1953), Harry Parsons Jr. papers.
2. Schoeffel oral history, NI, 6-351.
3. Clara Parsons interview, index 546.
4. Ashworth interview, Apr. 1969, 43.
5. Martha Parsons Burroughs interviews, 13. When interviewed, Lewis Strauss, chairman of the Atomic Energy Commission at the time of the Oppenheimer inquiry, voiced strong doubts that Deak Parsons could have heard the day before he died about the pending Oppenheimer inquiry. See Strauss interview, 8–12. However, Commissioner H. D. Smyth cites his notes of the time to refute Strauss' recollection of events. According to Smyth's notes, an order was widely distributed by the navy the morning of 4 Dec. establishing a "blank wall" between government-classified information and Oppenheimer. Smyth to author, 15 Aug. 1967, attachment to Strauss interview.
6. Mid-Pecos, *Living Water,* 196.
7. Peregrine White editorial, *Durham Morning Herald,* 7 Dec. 1953.
8. Bush and Schoeffel speeches, Parsons Auditorium dedication.
9. Mid-Pecos, *Living Water,* 196.
10. Comdr. Robert Morris, Prospective Commanding Officer, USS *Parsons,* to Mr. R. P. Burroughs, 28 Aug. 1967, Clara Parsons files; "Remodeled Destroyer Returns," *San Diego Union,* 7 Mar. 1968.
11. Nuclear Weapons Training Group, Atlantic, "Facility Dedication Ceremony," 30 May 1979, Clara Parsons files.
12. Mid-Pecos, *Living Water,* 195–96; Parsons speech before Undersea Warfare Symposium, 6 Apr. 1948.
13. Parsons speech, "Atomic Energy," 5 June 1947.

Bibliography

Unpublished Sources

Interviews by Author

Agnew, Harold. Jan. 1967. NHC.

Alvarez, Luis W. Mar. 1967. NHC.

Ashworth, Frederick L. 9–10 Apr. 1969. NHC. *See also* Henderson, J. E., and F. L. Ashworth.

———. 8 Sept. 1992, 28 Oct. 1993. Author's collection.

Bainbridge, Kenneth. 3 Apr. 1966. NHC.

Birch, A. Francis. 17 Feb. 1971. NHC.

Bowditch, Margaret (Parsons). May 1992. Author's collection.

Bradbury, Norris E. 23 Jan. 1967. NHC.

———. Sept. 1992. Author's collection.

Bramble, Charles C. May 1969. NHC.

Breslow, Arthur. Oct. 1966. NHC.

Burroughs, Martha (Parsons). 29–30 Apr. 1966. NHC.

Burroughs, Sherman E., Jr. Apr. 1966. NHC.

Carmondy, Hazel (Greenbacker). Jan. 1967. NHC.

Critchfield, Charles L. Sept. 1992. Author's collection.

Entwistle, F. I. Mar. 1967. NHC.

Fuller, Clarissa (Parsons). Jan. 1967. NHC.

Goss, Wilbur, and Henry Porter. 4 May 1967. NHC.

Granum, Alfred M. Jan. 1967. NHC.

Groves, Leslie R. May 1967. NHC.

Gunn, Ross. Apr. 1966. NHC.

Hafstad, Lawrence R. Feb. 1971. NHC.

Hayward, John Tucker. Aug. 1966. NHC.

Henderson, J. E., and F. L. Ashworth. Apr. 1969. NHC.

Henderson, Robert W. 23 Oct. 1993. Author's collection.

Hooper, Edwin B. Feb. 1971. NHC.

Hussey, George F., and L. T. E. Thompson. July 1966. NHC.

Jeppson, Morris R. Mar. 1967. NHC.

Kistiakowsky, George. 3 May 1966. NHC.

Lauritsen, Charles C. 4 Nov. 1964. NHC.

Loeb, Leonard B. Mar. 1967. NHC.

McKibben, Dorothy. Jan. 1967. NHC.

McMillan, Edwin M. Mar. 1967. NHC.

Parsons, Clara D. June 1992. Author's collection.

Parsons, Harry R., Jr. Feb. 1967. NHC.

———. Sept. 1992. Author's collection.

Porter, Henry. *See* Goss, Wilbur, and Henry Porter.

Ramsey, Norman. 3 May 1966. NHC.

Rivero, Horacio. May 1967. NHC.

———. Oct. 1994. Author's collection.

Root, Charles. May 1992. Author's collection.

Sawyer, Ralph A. May 1967. NHC.

Schoeffel, Malcolm F. 21 Apr. 1966. NHC.

Schreiber, Raemer E. Sept. 1992. Author's collection.

Schuyler, Garret Lansing. May 1969. NHC.

Smith, Levering. May 1967. NHC.

Stearns, Mrs. J. V. Jan. 1967. NHC.

Strauss, Lewis L. May 1967. NHC.

Thompson, L. T. E. Nov. 1965, May 1966, Nov. 1966. NHC. *See also* Hussey, George, and L. T. E. Thompson.

Tuve, Merle. May 1967. NHC.

Youngblood, Curtis. May 1967. NHC.

Oral History Transcripts

Ashworth, Vice Adm. Frederick L. Conducted by Paul Stillwell, U.S. Naval Institute, 1990.

———. Draft, "Postwar Washington." U.S. Naval Institute, 1990.

Chew, Vice Adm. John L. Conducted by John T. Mason Jr., U.S. Naval Institute, 1972.

Keith, Vice Adm. R. T. S. Conducted by Paul Stillwell, U.S. Naval Institute, 1987.

Riley, Vice Adm. H. D. Conducted by John T. Mason Jr., U.S. Naval Institute, 1971.

Rivero, Adm. Horacio. Conducted by John T. Mason Jr., U.S. Naval Institute, 1978.

Schoeffel, Rear Adm. Malcolm. Conducted by John T. Mason Jr., U.S. Naval Institute, 1979.

Withington, Rear Adm. Frederic. Conducted by John T. Mason Jr., U.S. Naval Institute, 1971

Video Interviews

Goldberg, Stanley, interviewer. Smithsonian Videohistory Program, Manhattan Project. Session 17 of 5–6 June 1990 and session 18 of 6 June 1990.

Speeches by Rear Adm. W. S. Parsons

(Crossroads and consequences). Meeting of Visiting Nurse Service Campaign, New York, 9 Oct. 1946. NHC.

"Results of Operation Crossroads." American Association for the Advancement of Science, Boston, Mass., 27 Dec. 1946. NHC.

(Atomic defense). Annual Dinner Meeting, Philadelphia Patent Law Association, Union League Club, Philadelphia, Pa. 23 Jan. 1947. NHC.

(Control of atomic energy). Seventh Session of the Science Talent Institute, Washington, D.C., 3 Mar. 1947. NHC.

(Effective research and atomic energy). Reader's Digest Forum, Pleasantville, N.Y., 20 Mar. 1947. NHC.

(Call for reason). American Whig-Cliosophic Society, Princeton University, Princeton, N.J., 1 Apr. 1947. NHC.

"Atomic Energy." Annual Convention of the Edison Electric Institute, Atlantic City, N.J., 5 June 1947. NHC.

"Atomic Energy—A Short Range Prediction." Society of the War of 1812 in Maryland, Baltimore, Md., 12 Sept. 1947. NHC.

(Atomic energy, New Mexico, and the future). Navy Day Address, Hilton Hotel, Albuquerque, N.Mex., 27 Oct. 1947. NHC.

(Military applications of atomic energy). Undersea Warfare Symposium, Washington, D.C., 6 Apr. 1948. (Remarks written at Eniwetok for delivery by proxy.) NHC.

(Naval power in the atomic age). Navy Day Address, El Cortez Hotel, San Diego, Calif., 27 Oct. 1948. NHC.

"Problems of Passive Defense." Eighty-first Annual Convention of American Institute of Architects, Houston, Tex., 15 Mar. 1949. NHC.

"Problems and Prospects of Atomic Energy." Navy Symposium, Naval Air Technical Training Center, Jacksonville, Fla., 26 May 1949. NHC.

(Technical interests of the modern navy). American Physical Society, Naval Ordnance Laboratory, White Oak, Md., 30 June 1949. NHC.

Speeches by Others

Ashworth, Frederick L. Dedication of B-29 aircraft display at National Atomic Museum, Albuquerque, N.Mex., 9 Oct. 1993. Ashworth papers.

Bush, Vannevar. Dedication of William S. Parsons Auditorium, Applied Physics Laboratory, Johns Hopkins University, 16 Oct. 1954. Thompson papers, NLCG.

Sawyer, Ralph. "Technical Side of Crossroads." Speech draft sent to Parsons for review, 16 Dec. 1946. Parsons papers, LC.

Schoeffel, Rear Adm. M. F. Dedication of William S. Parsons Auditorium, Applied Physics Laboratory, Johns Hopkins University, 16 Oct. 1954. Thompson papers, NLCG.

Thompson, L. T. E. "Robert Goddard and the Weapons Program." Fifth Joint Army-Navy Solid Propellant Conference, Naval Ordnance Test Station, China Lake, Calif., 23 Mar. 1949.

————. "After Forty Years—A Notable Occasion." (Thompson's memories of early life at Naval Proving Ground, Dahlgren.) Delivered at Dahlgren during retirement party for experimental physicist Nils Riffolt, 27 Jan. 1956. Thompson papers, NLCG.

Manuscripts and Informal Reports

Ashworth, Frederick L. "Back to Washington" chapter of life history, work in progress, 15 pp.

Hawkins, David, ed. "Manhattan District History, Project Y, the Los Alamos Project." Los Alamos Scientific Laboratory of the University of California, Los Alamos, N.Mex. Vol. 1, 375 pp., Aug. 1946; vol. 2, 237 pp., 15 Oct. 1947.

"History of 509th Composite Group, 313th Bombardment Wing, Twentieth Air Force, Activation to 15 Aug. 1945." Manuscript history prepared at Tinian, 31 Aug. 1945. 82 pp. LANL.

[Los Alamos Scientific Laboratory]. Manuscript draft, "Chapter One, History of the Atomic Bomb—Design, Assembly, and Delivery." Nov. 1945. File A23, box 6, unique doc. SAO 200.0945000, RG 38, NHC.

Mills, E. W. "Probable Advantages of the Use of a Substitute of Fuel Oil as a Power Source in Naval Vessels, from a Standpoint of Logistics." 30 May 1945. NHC.

Parsons, William S. "Summer 1939–Summer 1949, Summary of Activities for Family." Parsons papers, LC.

Ramsey, Norman F. "History of Project A." Manuscript draft transmitted 27 Sept. 1945 from Ramsey to Brig. Gen. T. F. Farrell. 19 pp. Doc. 29-6, LANL.

Robinson, Kenneth H. "Salt Wells Pilot Plant Story, 1945–1954." Naval Weapons Center, China Lake, Calif., July 1974. 72 pp.

"Transcript of Meeting on VT (Proximity) Fuze." Transcript of Annual Conference of the Radio Club of America, Inc., New York, 17 Nov. 1978. 100 pp. NHC.

Logs

Log book USS *Aylwin*—DD First Class, June 1936–Mar. 1938. Ships' logs, NA.

Log book USS *Idaho*—First Rate, Jan.–Dec. 1922. Ships' logs, NA.

Log book USS *Texas*—First Line, May 1930–May 1933. Ships' logs, NA.

Parsons, W. S. "Log of Actions Taken." Project Y, Los Alamos. 15 July 1943–4 Jan. 1944, doc. 37-1, LANL; 1 Jan. 1944–18 July 1944, doc. 37-3, LANL.

Published Sources

Books

Allison, David Kite. *New Eye for the Navy: The Origin of Radar at the Naval Research Laboratory.* Washington, D.C.: Naval Research Laboratory, 1981.

Alvarez, Luis W. *Alvarez: Adventures of a Physicist.* New York: Basic Books, 1987.

Badash, Lawrence; Joseph Hirschfelder; and Herbert Broida, eds. *Reminiscences of Los Alamos, 1943–1945.* Boston: D. Reidel Publishing Co., 1980.

Baldwin, Ralph B. *The Deadly Fuze: The Secret Weapon of World War II.* San Rafael, Calif.: Presidio, 1980.

Barlow, Jeffrey G. *Revolt of the Admirals: The Fight for Naval Aviation, 1945–1950.* Washington, D.C.: Naval Historical Center, 1994.

Baxter, James Phinney, 3d. *Scientists against Time.* Cambridge: M.I.T. Press, 1948.

Bowen, Harold G. *Ships, Machinery, and Mossbacks.* Princeton: Princeton Univ. Press, 1954.

Buderi, Robert. *The Invention That Changed the World.* New York: Simon and Schuster, 1996.

Bush, Vannevar. *Modern Arms and Free Men.* New York: Simon and Schuster, 1949.

———. *Pieces of the Action.* New York: William Morrow and Co., 1970.

Christman, Albert B. *Naval Innovators, 1776–1900.* Dahlgren, Va:. Naval Surface Weapons Center, 1989.

———. *Sailors, Scientists, and Rockets.* Washington, D.C.: Naval History Division, 1971.

Duncan, Francis. *Rickover and the Nuclear Navy.* Annapolis, Md.: Naval Institute Press, 1990.

Fermi, Laura. *Atoms in the Family.* Chicago: Univ. of Chicago Press, 1954.

Fiske, Bradley A. *From Midshipman to Rear-Admiral.* New York: Century, 1919.

Furer, Julius A. *Administration of Navy Department in World War II.* Washington, D.C.: GPO, 1959.

Furman, Necah Stewart. *Sandia National Laboratories: The Postwar Decade.* Albuquerque: Univ. of New Mexico Press, 1990.

Gerard-Gough, J. D., and Albert B. Christman. *Grand Experiment at Inyokern.* Washington, D.C.: Naval History Division, 1978.

Goddard, Esther C., and G. Edward Pendray, eds. *The Papers of Robert H. Goddard.* 3 vols. New York: McGraw-Hill, 1970.

Goodchild, Peter. *Robert Oppenheimer: Shatterer of Worlds.* New York: Fromm International, 1985.

Groueff, Stephane. *Manhattan Project: The Untold Story of the Making of the Atomic Bomb.* Boston: Little Brown and Co., 1967.

Groves, Leslie R. *Now It Can Be Told.* New York: Harper and Row, 1962.

Harral, Brooks J., and Oretha Swartz, eds. *Service Etiquette.* Annapolis, Md.: Naval Institute Press, 1959; 2d ed., 3d printing, Apr. 1969.

Hawkins, David. *Project Y: The Los Alamos Story.* Vol. 2 of *The History of Modern Physics, 1800–1950.* Los Angeles: Tomash, 1983.

Hewlett, Richard G., and Oscar E. Anderson, Jr. *The New World, 1939/1946.* Vol. 1, *A History of the United States Atomic Energy Commission.* University Park: Pennsylvania State Univ. Press, 1962.

Hewlett, Richard G., and Francis Duncan. *Atomic Shield.* Vol. 2, *A History of the United States Atomic Energy Commission, 1947–1952.* Washington, D.C.: U.S. Atomic Energy Commission, 1972.

Hoddeson, Lillian; Paul W. Henriksen; Roger A. Meade; and Catherine Westfall. *Critical Assembly: A Technical History of Los Alamos during the Oppenheimer Years, 1943–1945.* Cambridge: Cambridge Univ. Press, 1993.

Howeth, Linwood S. *History of Communications-Electronics in the United States Navy.* Washington, D.C.: Office of Naval History, 1963.

Jones, Vincent C. *Manhattan: The Army and the Atomic Bomb.* Special Studies, United States Army in World War II. Washington, D.C.: Center of Military History, 1985.

Kevles, Daniel J. *The Physicists.* New York: Alfred A. Knopf, 1978.

Kinetka, James W. *Oppenheimer: The Years of Risk.* Englewood Cliffs, N.J.: Prentice-Hall, 1982.

Knebel, Fletcher, and Charles W. Bailey II. *No High Ground.* New York: Harper and Row, 1960.

Kurzman, Dan. *Day of the Bomb: Countdown to Hiroshima.* New York: McGraw-Hill, 1986.

Lamont, Lansing. *Day of Trinity.* New York: Atheneum, 1965.

Laurence, William L. *Dawn over Zero: The Story of the Atomic Bomb.* New York: Alfred A. Knopf, 1946.

Lawren, William. *The General and the Bomb: A Biography of General Leslie R. Groves, Director of the Manhattan Project.* New York: Dodd, Mead and Co., 1988.

Livingston, Dorothy Michelson. *The Master of Light: A Biography of Albert A. Michelson.* New York: Charles Scribner's Sons, 1973.

McCollum, Kenneth G. *Dahlgren.* Dahlgren, Va:. Naval Surface Weapons Center, 1977.

Marx, Joseph L. *Seven Hours to Zero.* New York: G. P. Putnam's Sons, 1967.

Mid-Pecos Historical Foundation. *Living Water: Our Mid-Pecos History.* Fort Sumner, N.Mex.: Mid-Pecos Historical Society, ca. 1980.

Naval History Division. *Dictionary of American Naval Fighting Ships.* Washington, D.C.: Naval History Division, 1959–.

Naval Ordnance Station. *1890—Naval Proving Ground, Naval Powder Factory, Naval Propellant Plant, Naval Ordnance Station.* Indian Head, Md:. Naval Ordnance Station, ca. 1972.

New York Times. *Hiroshima Plus Twenty.* New York: Delacorte, 1965.

Nichols, K. D. *The Road to Trinity.* New York: William Morrow and Co., 1987.

Oppenheimer, J. Robert. *The Open Mind.* New York: Simon and Schuster, 1955.

Polmar, Norman, and Thomas B. Allen. *Rickover.* New York: Simon and Schuster, 1982.

Potter, E. B. *Nimitz.* Annapolis, Md.: Naval Institute Press, 1976.

Powers, Thomas. *Heisenberg's War: The Secret History of the German Bomb.* New York: Alfred A. Knopf, 1993.

Rhodes, Richard. *The Making of the Atomic Bomb.* New York: Simon and Schuster, 1986.

Rowland, Buford, and William B. Boyd. *U.S. Navy Bureau of Ordnance in World War II.* Washington, D.C.: GPO, 1959.

Russ, Harlow. *Project Alberta: The Preparation of Atomic Bombs for Use in World War II.* Los Alamos, N.Mex.: Exceptional Books, 1990.

Shurcliff, William A. *Bombs at Bikini: The Official Report of Operation Crossroads.* New York: William H. Wise and Co., 1947.

Smaldone, Joseph P. *History of the White Oak Laboratory, 1945–1975.* White Oak, Silver Spring, Md.: Naval Surface Weapons Center, 1977.

Smith, Alice Kimball, and Charles Weiner. *Robert Oppenheimer: Letters and Recollections.* Cambridge: Harvard Univ. Press, 1980.

Smyth, Henry DeWolf. *Atomic Energy for Military Purposes: The Official Report on the Development of the Atomic Bomb under the Auspices of the United States Government, 1940–1945.* Princeton: Princeton Univ. Press, 1945.

Stern, Philip. *The Oppenheimer Case: Security on Trial.* New York: Harper and Row, 1969.

Strauss, Lewis L. *Men and Decisions.* Garden City, N.Y.: Doubleday and Co., 1962.

Sweeney, Charles W. *War's End.* New York: Avon Books, 1997.

Taylor, A. Hoyt. *The First Twenty-five Years of the Naval Research Laboratory.* Washington, D.C.: Navy Department, 1948.

———. *Radio Reminiscences: A Half Century.* Washington, D.C.: Naval Research Laboratory, 1948; republished 1960.

Thomas, Gordon, and Max Morgan Witts. *Enola Gay.* New York: Stein and Day, 1977.

Tibbets, Paul W., Jr. *The Tibbets Story.* New York: Stein and Day, 1978.

Van Auken, Wilbur R. *Notes on a Half Century of United States Naval Ordnance, 1880–1930.* Washington, D.C.: George Banta, 1939.

Weisgall, Jonathan M. *Operation Crossroads: The Atomic Tests at Bikini Atoll.* Annapolis, Md.: Naval Institute Press, 1994.

Wyden, Peter. *Day One: Before Hiroshima and After.* New York: Simon and Schuster, 1984.

Zachary, G. Pascal. *Vannevar Bush: Engineer of the American Century.* New York: Free Press, 1997.

Yearbooks

Fort Sumner High School. *El Tepocate.* Fort Sumner, N.Mex., May 1918.

Naval Academy Class of 1922. *The Lucky Bag: Annual of the Regiment of Midshipmen, United States Naval Academy.* Annapolis, Md., 1922.

Articles

Allard, Dean C. "The Development of the Radio Proximity Fuze." *Johns Hopkins APL Technical Digest* 3, no. 4 (1982): 358–59.

Ashworth, Frederick L. "Rear Admiral William S. Parsons USN and the Atomic Bomb." *Shipmate*, July–Aug. 1986, 24–26.

Badash, Lawrence, and Richard G. Hewlett. "A Story Too Good to Kill: The 'Nuclear' Explosion in San Francisco Bay." *Knowledge* 14, no. 4 (1993): 356–71.

Christman, Al[bert]. "Deak Parsons, Officer-Scientist." U.S. Naval Institute *Proceedings*, Jan. 1992, 56–61.

———. "Making It Happen." *American Heritage of Invention and Technology* 11 (Summer 1995): 22–35.

Goldberg, Stanley. "Inventing a Climate of Opinion: Vannevar Bush and the Decision to Build the Bomb." *ISIS* 83 (1992): 429–52.

Hooper, Edwin B. "Over the Span of Two Hundred Years—Technology and the United States Navy." *Naval Engineers Journal*, Aug. 1976, 17–23.

Rosenberg, David A. "U.S. Nuclear Stockpile, 1945 to 1950," *Bulletin of the Atomic Scientists*, May 1982, 25–30.

Tibbets, Paul W. "How to Drop an Atomic Bomb." *Saturday Evening Post*, 8 June 1946, 18–19, 132–36.

Index

ABOUT THE AUTHOR

Al Christman proved his ability to humanize technical subjects in his previous books on science and the military: *Sailors, Scientists, and Rockets; Grand Experiment at Inyokern* (co-author); and *Naval Innovators, 1776–1900*. These books grew out of Christman's research as writer/historian for the Naval Weapons Center (China Lake, California) and later as historian of the Navy Laboratories.

As a combat engineer in the 99th Infantry Division, Christman saw World War II action at the Battle of the Bulge, Remagen Bridge, and the Ruhr Pocket. While attending the University of Missouri after the war, Christman received a commission in the U.S. Air Force reserves. He is now retired at the rank of major.

Like Deak Parsons, the author spent much of his early boyhood in New Mexico. His present home is in San Marcos, California.

THE NAVAL INSTITUTE PRESS is the book-publishing arm of the U.S. Naval Institute, a private, nonprofit, membership society for sea service professionals and others who share an interest in naval and maritime affairs. Established in 1873 at the U.S. Naval Academy in Annapolis, Maryland, where its offices remain today, the Naval Institute has members worldwide.

Members of the Naval Institute support the education programs of the society and receive the influential monthly magazine *Proceedings* and discounts on fine nautical prints and on ship and aircraft photos. They also have access to the transcripts of the Institute's Oral History Program and get discounted admission to any of the Institute-sponsored seminars offered around the country.

The Naval Institute also publishes *Naval History* magazine. This colorful bimonthly is filled with entertaining and thought-provoking articles, first-person reminiscences, and dramatic art and photography. Members receive a discount on *Naval History* subscriptions.

The Naval Institute's book-publishing program, begun in 1898 with basic guides to naval practices, has broadened its scope in recent years to include books of more general interest. Now the Naval Institute Press publishes about 100 titles each year, ranging from how-to books on boating and navigation to battle histories, biographies, ship and aircraft guides, and novels. Institute members receive discounts of 20 to 50 percent on the Press's nearly 600 books in print.

Full-time students are eligible for special half-price membership rates. Life memberships are also available.

For a free catalog describing Naval Institute Press books currently available, and for further information about subscribing to *Naval History* magazine or about joining the U.S. Naval Institute, please write to:

Membership Department
U.S. NAVAL INSTITUTE
118 Maryland Avenue
Annapolis, MD 21402-5035
Telephone: (800) 233-8764
Fax: (410) 269-7940
Web address: www.usni.org